PETER'S KEY

PETER'S KEY

PETER DELOUGHRY AND THE FIGHT
FOR IRISH INDEPENDENCE

Declan Dunne

MERCIER PRESS
IRISH PUBLISHER – IRISH STORY

MERCIER PRESS

Cork

www.mercierpress.ie

© Declan Dunne, 2012

ISBN: 978 1 78117 059 5

10 9 8 7 6 5 4 3 2 1

A CIP record for this title is available from the British Library

Printed and bound in the EU.

Contents

Acknowledgements 9

Introduction 13

1 Iron-Founder Moulded, 1882–95 17

2 Smoke Rises, 1895–1909 25

3 Flames Shoot, 1909–14 38

4 Fire Spreads, 1914–16 55

5 Kilkenny, 1916 62

6 Phoenix Flame Rekindled, 1916–18 81

7 The Road to Lincoln, 1918 95

8 Life in Lincoln, 1918 103

9 Escape from Lincoln – Thoughts Emerge, 1918–19 119

10 Escape from Lincoln – Peter's Key Turns, 1919 142

11 Escape from Lincoln – Aftermath, 1919 166

12 War of Independence, 1920 184

13 Fire Turns Inwards, 1920–21 199

14 Treaty and Civil War, 1921–22 213

15 Hatred Simmers, 1922 228

16 Catholic Church Brimstone, 1923–25 235

17 Founder Fights Back, 1926–31 251

18 No Rest, 1932–70 265

Endnotes   272

References   304

Bibliography   306

Index   309

To Mary Bridget Quinn (Nanny)

and

Master Oisín Barrett

(Northolt)

Acknowledgements

Little would be known about Peter DeLoughry, the author's grandfather, but for the care and attention given to his and other family documents held by Pádraigín Ní Dhubhluachra (the DeLoughry family papers) and Brenda and Giles Clausard (the Brendan Mangan papers). They gave me unlimited access to these papers and provided me with invaluable background material and wise counsel.

The spark that led to this biography being written was set off by Seán Flynn in a question posted on the internet asking if anyone knew anything about Peter DeLoughry. I contacted him and then relatives Eileen and Geoff Cartwright, Sheffield, England, who puzzled over why so little was known about Peter. Other forces of nature, both great and small, helped to bring this biography about, including Sheila Brennan, Kilkenny; Máire Burke, Claremorris, County Mayo; Jack, Anne and John DeLoughry, Talbotsinch, Kilkenny; Maeve DeLoughry, Orla DeLoughry, Nenagh, County Tipperary; Patricia DeLoughrey, Boston; Richard Deloughry, Manchester; and Aedine Mangan, Dublin. (Readers will notice the variety of spellings for the surname DeLoughry. In the text, the surname is spelled the same way as the individuals to whom it relates spelled it: Peter used DeLoughry. Some genealogists believe the surname is a corruption of Norman French, perhaps from De la Croix. Others, including Edward MacLysaght in his book *A Guide to Irish Surnames*, contend that it comes from the Irish Ó Dubhluachra and has as its synonym, Dilworth.)

Librarians and archivists helped to keep the blood flowing in the heart of this enterprise. I owe particular thanks to Damian Brett, Kilkenny Library; Diane Burnett, Upper Ottawa Valley Genealogical Group; Susan Ciccone, Research Librarian, Cambridge Public Library, Massachusetts; Kathleen S. Dodds, D.A. Archival Assistant, Msgr William Noé Field Archives and Special Collections Center, Walsh Library, Seton Hall University, New Jersey; Sharon Dahlmeyer-Giovannitti, Godfrey Memorial Library, Middletown, Connecticut; Caroline Herbert, Archives Assistant, Churchill Archives Centre, Churchill College, Cambridge, England; Gearóid O'Brien, Executive Librarian, Aidan Heavey Public Library, Athlone Civic Centre, County Westmeath; James Stuart Osbourn, Principal Librarian, New Jersey Information Centre, Newark Public Library; Áine Stack, Jesuit Library, Milltown, Dublin; and Catherine Stanton, Curator, Images, Department of History Collections, Museum of London.

This work demanded a trawl through many archives. The following people and institutions were the ones I visited most and therefore the ones who/which showed great patience and even greater assistance: Philomena Brant, Property Registration Authority, Registry of Deeds Branch, Henrietta Street, Dublin; British Library, Colindale; Catriona Crowe, NAI (in particular for assistance with copies of witness statements and archives related to Fenianism); Seamus Helferty, UCD Archives (in particular for assistance with the de Valera papers and the O'Malley papers); Yves Lebrec, Conservateur de la photothèque, Bibliothèque de Fels, Institut Catholique de Paris; Elisabeth Liber, Institut Pasteur, Paris; National Archives, Kew; National Library of Ireland; Gráinne Morton, Kilkenny Mental Health and Elderly Services, St

Canice's Hospital, Kilkenny; and Dr Joan Unwin, Archivist, The Cutlers' Hall, Church Street, Sheffield. The Bureau of Military History, Rathmines, Dublin, has custody of 1,770 witness statements, copies of which are held by the National Archives of Ireland. These statements were taken in the 1940s and 1950s from individuals involved in the movement for Irish independence from 1913 to 1921. They provided this biography with a wealth of material.

The historians listed here gave of their time and expertise: Anthony Begley; Turtle Bunbury; Mary Cassin; Tim Pat Coogan; Alan B. Delozier, University Archivist, Walsh Library, Seton Hall University, New Jersey; Glenn G. Geisheimer, Manalapan, New Jersey; Jim Herlihy; Eilish McShane; Jim Maher; Liam Ó Duibhir; Marta Ramón, a lecturer at NUI Maynooth; Tom Ryan, Old Trafford, Kilkenny; Jim Walsh, Slieverue, County Kilkenny; and Dr Walter Walsh, Kilfane, County Kilkenny.

David McCullagh unravelled and made sense of a complicated issue for me regarding events in Kilkenny in 1916, with the efficiency and flair for which he is known and respected as RTÉ's political correspondent. Dr Martin Holland provided me with translations of material into English from Irish and Latin that greatly helped the understanding of the depth of planning that went into the escape from Lincoln prison. The amendments suggested and advice given to me by Ray Burke, Senior News Editor, RTÉ, and Professor Tom Garvin, Institute of British-Irish Studies, UCD, were invaluable, and the reader will be as indebted as I am to them.

I was alerted to valuable material not found in official archives by the following people, who also showed me great kindness: Brother Damien Brennan, CBS, Kilkenny;

Tony Byrne; John Colivet; Dermot Curran, formerly of CBS, Kilkenny; Nicola Gordon Bowe; Melosina Lenox-Conyngham; Stan Purcell and the Milroy family; Blanaid Ó Brádaigh and Liam O'Dwyer, Lavistown, Kilkenny.

Each of these people gave me help and advice, but any errors or omissions in the text are mine alone.

I owe a great deal to my nieces and nephews: Cathy, who acted as my research assistant; Peter, who set up a website linked to this book (www.peterdeloughrytd.com); David and Laura. Their parents, my brother Conor and his wife Mary, along with my sister Win, went above and beyond the call of duty in listening to my ramblings as I tried to make sense of Peter DeLoughry's life, death and memory.

I am indebted to Mercier Press for their professionalism and understanding, especially Jennifer Armstrong, Patrick Crowley, Mary Feehan, Jenny Laing, Wendy Logue and Sharon O'Donovan.

Finally, Dennis Bannister, Tommie Gorman, David Hanly, Michael Murphy, Terry O'Sullivan, Angela and Vincent O'Hagan, Sinéad Barrett and Oisín Barrett gave me encouragement in abundance. For this and for their friendship, I am grateful.

Declan Dunne
Dublin, 2012

Introduction

On 3 February 1919, the mayor of Kilkenny, Peter DeLoughry, spent an anxious night in his prison cell in Lincolnshire in the East Midlands of England. A key he had fashioned from a 'blank' was being used by three inmates to escape and the most influential Irishmen of the time were gathered on either side of the prison wall: Michael Collins and Harry Boland were waiting for Éamon de Valera, Seán McGarry and Seán Milroy to emerge from captivity so that they could ferry them to safety.

The escape, in its preparation and execution, was the most audacious and spectacularly successful in the history of the conflict between Britain and Ireland. The plan drew on the skills of a baker, a linguist and a cartoonist. The merits of whiskey, candle wax and matches were demonstrated. Other curious additions included consultation with the stars, nerves of steel and cakes with more iron content than usual. But there is a tragedy to all this: within a few years, those who had worked together so closely on the plan would be fighting against each other in a civil war. That war broke out when the Anglo-Irish Treaty formed another dividing wall made of sterner stone and more bloody mortar than the one in Lincoln that had brought them together. Harry Boland and Michael Collins, who were at one time inseparable, took opposing sides and were shot dead within weeks of one another.

Another story emerges from Lincoln concerning one of the liberators, Peter DeLoughry, and one of the liberated, Éamon de Valera. They left the comradeship of prison life well behind them and, like Boland and Collins, took opposing sides in the Civil War. Unlike them, DeLoughry and de Valera survived, but their fractious relationship throughout the 1920s and up to DeLoughry's death in 1931 offers an insight into the tempestuous opening years of the new Free State of Ireland.

This story is not just about a key. Peter DeLoughry led a daredevil life in which his hands featured prominently. He rapped his fists on tables at local authority meetings to challenge opponents outside for a bare-knuckle fight. He used his hands to steer his motor-bike from Kilkenny to Clare to campaign for de Valera's election in 1917. During the War of Independence, his hands were tied behind his back by Black and Tans before they put a gun to his head and drove him around County Kilkenny. On another occasion, he was forced to raise his palms when cornered at gunpoint on a train, before jumping out, rolling down an embankment and making his way to safety. While facing an angry group of Redmondite Volunteers in Kilkenny city, he ordered those who stood for Ireland to stand to one side. He raised his hand against the Catholic Church several times during confrontations over censorship, divorce and religious discrimination. He used his right hand to accept congratulations for his election as mayor of Kilkenny on six successive occasions, as a member of Kilkenny County Council when he topped the poll, as a senator and as a TD (he was also director of elections for independent Ireland's first prime minister, W. T. Cosgrave). In Lincoln prison, Peter's hands became the greatest asset for the planned escape, when he used them to craft the special key.

Despite his varied career, it was my grandfather's role in the 'Great Escape' that was repeatedly mentioned when I was a boy. I remember playing in the front room of our house in Wexford when I was very young and looking up at a portrait of him in an oval frame. In time, I came to hear of his exploits. Now, as a man, my eye level and that of his image are the same. He looks away from me, smiling – at least, I think he is smiling.

This biography is written to a large extent from the perspective of Peter DeLoughry. I would ask readers not to make a final assessment of Éamon de Valera and Ernie O'Malley without getting a more rounded picture of their lives from biographies. Each of O'Malley's works and the biography of him by Richard English is worth a read, whether one is interested in history or not.

Peter DeLoughry was at various times an inventor, actor, judge, brigadier, fireman, cinema and theatre owner, industrial relations mediator, iron founder, engineer, locksmith, manager of a bomb factory and politician. He was irascible and generous. His close friend, E. T. Keane, the editor of the *Kilkenny People*, said that he lacked the arts and artifices of a politician because he laid all his cards on the table. Despite this, Peter lobbied successfully for the improvement of Kilkenny's water and electrical schemes. However, his regular and strong attacks on Catholic bishops and priests damaged his political career considerably.

His life raises a question that might be asked of many of his fellow revolutionaries. Why did he and his wife, who ran a successful business, decide to jeopardise their comfortable lives and those of their children by fighting for an independent Ireland? I will strive to answer that question and show how the achievements of Boland, Collins, de Valera and others rested on the shoulders of unsung heroes and heroines, many of whom are long forgotten, their stories entombed with their bones.

In telling the life story of Peter DeLoughry, we will see how the War of Independence and the Civil War held no glory. These were the worst of times, blanketed by cordite, which led to an envenomed atmosphere in Ireland that took decades to clear.

1

Iron-Founder Moulded, 1882–95

Peter DeLoughry was born into surroundings that inured him to the life he was to lead.[1] Noise and the power of fire, necessary for the family's foundry business, were his constant childhood companions. Dominating the space around his childhood home, in Rothe House in Kilkenny in the south-east of Ireland, was the blast furnace and all that went on around it: the blurring of the air as metals were heated to orange; clanging; bulls of men beating and bending, sweating and cursing; and the 'tish' sound of hot metal in water. His father, Richard, indulged a passion for blood 'sports' in the yard, which saw 'many an epic battle' in cock-fighting and badger-baiting, where badgers are forced to combat a succession of hounds.[2]

Rothe House had stood since the reign of Elizabeth I, but by 1882, the year of Peter's birth, it had lost its grandeur, having been divided into tenements. When Peter was two years old, the living quarters and offices in the building were described as being 'in a most filthy and dangerous condition. There is neither drainage nor privy accommodation; two portions of the yards are used as piggeries, and the whole place is full of heaps of pig manure and nuisance.'[3] Three years later, areas of the house were described as being in 'very bad repair' and 'almost a ruin'.[4]

Peter grew up among the squalor of animal waste, the spray of blood from spurred fighting cocks, the snarls of hounds and screams of badgers ripping at each other's flesh and the inferno of the foundry industry. Outside, another form of heat was making its presence felt: in the Corporation chamber, in the courts and, most of all, on the streets. This was a furnace of Fenianism, which was also fed and maintained to a great extent by his father.

Richard DeLoughry knew or was closely associated with some of the most important figures in Ireland, among them, the founder of the Land League, Michael Davitt,[5] the leader of the Irish Parliamentary Party, Charles Stewart Parnell,[6] and the co-founders of the Gaelic Athletic Association (GAA), Michael Cusack and Maurice Davin.[7] The *Kilkenny Journal* said Richard was 'numbered among the closest friends and most devoted comrades of the founder of the Fenians, James Stephens, [Jeremiah] O'Donovan Rossa and the rest of the old Fenians'.[8] Indeed Richard's cousin, John Breslin, was instrumental in the escape of James Stephens from Richmond prison, Dublin, in 1865.[9] Richard's life, associations and actions placed him under a category of Fenian described by the historian R. V. Comerford as one 'with a confident step and an independent air who refused to avert his eyes from the gaze of policeman or priest'.[10]

By the time of Peter's birth, Richard had led a full life. He had spent seven years in the United States where he married Bridget O'Brien, who was also from Kilkenny.[11] During his time abroad, Richard had maintained his nationalistic fervour. While in New Jersey, he joined Clan na Gael (the American arm of Fenianism) and attended a rally at Jones' Wood in New York at which James Stephens delivered an address.[12]

Following the couple's return to Kilkenny in 1872, Richard immersed himself in campaigns linked to the fight for Irish independence.[13] These included fund-raising events for the Manchester Martyrs, for nationalist Irish prisoners held in British jails, and for James Stephens, who ended up living in exile and penury in Paris.[14] Richard also became one of the founders of the GAA in Kilkenny, acting as referee, organiser of athletic competitions and treasurer.[15]

His association with the GAA and with the Working-men's Club (WMC) of Kilkenny, which offered Fenians an opportunity to band together, drew him into conflict with the Catholic Church and the Royal Irish Constabulary (RIC). The Catholic Bishop of Ossory, Dr Abraham Brownrigg, banned GAA collections and issued pastoral letters obliquely criticising the WMC.[16] Fr Fideles of the Capuchin Friary, Kilkenny, was not so restrained. He denounced the WMC from the pulpit, describing it as a 'council room of the devil' and called on St Patrick and all the saints of Ireland to put an end to this 'synagogue of hell'.[17]

Richard's association with the GAA and the WMC brought to the fore his strong character and his particular brand of nationalism. He campaigned and was successful in having a man admitted to the WMC despite protests from members that the applicant was unsuitable because he had played rugby.[18] As organiser of a GAA sports event in Kilkenny, he allowed the band of the 2nd Battalion of the Royal Irish Fusiliers to perform *God Save the Queen*.[19] Richard did not see the playing of the British national anthem as a threat. His target, as an Irish nationalist, was not the music, literature or royalty of Britain, but the British government.

The RIC kept a close watch on both the GAA and the

WMC. P. J. O'Keeffe, the founder of the WMC and its principal driving force, was charged with breaking around two dozen street lamps in Kilkenny city in 1888. Richard was called to give evidence against O'Keeffe, but refused to incriminate him and O'Keeffe was acquitted.[20]

The same year, the various strands of nationalism in Kilkenny organised their annual parade to commemorate the Manchester Martyrs. The event was banned and violence erupted in the city on the day it was to have been held. Despite a large police presence, the parade went ahead. The *Kilkenny Journal* recorded the role played by the St Patrick's Brass Band, of which six-year-old Peter was a member:

> The procession was headed by the Corporation boat. The forces were concentrated at Green's bridge weir and rowed down the river. The scene was impressive, the solemn strains of the *Dead March* in *Saul* being wafted across the waters, the flare of the torches reflected from the river, and the suppressed murmur of voices from the banks. The police became aware of the proceedings when it was too late to prevent them. They dashed down the quay and batoned all who came before them but objected to take a plunge into the cold and uninviting waters of the River Nore. They looked on the flotilla, and gnashed their teeth with impotent rage but even Head Meek [RIC Head Constable, Kilkenny city] refused to follow the example of *Horatio* and commit his sacred person to Father Nore and so the celebration in honour of the Manchester Martyrs was held under the very noses of Her Majesty's forces.[21]

Peter and other children shared the relish of their Fenian fathers who had outwitted the authorities, but the movement was to receive a most telling blow shortly afterwards, during a confrontation in Kilkenny that attracted worldwide attention. This took the form of a by-election in 1890, contested by those for and against Parnell. The atmosphere was charged with the reaction of Parnell's opponents to the divorce proceedings that followed his scandalous relationship with Kitty O'Shea and, by extension, to Parnell's continued leadership. There was also the issue of the intractable position adopted by those seeking home rule. The campaign was marked by verbal savagery and violence.

During one of the many hot exchanges of the campaign, Richard, a staunch Parnellite, and Michael Davitt, who supported the anti-Parnellite candidate, rowed over the merits and demerits of their respective candidates. Afterwards Davitt said of Richard, 'I might as well bend an iron bar as change his views.'[22]

The Catholic Church became heavily involved in the campaign. Some priests supported Parnell, but the majority worked unceasingly for his opponents. In a letter to Archbishop William J. Walsh, Bishop Brownrigg lamented that those who supported Parnell were 'some of those who always professed greatest friendship for me'. He continued, '*The ladies* (so-called) were the most demonstrative of all, the lowest dregs of the people, the Fenian element, and the working classes are all to a man with Parnell ... in a word, everything bad or corrupt has come to the surface in favour of Parnell.'[23]

The Parnellite candidate lost and any immediate hope of home rule disappeared. Peter, at the impressionable age of eight, saw the viciousness of Irish politics played out on the streets of his city.

Two months after the by-election, he, as usual, accompanied members of his family to mass and listened to the Lenten pastoral from Bishop Brownrigg that was read by priests in all Catholic churches in the diocese:

> I must not omit to make known to you the joy that fills my heart at being able to announce the gratifying intelligence that not a single 'mixed marriage' took place during the last twelve months within the confines of the Diocese of Ossory. You will recollect that one of the very first acts of my administration when I came amongst you was to declare war on these unholy alliances, which are fraught with such evils for those who engage in them, as well as for their offspring.

The bishop warned his flock against bad and dangerous reading, during which he took a swipe at Parnell, though without naming him:

> It is found in many of our public prints and newspapers, which give in detail the scenes of scandal and debauchery from the English divorce courts, and which propagate amongst our simple people unsound maxims of morality and anti-religious principles, which are still worse.[24]

The Parnellite split had a very damaging effect on the GAA football and hurling championships in Kilkenny, where they faltered in the early 1890s. Apart from internal disputes and the obstacles raised by the rupture, the association was also harried by the Catholic hierarchy. An RIC officer reported to Dublin Castle in January 1893 that 'the Roman Catholic clergy are opposed to the [GAA] which, accordingly, has not made much advance in this city'.[25] However, the beginnings of a revival occurred in 1893 when the championships resumed.

Peter's twenty-one-year-old brother, John, played on the Confederation club teams that won the Kilkenny County championship in 1893 and 1894.[26]

Even though the championships had resumed, the GAA in Kilkenny was not on a sound footing. Richard and his son John led a charge at a convention at which Richard gave an impassioned speech for revival and re-organisation.[27] His appeal had the desired effect and the GAA began its resurgence and blossomed. Richard thus became a unique figure in Kilkenny GAA history, having not only been a founder of the association in the county, but also one of its saviours.

The changes that had pervaded Peter's life in the first half of the 1890s enveloped his entire family. In 1894 Richard's business acumen allowed him to move his family just a few doors down from Rothe House to a townhouse at 18 Parliament Street to which was attached a yard for his foundry business.[28] By December of that year, Richard was advertising his latest wares. Under the slogan 'Support Irish Manufacture', the stock listed included 'every description of household goods', 'all classes of agricultural machines' and 'Tolch's patent capitaine oil engine', one of which could be seen working on the premises.[29]

Another change came just two months later. Peter, now twelve years old, along with his brothers, Richard Junior, twenty-four, John, twenty-three, Francis, sixteen, David, ten and Larry, six, filed into a pew for the funeral mass of their father.[30] Richard had taken ill five weeks earlier and died at his new home, at the age of fifty-one, of complications arising from kidney failure.[31] As he sat through his father's funeral mass, the only certainty for Peter was that the hand which had led him to sporting events, which had introduced him to the skill of an iron founder, which was used on playing pitches to calm upset or silence rancour, was gone. The furnace had gone cold. His father, the founder, was cast to ashes.

2

Smoke Rises, 1895–1909

Colourful characters and events combined to distract Peter and his siblings from their grief in the aftermath of their father's death. The life of the city was much shaken up by E. T. Keane and P. J. O'Keeffe, who went into partnership to set up the *Kilkenny People*, which supported and encouraged both the GAA and the cause of Irish nationalism. Peter became more attracted to both movements once he had completed his formal education with the Christian Brothers at the age of fourteen in 1896, after which he began his apprenticeship as a founder in the family business, under the supervision of his brother John.

Both Peter and his brother Larry became enthusiastic members of the Gaelic League, a branch of which was set up in Kilkenny in 1897, attending Irish-language classes in their former home, Rothe House. Through the Gaelic League, they met and became lifelong friends with Captain Otway Cuffe and his sister-in-law Ellen (Countess of Desart). The captain dressed in the old Irish costume of knee-breeches to 'give a lesson to the people who saw him, on the duty they owed to home-made goods'.[1] From a German-Jewish banking family, the fabulously wealthy countess used her money to erect several important buildings in Kilkenny, to help the sick, to promote education and to spread appreciation of the arts. She included among her eccentricities an opposition to women being given the vote.[2]

As the Irish-Ireland movement, including the Gaelic League, blossomed, so too did the reputation of P. J. O'Keeffe for extravagant and violent acts of extreme nationalism. Following a debate at a Kilkenny Corporation meeting in October 1896 on commemorating the Battle of Trafalgar, O'Keeffe and a mob smashed their way into the chamber. The *Kilkenny Moderator*'s headlines summed up what followed:

Night 'Scenes' in Kilkenny

The Mayor Burnt in Effigy

The British Flag Reviled

The Tholsel[3] Broken into

Disgraceful 'Scenes' in the Corporation

The Mayor's Nose Pulled by a Councillor

A Beer Barrel Put in the Chair

His Worship Not Allowed to Speak[4]

Over the next few years, Peter's life was again touched by sadness: his sister, Lil, left home to pursue a teaching career in Castledermott, County Kildare, and their mother, Bridget, died at Kilkenny District Lunatic Asylum in 1901, at fifty-one, having suffered epileptic seizures for three days.[5] Two of his brothers emigrated, Richard Junior to England and Francis to the United States. The challenge facing Peter's brother John, who remained at home, was formidable. Aside from the loss of his parents within a relatively short space of time, he had to deal with comforting his younger brothers, Peter, David and Larry, while ensuring their physical, moral and spiritual well-being and seeing off any opportunistic business competitors. However, he seems to have risen to the occasion.

Shortly after his father's death, John was advertising the foundry in a local newspaper.[6] In 1897 the *Kilkenny People* noted:

Messrs DeLoughry & Sons are agents for some first-class machines, and the customer who pays a visit to their workshop will be sure to find a suitable 'mount'. The Messrs DeLoughry are practical mechanics … They buy second-hand machines at highest prices and have ladies' and gentlemen's machines on hire.[7]

A subsequent article in the same newspaper reported that the foundry 'conducted by John DeLoughry' was employing 'many hands', that castings were being turned out in an efficient manner and that repairs were being competently executed.[8]

Peter's continued membership of the Gaelic League brought him into contact with many important figures, such as Dr Douglas Hyde, the future first president of Ireland; Thomas MacDonagh, one of the seven signatories of the 1916 Proclamation;[9] and Standish O'Grady, a unionist who, as editor of the *Kilkenny Moderator*, did much to push forward the Irish-Ireland movement. Despite the differing religious and social backgrounds of the people Peter encountered, they were all linked by the Gaelic League. This gave him and other league members an invisible uniform of patriotic green and allowed them to savour being Irish. Previous to this period in history, antagonism towards the British Empire was born out of land wars, discrimination, starvation and cruelty. Irish identity was inextricably linked to and defined by how one acted within or against the empire. Now, the assertion of identity, an Irish identity, could be found in language, literature, dance, and – with the GAA – sport. The invisible uniform of the Gaelic League showed that Irish people were unique:

> The Gaelic League was in many ways the central institution in the development of the Irish revolutionary élite. Most of the 1916 leaders and most of the leading figures in the Free State, whether pro-Treaty or anti-Treaty, had been members of the league in their youth and had imbibed versions of its ideology of cultural revitalisation.[10]

The theatre provided another forum in which Peter could express his Irishness. His sister, Lil, married Henry Mangan, a Dublin Corporation official, journalist, playwright and historian, who encouraged Peter, David and Larry onto the stage. The brothers took part in plays produced by Captain Cuffe, greatly encouraged by Ellen, now Dowager Countess of Desart. The plays were performed at the Kilkenny Theatre, Patrick Street, which was built by Cuffe in 1902, and were of a distinctly Irish flavour: they included *The Whiteboys* (1903) and *The Masque of Finn* by Standish O'Grady (1907), which was performed in the open air at Greenvale, Kilkenny. The reviewer for the *Kilkenny People* was not impressed with *The Whiteboys*, describing it as 'a gross caricature as was ever hissed off the stage'.[11] Unfazed by this, Peter, David and Larry extended their involvement in the theatre by organising and appearing at the annual Banba fancy dress balls.

The DeLoughrys also displayed a skill for invention. In 1901 Peter was complimented by each of the Kilkenny newspapers for his 'skilful manipulation' of a magic lantern during a show to entertain young boys from the Kilkenny National Guard.[12] At an industrial exhibition in Kilkenny, the DeLoughrys' stand had 'an ingenious and well-constructed printing machine in working order, made by themselves'.[13] The firm took a stand at a feis where 'one dray was entirely occupied by a casting of the centre part of a water-wheel, weighing upwards of six cwt. This piece attracted much interest and the whole display indicated that the firm may be safely entrusted with orders for castings of the smallest or largest proportions'.[14]

The inventiveness and indeed pluck of Peter and his brother David were called on to assist in fighting four fires in the city during the first decade of the new century. Following one of these fires, members of Kilkenny Corporation noted that Tom Stallard and Peter had arrived at the scene with keys for the hydrants which they knew how to work. When it was found that the water pressure was not strong enough, Peter rushed to the Castlecomer Road to cut off the supply to John Street and solved the problem.[15]

Peter appeared unthreatening to the local RIC, who sent monthly reports to their superiors in Dublin Castle on the activities of dangerous nationalists. He was regarded as a local boy who worked hard, dabbled in theatre and spent his free time putting out fires, inventing curious machines, learning Irish and socialising with Jews, unionists and intellectuals. However, there was another hidden side to Peter.

On 10 April 1904, at Dunbell in County Kilkenny, a big meeting was called by the United Irish League to protest against the most detested creature in Irish society, the land-grabber. Lengthy speeches were made in a charged atmosphere. However, Fr Patrick Hipwell of Goresbridge deviated from the subject of tenant rights to speak about the forthcoming visit of the British monarch:

> I say you are rotten to the core if you give the king a reception in Kilkenny ... I say float the black flag over in Kilkenny when he comes there ... Are you so forgetful of the oath of England? Are you forgetful Catholics, that no matter how enlightened you are you can never succeed to the throne of England because you are Catholics? Fellow country-men, you are rotten to the core again if you give an address to the king.[16]

The *Kilkenny People* printed the oath taken by the king, which led to members of Kilkenny Corporation proposing a motion expressing its 'indignation and detestation at the outrageous insult offered to us as Catholics by the abominable and insulting language put into the mouth of King Edward VII, on the occasion of his taking the Coronation oath, whereby he declares some of the most sacred dogmas of our faith to be idolatrous and superstitious'.[17] Despite all this, Kilkenny Corporation and County Council voted in favour of making presentations to the king.

On the evening of the arrival of King Edward, Queen Alexandra and Princess Victoria to Kilkenny, Peter and three brothers, Jack, Tom and Peter Stallard, erected a black flag on top of one of the city's landmarks so that it would be visible from Kilkenny Castle, where the royal party was staying.[18] For good measure, Peter, along with some other Kilkenny residents, also posted a black flag outside their family homes. In spite of all the standard-bearing and denunciations about oaths and votes at local authority meetings, the people of Kilkenny gave the royal party a warm reception.

Further evidence of Peter's early adherence to a fiery brand of nationalism was given by Timothy Hennessy and James Lalor. They recounted that he swore them into the Irish Republican Brotherhood (IRB) at his family home in Parliament Street in 1905, showing that he had risen to a high level in the local organisation by his twenty-third birthday.[19]

In the same year, Peter became involved in a campaign that saw him declaring his political credentials publicly. A young Kilkenny man, Michael Dwyer, was arrested in Kilmacow and charged with distributing seditious literature. Evidence was given at Kilkenny courthouse that Dwyer had given out leaflets calling on Irishmen not to join British forces and the court heard that the literature urged Irishmen not to 'become armed robbers for English money-lenders. You would get the bullet. They would get the gold. Remember always, an Irishman who enlists in the Army, Navy and Police Force is a traitor to his country.' Dwyer was accused of handing one of the leaflets to an RIC officer named Slevin, who was in plain clothes. He was returned for trial to the winter assizes and was granted bail in his own surety of £100 and independent sureties of £50 each from George Stallard and E. T. Keane.[20]

A meeting was called by Peter, Keane, Stallard, Pat Corcoran, Edward O'Shea (the mayor of Kilkenny) and others, to set up a defence fund. Alderman Joseph Purcell, who chaired the meeting, said the incident was 'an eye-opener to the young men of Kilkenny to beware of policemen'. Peter was appointed secretary and seconded a motion proposed by Fintan O'Phelan of the *Wexford People* 'that we call on our fellow-townsmen to disassociate themselves by every means in their power from anything connected with constabulary functions or other functions connected with the British force in this country, or which has the slightest taint of the Union Jack. That applied, he said, to their dances and to their sports as well.'[21]

The fund raised almost £50. Subscriptions were made to Peter by his brother-in-law, Henry Mangan, and by Patrick O'Brien MP, who raised the issue in the House of Commons. Sums were also given by Peter's brother Francis in the United States and by John Sweetman, a financial supporter and one of the founders of Sinn Féin.[22] When the case came before court, the Waterford grand jury threw it out.[23] The money left over from the subscription fund was donated to other causes, including one for a Kilkenny ex-prisoner of war who had deserted the British army to fight with the Boers.[24]

Peter extended his reach into the community by associating himself with initiatives by Captain Cuffe and Ellen, Countess of Desart, to build up industry in the county. These resulted in the setting up of the Kilkenny Industrial Development Association in November 1905.[25] The organisation began around the same time as the two set up a tobacco farm and led a campaign to open up Kilkenny woollen mills. Peter attended meetings to set up the mills, which opened in April 1906.[26]

His involvement in the campaign to encourage local industry proceeded on a parallel track with his consolidation of his position as a Republican leader in Kilkenny. James J. Comerford recalled celebrations in Kilkenny when the team won the 1904 Hurling All-Ireland, its first of many (the final was actually played in 1906):

For the first time in Kilkenny city, a Sinn Féin flag was seen in public as it was held high by a stalwart young Kilkenny hurler over the heads of a crowd of celebrants who gathered on the Parade at dusk to hear Peter DeLoughry of Kilkenny city and Seán Gibbons of Clonmantagh praise the Kilkenny hurling team for bringing the All-Ireland to Kilkenny.[27]

Despite Peter's deep involvement in Kilkenny's political and social life, in late 1906 he emigrated to Manchester, where he joined his brother Richard Junior and secured employment in the Westinghouse Engineering Works.[28] However, he did not sever his political links with Kilkenny, and in early January 1907 he returned temporarily and attended a meeting in Thomastown to set up a branch of the National Council in connection with the 'Sinn Féin Policy', as set out by Arthur Griffith in 1905, advocating the right of Irish people to govern themselves. He told the gathering he hoped that a similar branch would be set up in Kilkenny city and that before the year was out there would be at least twenty such branches in the county.[29] The move marked a shift in his political affiliation, as exactly a year before, he and his brother John had signed nomination papers for the Irish Parliamentary Party candidate, Patrick O'Brien, to secure a seat at Westminster.[30]

Peter also stood as a witness for the marriage in Kilkenny of his brother John to Margaret Donnegan on 29 January 1907. Tragically, just three months later John died, at the age of thirty-one. He had got a drenching during a downpour at a hurling match and his death was brought on by influenza and acute laryngitis.[31] His obituary in the *Kilkenny People* recalled the death of his father, twelve years earlier, which:

… left him to face the world alone and unaided with younger brothers to provide and care for, and the pluck and perseverance with which he entered on the fight, overcoming difficulties that would have conquered men of weaker purpose. [He] lived for others quite as much as for himself [which] won for him the respect that the world always willingly accords to the brave fighter.

An incomplete list of mourners took up an entire column. The wreaths included ones from the Confederation club 'In loving memory', from his loving comrades 'With sincere regret' and from the Gang 'With deepest sympathy'.[32]

Whether he intended it to be temporary or permanent, Peter's time in Manchester was over. At twenty-four, he took up the reins of the family business with Larry.

The hope expressed in 1907 at the Thomastown meeting, for a branch of the National Council to be set up in Kilkenny city, was realised in April the following year. (In this month the National Council merged with the Sinn Féin League to form the Sinn Féin party.) The provisional committee appointed included Alderman Joseph Purcell, chairman, E. McSweeney, treasurer, and Michael Dwyer and Peter as honorary secretaries. Apart from those mentioned above, the movement attracted powerful figures in Kilkenny, including Pat Corcoran, James Nowlan and Tom Stallard.

Seán MacDermott, a Sinn Féin organiser and later signatory of the 1916 proclamation, addressed the first meeting in Kilkenny to explain the party's policy. He rubbished the role of the Irish Parliamentary Party at Westminster, describing its presence there as a waste of money. While cautioning that he was not advocating physical force as an alternative to parliamentary lobbying for Irish independence, he credited the introduction of the Land Act of 1870 and the Disestablishment Church Act of 1869 to the Fenians. His speech was short on specifics, other than to urge people to buy Irish-made goods. Alderman John McCarthy went further in his criticism of the Irish Parliamentary Party, describing the speeches of its MPs as 'very oily' and 'disgusting' and claiming that these representatives had 'nothing like manliness in them'.[33]

The Kilkenny city branch of Sinn Féin took up a campaign to buy Irish goods with vigour. At meetings held throughout the latter part of 1908, the branch launched a campaign for city traders to sell locally made Christmas cards; received a written undertaking from one shopkeeper that he would no longer stock foreign-made margarine;[34] complained that Irish-made buckets bore no mark to prove they were genuine;[35] and objected to the decision by Kilkenny County Council to import brooms from Birmingham.[36] They referred these complaints to the Kilkenny Industrial Development Association, of which Peter was also a member.

Debates and arguments at these meetings showed assertiveness in Peter's contributions. During a row about the Kilkenny woodworkers not using coal from Castlecomer mines, E. T. Keane suggested that the matter should be left to Kilkenny Corporation, to which Peter retorted that the matter was 'more our business than that of the Corporation'.[37] At a subsequent meeting, a letter was read from Peter in his capacity as secretary of the Kilkenny Sinn Féin branch:

I am directed by the committee above to draw your attention to the importation [from Glasgow] of school desks by the trustees of St Kieran's College, and also to the fact that a letter from me to the president on the subject elicited no reply. I am to add that my committee requests you will be good enough to write to the trustees of St Kieran's College, with the hope of obtaining a reply before next meeting of the Industrial Development Association. I enclose replies received from local manufacturers, who were not given an opportunity to quote for the school furniture referred to. I am, further, to request that your association will take vigorous and immediate action in the matter.[38]

During a discussion on what action should be taken, Peter drove forward his argument:

St Kieran's College was built by the public money, and they should get furniture, when they wanted it, from the local people who helped to maintain it. The people, it seemed, who preached most about emigration were those who encouraged it by buying foreign manufacture, while their own countrymen were idle.[39]

Peter's assertiveness was helped by his thorough preparation for the debate: he not only raised the issue, but went out of his way to find proof that local traders had not been given the option to tender.

Aside from a skill for debate, he was also showing a keen talent for organisation, which manifested itself in his success in mounting the annual Manchester Martyrs' parades[40] and in establishing separate committees to fund a monument to Parnell in Dublin[41] and a memorial to James Stephens.[42] He saw the campaign to buy Irish as a task for the civilian Kilkenny Industrial Development Association, not for the corporation. He and others played a prominent part in putting out fires in the city, a duty that should strictly have been the preserve of the authorities. The teaching of Irish was spearheaded by the Gaelic League and, at its behest, was introduced to schools. In a different society, such educational initiatives would have been led by elected politicians and implemented by a civil service.

All this went to highlight the failure, in the eyes of many nationalists, of both the local authorities and the Dublin Castle administration to govern the country. The gap was being filled by people like Peter and the more that IRB members filled it, the more they saw Dublin Castle – which was the representative of the British government – as unaccountable, useless, uninterested in the day-to-day governance of Ireland and, above all, ripe for eradication. It was only a matter of time before this local self-sufficiency developed into a drive for national self-sufficiency.

3

Flames Shoot, 1909–14

Thomas Furlong was sworn into the IRB by Seán T. Ó Ceallaigh and moved from Wexford to Kilkenny in 1909.[1] At the behest of Seán MacDermott, he contacted Peter DeLoughry with a view to re-invigorating the IRB there.[2] Peter called a meeting and was elected as head centre.[3] In June 1910 the Kilkenny RIC reported to Dublin Castle that the Sinn Féin branches in Kilkenny city and Thomastown had collapsed.[4] The local IRB was similarly dormant, so Peter set to work.

Another side of Peter's personality emerged at this time. His attitude to religion showed that he had been more influenced by his father than the protestations of Bishop Brownrigg – he did not share the bishop's antagonism towards those of other faiths. Indeed, he was animated more by religious intolerance than by other issues. His position was clearly demonstrated when he became a member of the organising committee charged with the establishment of the Carnegie free library in Kilkenny, a facility brought into being by the generosity of Ellen, Countess of Desart. During a discussion on the make-up of a committee to decide on the books that would furnish the library, Peter took exception to the number of Catholic priests on it: 'In my opinion, the representation of clergymen should be equally divided between Catholic and Protestant.

If Canon Doyle's proposition is passed, you will have three Catholic clergymen and only one Protestant. That wouldn't be a fair proportion.'[5]

The opening of the library was a grand affair attended by the great and good of the city, although Bishop Brownrigg and Canon Doyle both sent letters of apology that they would be unable to attend.[6] A month later, Kilkenny Corporation awarded Ellen, Countess of Desart, the freedom of the city. During her acceptance speech, she described her elation at being the first woman to have been given such an honour in Ireland and at being, she believed, the first Jewess to receive the freedom of a city anywhere in the world.[7]

In early January 1911, Peter's decision to seek public office was announced in local newspaper advertisements. Describing himself as a working man, he pledged that he would strive towards making Kilkenny a centre of industrial importance and that he would support campaigns for proper housing, fair rents and the proper maintenance of streets and public property. His announcement referred to his coming from a Kilkenny family that had been honourably connected with the city for a century. He already had a solid base of support among IRB members, the Gaelic League and the GAA, and was known for his community service in helping to deal with fires.[8] His election in January for St John's Ward marked the beginning of a career in public office that continued unbroken until his death.[9] He secured a seat on the municipal fire brigade committee and was among thirteen Kilkenny Corporation members who elected the incoming mayor, Thomas Cantwell.[10]

One of those who attended the mayoral banquet was E. T. Keane, in his capacity as editor of the *Kilkenny People*. Keane later wrote that Peter's favourite song was the *Boys of*

Kilkenny and that 'he could give points to the best American city "booster" and beat him'.[11] At the banquet several guests, including Peter, 'sang their favourite numbers in the very best style, and to the intense pleasure of the company'.[12] Indeed, singing had led Peter to join St Patrick's church choir some time earlier, where he met his future wife, Winifred (Win) Murphy. They married on 25 April 1911, becoming not only a devoted couple, but a partnership focused on the campaign for Irish independence.

Win was born in the Kilkenny workhouse on 5 May 1888 to Thomas Murphy, master of the workhouse, and Ellen (*née* Kelly), its schoolmistress.[13] Growing up in the master's house, Win witnessed, more than most, the misery and desolation to which the human character is capable of descending.

The family itself was not immune from tragedy or bad luck. Thomas Murphy's first wife had died. Shortly after his second marriage in 1883,[14] he attempted to secure a better job as master of the workhouse run by the North Dublin Union Board of Guardians. However, despite having nine years' experience and receiving the greatest number of votes from the interview board, he was passed over in favour of James Jenkinson, an ex-petty officer of the Royal Navy who had no experience of running a workhouse but whose contacts were better. The issue was raised by Justin McCarthy MP in the House of Commons, who asked the chief secretary, Sir George Trevelyan, to urge the Local Government Board to intervene. The response was that the board had power only to sanction appointments, not to make them.[15]

During an outbreak of rabies in Kilkenny, Murphy experienced once again the failings of authority. (It is likely that this particular episode coloured Win's viewpoint in later life, where she showed a remarkable willingness to support Peter when he confronted authority.) An infected dog bit three children and an adult in June 1891. All four went to Paris to be treated at the Pasteur Institute.[16] As he accompanied one of the young patients, Mary Mulrooney from Goosehill in Kilkenny, to Pasteur's clinic, Murphy's employers, the Kilkenny Board of Guardians, squabbled over the cost and whose responsibility it was. While the child was being treated, the Kilkenny Board of Guardians complained that the infected dog had made its way in from Castlecomer and that the board of that town should bear the costs. One member fumed that the mad dog had a right to stay where it was from.[17]

Thomas and Ellen did their best to make the lives of their charges as pleasant as possible. Shortly after their marriage they instituted a Christmas party for the workhouse children.[18] Yet behind this happy scene lay an unhappy string of events for the Murphy family. Of the couple's six children only Win, John and Thomas Francis survived. Two of Win's brothers died before she was born and when she was five years old her three-year-old brother, Laurence, died.[19] In January 1900, when she was twelve years old, her father took ill and died shortly afterwards. Ten days later her mother died.[20] The children were sent to live with relatives; Win and her brother Thomas lodged with Patrick and Jane Lalor on the Ormonde Road in Kilkenny. Their arrival swelled the number of occupants of the house to nine. In her teens, Win became an apprentice shop-assistant in the Monster House[21] and later sang in the St Patrick's church choir in the evenings where she met and fell in love with Peter.

The couple's first child was born in 1912 and christened Richard after Peter's father.[22] His birth brought a petite woman into the family, to whom this book is co-dedicated, and who remained with them for more than half a century. Her name was Mary Bridget Quinn, but to anyone in the DeLoughry family she was known as Nanny. She and Win were devout Catholics and daily communicants. They intoned the Angelus and the Rosary every day. Nanny wore a snow-white blouse, buttoned to the top – not a crease in sight – ankle-length black skirt, small-sized boots and, on journeys out, a black cloche hat held in place by a pin. She smelt of soap. As more and more children arrived she took over the duties of bathing, scrubbing, shoe-polishing and playmate. On trips to the cinema, her charges were distracted from the genius of Chaplin, Lloyd and Keaton by Nanny's uncontrolled laughter that turned to tears and made her sway back and forth. In the evenings after the Rosary, Nanny took herself down from the kitchen to the closed shop where the smell of paraffin pervaded the air. She sat on a chair with a prayer book, put on her rimmed spectacles and read, after pulling the window-shutter ajar to glance out at the bustle or the quiet of Parliament Street. She could not be seen by passers-by, but those who knew her habits waved at the window. Nanny, still hidden from the street, would wave back.[23]

Win quickly established close friendships with David and Larry (who continued to lodge in the family home and who were, by this time, immersed in the theatre),[24] and her sister-in-law, Lil, and Lil's husband, Henry Mangan, during their occasional visits from Dublin. Peter and Win had similar life histories, with tragedy always lurking around the corner. Their marriage gave Win a view into another world where she came into contact with important figures visiting Kilkenny, including The O'Rahilly,[25] Dr Hyde[26] and journalist and leading member of the Irish Volunteers, Bulmer Hobson.[27]

The couple's second child, Thomas Francis, was born on 13 November 1913. Their joy at the birth was quickly turned to sorrow two days later, following the arrival of a telegram from the United States announcing the death of Peter's brother Francis in a road accident in New York.[28]

The dramatic productions in Kilkenny involving David and Larry give an insight into Peter's capacity to raise funds for political causes. The proceeds from stagings of *Robert Emmet* and *The West's Awake* went towards the James Stephens Memorial Association. As joint honorary secretary of the association with Tom Stallard, Peter organised a convention in Kilkenny that drew large numbers of people from all parts of Ireland. Private subscriptions, fund-raising at GAA tournaments, dramatic entertainments and dividends from shares invested had raised almost £200. The convention heard pledges of support from MPs Matthew Keating and Patrick O'Brien, from the MP John Redmond's daughter, Johanna, who had given her permission for the production of one of her plays in London for the benefit of the association, and from James Glover, conductor of the Drury Lane theatre orchestra in London. Fund-raising for the association stretched as far as New York, where the Kilkennymen's Association set up a committee to collect subscriptions.[29]

However, the main focus of Peter's career remained the establishment of an independent Ireland. When Kilkenny Corporation held a meeting to discuss the Home Rule Bill, members complained that it would lead to the city losing one of its two MPs. Peter adopted a theoretical argument that no English parliament could disenfranchise Kilkenny under the Act of Union. He took issue with attempts to stifle debate on the bill in the national newspapers and in particular with a comment by T. P. O'Connor that anyone who criticised the bill would be guilty of treason. Peter accepted that the bill might be a good one, but then qualified his remark by saying that he did not see where Irish independence would come from if the English parliament was going to control taxes in Ireland.[30]

Peter also turned his attention to the scouting movement, which he saw as a way of harnessing boys into the campaign for Irish independence. He was not alone. The *Kilkenny Journal* also decided to place some of its faith in the future of Ireland in the organisation, a branch of which was established in Kilkenny in 1912. The *Journal* praised the movement for its objectives in moulding Irish boys into manly, clean-living, honest and sober members of the community, but added 'the boy scout movement had, of course, its national side. Members must always remember that they had, above all things, a duty to their country.'[31] Peter played a leading part in the establishment of the Boy Scouts in Kilkenny.[32]

Four months later the Scouts and others attended the annual Manchester Martyrs' commemoration in Kilkenny at which The O'Rahilly was invited to speak. Peter again took a prominent role in this event and it is likely that the decision to have them attend was at least partly his responsibility. The O'Rahilly delivered a lengthy address in which he recounted the fate of the martyrs, IRB members William Philip Allen, Michael Larkin and Michael O'Brien, who were executed in 1867 for the murder of a police officer in Manchester, England. However, he also told his audience that there was one lesson to be learned from the episode: the most powerful of all human agencies was the man with a gun in his hand.[33] The following year the address was given by Bulmer Hobson, who asked his audience if they knew of a single prosperous nation that was not armed and that was not prepared to enforce its wishes by force of arms. He spoke of Kilkenny city being full of ruined mills and suggested that if the Irish people armed Volunteer companies they would show that they meant business.[34]

Peter's aptitude for business management did not go unnoticed by his colleagues in Kilkenny Corporation, who elected him to its Finance and Leases Committee.[35] At a meeting of the municipal authority Peter used an aerial display in Kilkenny by the pilot Richard Corbett Wilson to underline the importance of promoting local industry and to take a swipe at what he saw as the blinkered economic policy of Dublin Castle:

> Having regard to the fact of the very important part the aeroplane would play in the future, [Mr DeLoughry] thought they should hail Mr Wilson's feat with delight, because they should try and encourage aviation in Ireland ... Mr DeLoughry said Ireland lost a good deal by not taking up the motor car business more enthusiastically. In Ireland, they were manufacturing nothing in that line whilst other countries were reaping immense benefits from an important industry by being more alert than they were and he hoped it would not be the same with the manufacture of aeroplanes, and that the Irish people would make themselves acquainted with the science of flying.[36]

Peter's contributions at meetings of the local authority in his early political career bear out a later description of him by E. T. Keane that he was a 'plain blunt man – blunt to the point of brusqueness' and that those who did not know him well viewed him as a 'dangerous intransigent'. According to Keane, Peter was 'either up or down, never just half-way between'.[37]

The two regularly disagreed at meetings of the local authority to which Keane had also been elected. During a row over reports that the corporation was taking legal action against an individual for allegedly selling horses without a permit, Keane asked Peter if he was the only 'Simon Pure' in the room to which the retort was: 'I suppose you are the only Lord chief high dictator.'[38] Two months later they rowed over the rates for water meters:

> Mr Keane – It is most unjust to have meters on poor traders whilst those well able to afford it are not asked to pay.
>
> Mr DeLoughry – That is wrong. He pays according to the valuation of his house.
>
> Mr Keane – But he does not pay by meter.
>
> Mr DeLoughry – He would not be paying as much.
>
> Mr Keane – My point is clear. There is no use jumping on me.
>
> Mr DeLoughry – I am not jumping. You do all the jumping here.
>
> Mr Keane – I do not.
>
> Mr DeLoughry – You jump more than anybody here. You are like a Jack-in-the-box. Nobody can say anything but you I suppose.[39]

Peter's failings were also exposed through issues that arose at these meetings. While he showed foresight in identifying the opportunities Ireland should grasp in establishing automobile and aviation industries, he displayed a distinct lack of vision when it came to tourism: 'Mr DeLoughry said he did not like to see tourists coming to Ireland at all because they were only making beggars of the Irish children. Down in Killarney and Cashel, he said, visitors were always followed by children begging pennies.'[40]

On another occasion the corporation was invited to enter examples of Irish industry to a trade exhibition in Turin to promote their wares. When the matter came before Kilkenny Corporation, Peter objected to any involvement because the exhibits would be categorised under the British section. He argued that the invitation was 'only to try and get us under the Union Jack'.[41]

Peter's obduracy was apparent during another discussion at the corporation on a movement set up in Limerick aimed at preventing the sale of immoral literature, particularly English Sunday newspapers. The movement rejoiced in the name 'Campaign Against Immoral Literary Garbage'. Peter declined to join the committee because some of its other members had refused to buy publications that supported Irish nationalism.[42]

However, his most glaring error as a nationalist came in 1913 at the start of the Dublin Lock-out, when some 20,000 workers were fighting for the right to unionise against around 300 employers, chief among them being William Martin Murphy, chairman of the Dublin United Tramway Company. Peter had earlier described Murphy as a 'good financier',[43] and urged fellow corporation members to have nothing to do with the dispute, saying that if the corporation could be convinced that Jim Larkin was in sympathy with the Irish working man, they would support him but that he, for one, did not believe it.[44] He failed to see the importance of the Labour movement in the fight for Irish independence.

The inflexibility of Peters' nature was also apparent in the way he used every opportunity to attack the RIC. When the corporation was asked to support a motion calling for an inquiry into the pay and conditions of the RIC, he suggested any decision should be deferred:

> Mr DeLoughry – We will postpone that until we see the Home
>   Rule Bill – until we see will we have control over them. None
>   of us knew they were badly paid before. I propose that it be
>   marked 'read'.
>
> Mr Tom Stallard seconded.
>
> Mr Magennis – I think it would be no harm to adopt it. It would
>   be nothing out of our pockets.
>
> Mr Stallard – There will be no police after a few years.
>
> Mr DeLoughry – We won't want them when we get home rule.
>
> Ald. Michael L. Potter – That is the time we will want them.
>
> Mr DeLoughry – That is the English version – that we will eat
>   each other when we get home rule.[45]

Peter showed his animosity towards the police more emphatically during a local authority meeting where he objected to RIC officers making private use of telephones at the fire station. He proposed that the council instruct the fire chief to turn off the telephones at night, adding that 'surely there was enough of money spent on the police in this country without giving them telephones *gratis*'.[46] There followed a series of exchanges illustrating his determination and stubbornness:

> Mr E. Kenna – I hold that until the previous resolution is
>   rescinded the motion is out of order.
>
> Mr DeLoughry – It comes well from a member of the Gaelic
>   League, to stand up and ask that telephones be given to police
>   and soldiers.
>
> Ald. M. Potter – I feel bound as Chairman to put this matter
>   clearly before the Corporation … As for the private use, the
>   police force is established for the public good.
>
> Ald. Purcell – I beg to differ with you.

Mr DeLoughry – So are the military – for chasing nuns …

Ald. Potter – Any time the police use the telephone it is not for private use; but for the public good. I don't suppose they would use it except in case of necessity. They would have no other use for it.

Mr DeLoughry – I disagree altogether. The police in this country are the garrison of the country and I hold that we should not assist them at all.

Ald. Potter – I am sorry I cannot agree with you.

Mr DeLoughry – I don't care whether you do or not. There is enough of them in it to do all their messages without having the use of a telephone … The country has nothing to do with them.

Ald. Potter – Our property would not be safe in the country only for the police.

Mr DeLoughry – We are a dangerous lot of robbers …

Ald. Potter – It is hardly fair to say the police use the telephone for private use. The police are the servants of the public.

Mr DeLoughry – They are not the servants of the public. They are masters of the public. How are they the servants of the public? …

Mr Kerwick said he did not think they would find the charges well founded.

Mr DeLoughry – We all know the way you will vote. I don't mind you.[47]

Peter applied the same scrutiny to the family enterprise. Larry became 'cycle agent' for the business. Advertisements were placed in national newspapers.[48] In the local press, the firm's longevity was played up. During the First World War, notices from DeLoughry's foundry reminded farmers of their duty to economise and 'keep their money at home by buying Kilkenny made plough parts'.[49]

In 1914 Peter had another confrontation with the RIC at a stormy meeting of members of the suffragette movement in the Tholsel that was reported in the *Kilkenny People*. A large crowd turned up 'eager to see a suffragette in the flesh'.[50] RIC constables were stationed in each corner of the room. When Dr Mary Strangman of Waterford attempted to open proceedings, there were loud cheers and shouting. The noise showed no signs of abating. Dr Strangman used the leg of a chair to beat the table and call for order, but without success. E. T. Keane and the RIC Head Constable Frizelle once more failed to quieten the crowd. Several bangers were let off. Head Constable Frizelle mounted a chair and warned that anyone could be arrested if there were any more interruptions. At this point, Peter, who was standing at the back of the hall, addressed the RIC officer:

> 'You are not going to do any good for the cause.' At this remark there was loud applause and it was re-echoed when Mr E. Kenna, T. C. remarked in a loud voice, 'I think any man is entitled to speak here. It is a public meeting.'
>
> At the conclusion of the cheering which the latter remark provoked, the Chairman [Dr Strangman] intervened and said, 'If any of you want to speak, you will have full permission, and you can also ask questions if you wish. Give [us] a fair hearing and then you can do what you wish.'
>
> Mr DeLoughry then told the Chairman, 'Police at public meetings in Ireland have never been favourable or popular, and if you are responsible for the presence of the police here to protect you I may tell you that there is no necessity for it.'
>
> Chairman (Dr. Mary Strangman) – Give us fair play.
> Mr DeLoughry – You would have got fair play without police protection (cheers).

Chairman (Dr. Mary Strangman) – If you would keep order yourselves, the police would leave you alone.

Mr DeLoughry – There is no disorder here, my lady.

The cheering and loud talk continued, and the chairman remarked 'I am absolutely ashamed of you.'

Mr DeLoughry – You must not know Ireland.

Chairman – Why don't you let us go on?

Mr DeLoughry – Everyone is in sympathy with you, but they are against the police coming in and interfering with a public meeting (cheers).

Head Constable Frizelle still stood on the chair and surveyed the scene with the utmost calm. When Councillor DeLoughry had concluded his last remark, the head constable said: 'I did not interfere until I saw the crush. It was as much in your interest as in mine. I am not a man to interfere with the public.'

Mr DeLoughry – You seemingly are. I am very much in favour of the arguments put forward by the ladies but I am against the police interfering.

Head Constable Frizelle – There are ladies here who are being crushed.

Mr DeLoughry – If you were trying to keep back the crowd it would be better.

Chairman – Before the police interfered at all or even uttered a word, several people as you saw yourself left the room as they were afraid.

Mr DeLoughry – It is some young kids at the back who are kicking up disorder. If the police went to the back and put those out you would have good order. (Cheers). There is no use in trying to intimidate people. (Loud cheers).[51]

The Kilkenny Corporation was divided into two factions. One included Peter, James Nowlan and Tom Stallard who were IRB, the others were supporters of the Irish Party and included Joseph Purcell and John Magennis, with E. T. Keane somewhere in the middle, but more inclined towards the Irish Party. On local issues, the dividing line between the two camps could disappear. However, the marker was clearly laid down during the mayoral elections. Peter rarely missed an opportunity to have a go at the Irish Party or to scoff at the measures contained in the third Home Rule Bill which was introduced in the British parliament on 11 April 1912. This widened the divide and exploded in a storm of anger at the meeting to elect a new mayor in January 1914.

Peter went forward for election, but was defeated by John Magennis, as reported in the *Kilkenny People*. Both contestants gave courteous speeches complimenting each other on their campaigns. However, a speech by the outgoing mayor, Alderman Joseph Purcell, changed the tone of the proceedings. He said it gave him great pleasure to declare Magennis elected because he would 'break up the ring that is trying to run Kilkenny (applause). You see them night and day; you could not walk the streets of Kilkenny but you would find those men in corners and alleys plotting to get a certain man in, and they sat on that man there, Mr [R. H.] Smithwick.'[52]

In his speech, Peter said he had put his name forward not as a member of any party or clique. Alderman Purcell then accused Peter of 'dodgery and trickery'. During the exchanges that followed, Peter and James Nowlan accused Alderman Purcell of attempting to rig the vote, additionally claiming that he had wanted to be re-elected as mayor but then found out that Peter had more support. They also said that Purcell had called to Smithwick's house earlier that week to pledge support for him to keep Peter from becoming mayor. When Smithwick refused to do this, they claimed, Purcell got Magennis to stand instead. Purcell denied all this vehemently and called on Smithwick to make a statement:

> There was now a lull of expectation, and as Mr Smithwick rose to speak there was absolute quietness. He asked, 'May I speak' and Ald. Purcell answered, 'You may.'
>
> Mr Smithwick then said: 'Ald. Purcell came to me and said he would give me his vote and the votes of his supporters.'
>
> Loud and continued applause greeted Mr Smithwick's statement and above the noise could be heard the exclamation, 'Now we know who are the dodgers!'
>
> Several of the members now stood up to leave the meeting and Mr DeLoughry remarked, 'Now that shows who is the dodger!'

> Ald. Nowlan – Yes that shows the dodgers and tricksters.
> Ald. Purcell – Where did I do this?
> Mr Smithwick – In my own house.

> Practically all Mr DeLoughry's supporters had now left their seats and were moving towards the door. The mayor loudly appealed for order, but it was useless and Ald. Cantwell made an attempt to speak. Ald. Purcell interrupted and, pointing to the members leaving the room, shouted, 'Now look at the ring they have there – look at the ringleaders now!'

Mr DeLoughry – You can shout to the gallery as long as you like; you are well shown up now anyway. The public now know who is the trickster and the dodger.

Ald. Cantwell, having succeeded in gaining a hearing, said: 'The ringleading is much the same as always. (To Ald. Purcell) We have borne with you a long time, but we won't bear with you any longer.'[53]

4

Fire Spreads, 1914–16

The formation of Irish Volunteer companies from late 1913 followed the setting up by Sir Edward Carson of the Ulster Volunteers, whose opposition to the Home Rule Bill was as vocal as it was armed. Charles Townshend observes that the Ulster Volunteer Force 'was the decisive spur to the militarisation of nationalist politics'.[1]

Sir Roger Casement and Thomas MacDonagh spoke at the Irish Volunteers' launch meeting in Kilkenny on 5 March 1914. Peter attended this rally and enlisted. Sir Roger told an enthusiastic crowd that 'no nation could ever win its freedom without fighting for it. They could not pay the price without making a sacrifice and they would have to make that sacrifice before they could ever realise what it was'.[2] More than 200 men enlisted.

It was decided that the Market Square and sheds were to be used as the Volunteers' drilling station. Thomas Connolly of Michael Street, Kilkenny, a former sergeant of the Kilkenny militia, was the drill instructor. Drills, without arms, took place three nights a week. The local RIC recorded that the Irish Volunteers drew people from the labouring classes, but that 'the merchants and more respectable classes have held aloof from the movement'.[3]

Reports that Ulster was to be excluded from an independent

Ireland in the Home Rule Bill sent many nationalists into a frenzy. According to a report in the *Kilkenny People*, Peter told a meeting of Kilkenny Corporation that Irish people were being called on to make too great a sacrifice and that it would be 'a miserable thing if we were to part with 300,000 of the best nationalists in Ireland'. Again, turning to folklore, he described Ulster as the 'trysting place of the Red Branch Knights and of mighty Finn and his companions. Surely, we are not going to part with the counties that hold memories of Cave Hill, Wolfe Tone and that was [*sic*] the birthplace and nursery of the ninety-eight movement'. Peter continued to mix folk memory with present-day political argument:

> I think if this is to be the fruition of all our work and if the ideal of every Irish patriot from Brian Ború to Thomas Davis is to perish now simply to please English political parties, it is a monstrous thing. I think we should give the Orangemen every guarantee of fair play, but at the same time we should hold our country whole and entire; we should not part with a single sod of it. I think Mr Redmond should assert himself more.

Once more, the meeting descended into an argument between those who supported Sinn Féin and those who supported the Irish Party and the United Irish League. During one exchange, Councillor Kenna criticised leading Sinn Féin figures. Peter retorted that not very long ago Kenna had been a great admirer of the Sinn Féin party:

> Mr Kenna – Certainly, and I am so today. I say there are still honest men in the Sinn Féin party.
> Mr DeLoughry – That is a wonder, when you are left it.[4]

Peter's language was as sharp, if not sharper, when he delivered a speech at a Volunteer rally held at Limetree, Cuffesgrange, two months later:

> We are all brothers in this great movement. We would die for each other. We are linked together with bonds stronger than steel (hear, hear). We are all, as I say, in one common cause, and ready to shed our blood (hear, hear).[5]

In between speech-making and political arguments, he was busy helping to establish Volunteer corps in the county areas. Courses in first-aid were held in Rothe House.[6] Bandoliers and haversacks were acquired for recruits.[7] Shooting ranges were set up at the Long Wood on the Lower Dunmore Road and at the Volunteer Hall in Kieran Street. Tom Treacy, captain of the 'A' Company Volunteers, said drilling was held with clock-work regularity. In addition, Irish classes were organised, lectures on military and historical subjects were given, and discussions and criticisms on each manoeuvre and operation were held.[8] British intelligence reports estimated that there were 2,000 Volunteers in the county by June 1914.[9]

As honorary treasurer of the Kilkenny Volunteers, Peter set up a subscription to an equipment fund that was primarily used for the purchase of arms.[10] Some of the guns were bought directly from The O'Rahilly. Patrick O'Brien, MP, presented the Kilkenny Volunteers with 100 rifles. The recruits were bemused by some of the guns and nicknamed the Martini Henry rifles they had been given as 'gas pipes' because of their length. James J. Comerford spoke about the arms he had seen in the possession of the Kilkenny Volunteers:

Among them they had a few of the European rifles landed on 26 July 1914 at Howth, County Dublin from Erskine Childers' yacht named the *Asgard* and a few rifles which were landed at Kilcoole, County Wicklow on 1 August 1914. These rifles were landed from [mainland] Europe by a 'gun running event' and were taken possession of by Dublin Irish Volunteers. Peter DeLoughry got some of them for his Kilkenny men.[11]

The outbreak of the First World War in July 1914 resulted in the enactment of the third Home Rule Bill being delayed. John Redmond then had to decide whether or not to encourage Irish people to enlist in the British army. He announced his decision in Woodenbridge in County Wicklow on 20 September 1914, when he called on the Volunteers to join up. This split the movement into those who supported Redmond (the National Volunteers) and those who did not (the Irish Volunteers, led by Professor Eoin MacNeill). The split in Kilkenny was indicative of the rupture in the movement throughout Ireland. Tom Treacy gives this account of a meeting held in early September 1914 in the Market Yard, Kilkenny, which was attended by all the city companies:

There were about 650, counting officers, NCOs and men on parade on that occasion. All assembled were addressed by Rev. J. Rowe, St Mary's, James' Street, Kilkenny, and Rev. Philip Moore, St John's, Kilkenny, the trend of whose addresses favoured the policy of the Redmondites and the Ancient Order of the Hibernians. They were very vigorously replied to and opposed by Peter DeLoughry, Pat Corcoran and Ned Comerford on behalf of the Irish-Ireland side (otherwise Sinn Féin and IRB). After numerous very hot exchanges by the speakers referred to and the parade moving towards a riotous state, Peter DeLoughry called on all those who stood for Ireland and the green flag to fall out and line up at a point indicated by him, near the poultry sheds in the Market place; and all those who stood for England and the Union Jack to stand where they were. Twenty-eight men left the ranks and lined up at the point indicated for those who stood for Ireland and the green flag: and the balance on parade (over 600) stood on the Redmondite side. I was put in charge of the twenty-eight men who stood for Ireland on that occasion and I formed them into company formation and marched them out of the market amidst a most hostile demonstration. Tempers on both sides were very frayed and a feather could have turned it into a riot. I marched the twenty-eight to what was then known as the Banba Hall (formerly Kyteler's Inn, Kieran Street,[12] which was, at the time, occupied by Fianna Éireann).[13] This hall was from that time onwards the Volunteer Hall and was the headquarters of the only company of Irish Volunteers in the city of Kilkenny up to 1916.[14]

The Irish Volunteers were in a minority. Indeed, a month later an estimated 5,000 people turned out to welcome John Redmond to Kilkenny, where he was given the freedom of the city. Yet the RIC county inspector, Pierce C. Power, wrote of his fear that a large majority of eligible young men were not inclined to enlist in the British army and that 'I have no doubt that this spirit is to some extent fortified by the subtle influence which is being exercised by the Sinn Féin party.'[15] Over the next two years, Power issued reports to his superiors on the Irish Volunteers. He described them as 'a small clique in the city [which is] discountenanced by every person of any influence or standing'.[16] He said they were looked upon with contempt by respectable citizens and, in another report, deemed them to be a rabble.[17] In a communication in August 1915, Power reported that the branch of the Irish Volunteers still existed, but that 'its few members are confined to the very lower orders who are without influence and are generally regarded as "cranks"'.[18]

The RIC reports are indicative of the sharp focus the force kept on both Volunteer groups. The comings and goings of drilling officers occupied a large portion of its time. J.J. 'Ginger' O'Connell, a prominent member of MacNeill's Volunteer staff, was deployed to Kilkenny, arriving on 25 September 1915. Power issued a report that O'Connell 'appears to have got a few sympathisers at Clomanto, Paulstown, etc., but these are people of a very ignorant class and have no influence'.[19]

O'Connell organised a training camp for local Volunteers at Galbally in County Limerick and Larry DeLoughry took part in this week-long exercise.[20] Indeed Larry and Peter's activities are likely to have prompted the British authorities' decision to remove their brother David from the war signal station at Carnsore Point, County Wexford, in September 1914, and to return him to ordinary duties at Kilkenny post office.[21]

The fear that the British government might impose conscription in Ireland changed attitudes to the Volunteer movement. Fr P. H. Delahunty, who had opposed Peter during the split in the movement, changed course completely when he addressed his parishioners in Callan in November 1915. County Inspector Power said the cleric 'delivered a rather violent speech, mainly antagonistic, to recruiting and conscription which, he said, would be resisted by armed force'.[22] The threat of conscription boosted support for the Irish Volunteers, but they remained a much smaller force than the National Volunteers.

The militarisation of nationalism led to an improvement in intelligence gathering. Thomas Furlong, a member of 'B' Company, Irish Volunteers, Kilkenny, told of how he stole a document from Kilkenny military barracks while he was decorating the officers' quarters. The operation also involved Peter, Pat Corcoran, Seán MacDermott, Liam Mellows and 'Ginger' O'Connell:

> The documents included a secret code with instructions on how to use it, and the key for deciphering it. O'Connell told me it was the most important thing they had got and that they had been trying to get it for a long time. I heard later that Volunteer headquarters used the key and, by means of it, learned of the orders which had been issued for the arrest of Mellows.[23]

The young men of Kilkenny had reached a point where they were formed into an army, where they were angered by the substance and path of the third Home Rule Bill, and where the looming menace of conscription needled their Irishness. They had in their minds the stories of the Red Branch Knights, of Fionn MacCumhaill and of more recent heroes such as Wolfe Tone and O'Donovan Rossa. This mythological motor was driving towards a revolution against all the king's men.

5

Kilkenny, 1916

In March 1916 Peter embarked on confrontations with two institutions. The first was a row with the Catholic Church authorities in Kilkenny, the second was his involvement in the Rising of 1916 through which Irish Republicans aimed to end British rule in Ireland.

In 1914 Peter, with Tom Stallard's father, George, had set up the Kilkenny Cinema Company in Parliament Street.[1] Two years later a dispute with the Catholic Church arose over this establishment. Catholic priests at masses in Kilkenny condemned the showing of films on Sundays, a move that was endorsed by Bishop Brownrigg:

[The priests] made it quite clear that, apart from the Sunday shows, there was no other ground of objection to the cinema, the pictures presented in which appear to have been carefully supervised. At the same time, parents were requested not to permit the frequent attendance of their children at the pictures, as, although unobjectionable to adults, they were not calculated to exercise a healthy influence on youthful minds. Attention was also drawn to the fact that in Wexford – where the bishop of Ferns and the Corporation had taken action – the two cinemas in that town had agreed to close down on Sundays during Lent.

It has been stated that in Clonmel and Waterford there are no Sunday openings during any part of the year.

The Kilkenny cinema was open last Sunday night as usual.[2]

Peter's involvement in the 1916 Rising was more complex and dangerous. In Kilkenny, one of the first indications of a planned military action came on 23 November 1915 after the annual Manchester Martyrs' parade. The oration was given in the Gaelic League rooms of Rothe House by Thomas MacDonagh. James Lalor, later vice-commandant, Kilkenny Brigade, IRA, said that after the commemoration MacDonagh informed him that a rising would take place shortly, but that a date had not yet been fixed. Lalor said MacDonagh told him that 'it would be soon and some of us must go down in it'.[3]

In Kilkenny 1916 began with a mayoral election. The incumbent, John Magennis, was a strong supporter of the Irish Party, and had taken part in a recruiting conference at Waterford attended by John Redmond and the Lord Lieutenant, Lord Wimbourne. He had risen to the rank of colonel with the Irish Volunteers and, after the split, sided with the National Volunteers (Redmondites). He was re-elected unopposed and, without naming Peter, who had decided at the last minute not to enter the contest, thanked him for his 'honourable, fair and square fight', referring to their debates up to the point where Peter had decided not to stand for election.[4]

In February the Irish Volunteers were given a boost by the arrival of Lieutenant Edward O'Kelly from Volunteer headquarters in Dublin, whose organisational skills were used to strengthen the city and county corps.[5] By this time, Larry DeLoughry, who had completed a military training course at Galbally, County Limerick, was Section No. II commander of the 'A' Company (Kilkenny city), a position that put him in charge of his older brother Peter, Tom Stallard and twenty-three others.[6] The local RIC head constable, George Frizelle, noted in mid-February, that Larry had left a dance held at the Desart Hall because a young British officer was present in uniform.[7] The DeLoughry business on Parliament Street became the unofficial 'post-office' for messages from Dublin and the focal point for revolutionaries stopping in or travelling through Kilkenny. Joseph Plunkett stayed in the house and became very friendly with the DeLoughrys, as did J.J. 'Ginger' O'Connell.[8] The frequency of visits and messages increased in April 1916 as Tom Treacy recounted:

> About a fortnight before Easter, 1916, Pat Corcoran (a member of the controlling committee of the Irish Volunteers) called me out from the Irish Volunteer Hall, saying someone wanted to see me outside in [Kieran Street]. On arriving outside, he introduced me to Cathal Brugha. I was not personally acquainted with him previous to this, but I knew him by sight as a commercial traveller coming to Kilkenny.[9] Pat Corcoran told me that Cathal Brugha had something very secret and important to tell me as Captain of 'A' company, and then Cathal Brugha told me that the Rising was coming off at Easter, and the instructions he gave me were:
>
> (a) General manoeuvres were to be arranged for Easter Sunday.
> (b) When my company paraded for the manoeuvres referred to in (a) with whatever arms and equipment we possessed it was to proceed by way of Borris, County Carlow, to the Scallop Gap on the Wexford border, where we would link up with Wexford.
> (c) No operations were to be commenced until we linked up with Wexford.

(d) Captain J. J. 'Ginger' O'Connell from GHQ would be in command of all units in the city and county and all orders for the carrying out of operations and tasks were to be taken from him, and this would hold when we linked up with Wexford at the Scallop Gap.

The above information and instructions had been given by Cathal Brugha to Pat Corcoran and Peter DeLoughry, our contacts with GHQ.

Treacy told Brugha that 'A' Company numbered sixty men, but that there were only arms for twenty-five. Brugha assured Treacy they would be able to collect arms from Dr Edward Dundon of Borris, County Carlow, on Easter Sunday and that a further supply would be available so that the men would be adequately armed.[10]

W. T. Cosgrave, who had thrown himself heart and soul into the Volunteer movement, was briefed about the feelings of the Kilkenny Volunteers:

> Early in Holy Week, a priest from Kilkenny came to see me and told me that the Volunteers there were against an early rebellion as they were without arms or ammunition. He said that they were preparing but needed time and equipment and that an early Rising would be fatal as they were willing to take part but were helpless without munitions.[11]

In a letter to his sister, Dr Josephine Clarke, a Cumann na mBan member, Tom Stallard said that, after Treacy's encounter with Brugha, the Kilkenny Irish Volunteer leaders held a meeting at which it was decided to seek clarification about the orders given. Pat Corcoran and Peter went to Dublin where they met Eoin MacNeill, who said 'the first he knew about it himself was when a few more lads from other parts of the country went to him on the same mission. Anyway they came to an agreement that if MacNeill did not give orders to Kilkenny to rise, Kilkenny would not rise'.[12]

For Kilkenny city and county this meeting was very important as in the week preceding the Rising, three women visited Peter at Parliament Street with letters from nationalist leaders in Dublin. Dr Clarke delivered one from Lieutenant O'Kelly, the contents of which were never made known to her. However, the details of the orders given in the other two despatches are known and came from opposing camps in Dublin between those wanting or planning a rising (including Thomas MacDonagh, Pádraig Pearse, Seán MacDermott and Thomas Clarke) and those either reluctant to stage what in their minds would be an unprovoked military assault, or who required sufficient evidence that such an operation would be successful. MacNeill and Bulmer Hobson were in the latter camp. This tension resulted in some of those who were zealous for action attempting to fool the MacNeill camp.

One of the more concrete measures they adopted was the circulation of what became known as the Castle Document, which purported to show that the British military was on the verge of arresting Sinn Féin leaders, to bring MacNeill and like-minded people over to the side of those who wanted to take immediate military action against the British forces in Ireland. (Historians are divided on whether or not the document was a forgery.)

Bulmer Hobson sent the Castle Document to Irish Volunteer leaders before Easter Week 1916, at the behest of

MacNeill, who believed the document was legitimate. Hobson's wife, Claire, delivered it to Peter on the Wednesday before the Rising. In her statement, she describes Peter as reserved, an observation that is consistent with other accounts of him:

> Bulmer gave me the envelope and told me the document was in it … I am not sure now what train I caught [from Dublin] but judging from the fact that I went to the station from the office it was probably either late in the morning or early in the afternoon … I must have gone to DeLoughry's place of business and I gave him the envelope. He did not tell me what was in the letter. I conveyed to him that I knew about the document and we started to talk about the dangerous times. I never knew whether there was a letter with the document or not, but I have no recollection of typing one.
>
> I think I met DeLoughry before that. My impression of him was that he was a reasonable, controlled type of man. If he said anything of importance, it has certainly not stuck in my mind. He gave me the impression that he assented to whatever was suggested. He gave me no reply either verbal or written to bring back. He said something like, 'That will be all right, I will see to things' or words to that effect.[13]

Peter indicated that he would make contingency plans to deal with a possible round-up of suspects as outlined in the Castle Document.

The next message was delivered to him by Kitty O'Doherty, quartermaster, Cumann na mBan, Dublin, who opened the account of her meeting with Peter in her witness statement by recalling a meeting she had with Thomas Clarke at his home in Richmond Place, Dublin. She had been asked to go to Clarke's house by Seán MacDermott. Clarke asked her if she would be willing to travel to Kilkenny the following morning (Holy Thursday). When she consented he explained the purpose of her journey:

'Don't say that either Seán [MacDermott] or myself sent you. Say Pearse sent you.' He repeated it ... then he gave me a blue envelope. This was a written message for DeLoughry. I did not see the message. Tom said: 'Tell him that you are to bring the samples. Say you will take the samples.' In the light of after events, I know I was supposed to get hand grenades but I did not know then ... I am not very good at praying but that [Holy Thursday] morning I was praying that I might find the iron foundry without having to ask directions.

I walked from [Kilkenny] station, and, walking along, the first thing I saw was 'iron foundry'. It was a dingy looking place. To whoever was behind the counter, I said: 'I want to see Peter DeLoughry.' He bowed and I said: 'I have just come off the train from Dublin and I have a message for him.' He was immediately antagonistic. He said: 'Who sent you?' I said: 'Pádraig Pearse.' He took the letter which I handed to him and he went to an inner room and he was out again in a minute. No one asked me to sit down. He said: 'Who sent you?' I said: 'Pádraig Pearse.' He said: 'It was not. It was Clarke and MacDermott. I have my instructions and I am going to act on them.' I said: 'I was told to take the samples.' He said: 'I have my instructions, and I am going to act on them.' He was just as short as that.

O'Doherty said that, at the time, she was aware Hobson had sent messages to the provinces asking local Irish Volunteer leaders not to fall in line with arrangements for Sunday. When she returned to Dublin she reported to Thomas Clarke what Peter had said to her:

Tom's eyes lit up. He said: 'Just as I expected.' He used to stare and look right through you with the most extraordinary eyes. You would know he was not thinking about you. He said: 'Just as I expected.' That was Holy Thursday.[14]

The exchanges show that Peter was sure it was Clarke and MacDermott who had sent the despatch and illustrates how well informed he was of the internal wrangling going on at Volunteer headquarters.

The conflicting messages from Dublin signalled the disunity that was to emerge publicly and was formed from opposing military agendas advocated by individuals with a firm or unfirm resolve. Some had a passionate will to set off a conflagration, others were in two minds, still more were firmly against a rising. The complicated web of people struggling for power included the IRB, cabals within the Irish Volunteers and unlabelled groups whose lack of a brand name did not diminish the power they might wield.

In Kilkenny the divisions between the nationalist forces were as muddy. Tom Treacy, for example, let it be plainly known in his witness statement that he was not a member of the IRB and never had been. Tom Stallard and Peter were. Whatever the conflicting agendas between these groups in Kilkenny, they were united when it came to obeying orders and these they took from the chief of staff of the Irish Volunteers, MacNeill, not from anyone else. The Irish Volunteers in Kilkenny decided, in any case, to prepare for a possible call to arms.

On the Tuesday before the Rising, Peter, Éamon Fleming (The Swan, County Laois)[15] and James Lalor collected explosives at Wolfhill colliery and delivered them to Patrick

Ramsbottom, Portlaoise. They understood the explosives were destined for Dublin. Lalor said that it was during this trip he learned from Peter that the Rising was fixed for Easter Sunday. On Good Friday, Peter, Pat Corcoran, Tom Furlong and James Lalor travelled to Skeeter Park, Cleariestown, County Wexford, in Peter's car and collected more gelignite, fuses and detonators from Furlong's brother, an overseer in Wexford County Council. The ordnance was packed in butter boxes and brought back to Kilkenny where it was despatched to Volunteer headquarters in Dublin labelled as 'castings' from De-Loughry's foundry.[16]

The day of the planned Rising, Easter Sunday, arrived. The Kilkenny Irish Volunteers assembled at the Volunteer Hall with arms, twenty-four-hour rations and field-dressings, only to learn that MacNeill had called off the manoeuvres in a notice printed in the *Sunday Independent*.[17] Word reached Kilkenny directly shortly after ten o'clock on Sunday night, when Captain J.J. 'Ginger' O'Connell and Pat Corcoran arrived from Dublin to give the order that 'everything was off'.[18] On Easter Monday, Peter drove Corcoran to Dr Dundon's house in Borris, where they collected arms which they deposited later that day in Tom Stallard's garden at Asylum Lane, Kilkenny. Here they met Tom Treacy, who told them that hostilities had broken out in Dublin but that the situation was confused.[19]

The Volunteers assembled in their hall each night waiting for orders, but nothing came. On 26 April Captain O'Connell sent James Lalor with a despatch to James Leddon in Limerick.[20] Lalor returned by motor-bike with the news that Limerick was 'not out'.[21] The waiting ended on 3 May when the British military, accompanied by the RIC, cordoned off the streets of Kilkenny and began making arrests. Captain O'Connell was apprehended at Peter's house where he had been staying. The following day Peter was arrested and later that evening James Nowlan was taken into custody as he arrived in Kilkenny on the Dublin train. On 5 May twenty-six suspects were apprehended[22] and another four were arrested the following day.[23]

All the prisoners were lodged in Kilkenny jail, where the conditions, according to Tom Treacy, were very rough.[24] James Lalor recalled a visit they received from a local Capuchin friar:

> He appealed to us to arrange to have the arms belonging to the Volunteers handed over to the British forces. The poor man appeared to have been well primed with British propaganda, for he stated that in return for the handing over of the arms, the British authorities had assured him that we would be dealt with leniently. Peter DeLoughry replied on behalf of the prisoners by simply suggesting to the priest that he give us his blessing and let the matter rest at that.[25]

On 9 May the prisoners were marched to the train station:

> On the way ... John Kealy, one of the prisoners, who was ill when he was arrested, had no strength to complete the journey to the station and he collapsed and died in Upper John Street, about thirty yards from his own door. He was at the extreme rear of the line of prisoners and gradually those in front of him – without noticing it – let him tail off, and, when he collapsed, the military closed the gap between him and the prisoners in front, and in that way, the prisoners did not know what happened to him.[26]

John Kealy's brother Martin, who was among them, described what happened when they arrived in Dublin:

> We were marched to Richmond barracks where a large number of prisoners, both from Dublin and various parts of the country, were assembled. Naturally, I missed my brother, but no one from whom I inquired could give me any information about him. At this time we were not permitted any visits or letters, but the other Kilkenny prisoners learned of John's fate from a newspaper which was smuggled in. Out of consideration for me, none of these men told me the sad news, and when, eventually I did get the newspaper, the portion reporting his death had been cut out.

Kealy was deported to England and incarcerated in Wakefield prison. He was released on 7 June 1916:

> On the train journey back, I was accompanied by a number of other released prisoners one of whom, whose name I cannot now recall but who I believed was from the County Wexford, remarked that it was very sad about the prisoner who died on the way to the railway station in Kilkenny. I immediately replied, 'That must have been my brother.' He was nudged by the man sitting next to him and no further conversation on the matter took place.[27]

In the aftermath of the Rising and the arrests in Kilkenny, County Inspector Power was keen to tell his superiors in Dublin Castle of his disdain for the rebels and of the contingency plans he had put in place:

Kilkenny
Confidential report for April 1916
Part I

I beg to report that the general condition of this county is peaceable so far as ordinary crime is concerned … No persons, so far as can be ascertained, took an active part in the recent Rebellion and disgraceful scenes in Dublin or elsewhere but the local Sinn Féiners appeared to be in thorough sympathy with it, and I venture to say, were restrained from overt acts by fear and from the fact that I had made adequate police arrangements to deal forcibly and probably effectively with any hostile movement. During the Rebellion, suspect J. J. O'Connell No. 23, war B list was in the city … he actually stopped as a guest with Peter DeLoughry and was arrested in his house.

There appears to be an undercurrent of sympathy with the prisoners, many of whom were personally popular and some of them were members of the Kilkenny Corporation and other local bodies. So far as public expression of condemnation of the Rebellion has been made, none of the arms and ammunition which undoubtedly were introduced into Kilkenny has been surrendered. The people here are a curious lot and it is impossible to accurately gauge their real opinion. Reticence and a selfish regard for their trade interests are their prevailing characteristics.[28]

In his evidence to the British parliamentary inquiry into events surrounding the Rising, Power said that after Peter's arrest, the RIC found in his house a Lee Enfield .303 rifle and a 'dangerous pattern of an automatic pistol'.[29]

On 12 May most of the prisoners, including Larry, were transferred to jails in England. Peter and Tom Treacy were kept in Richmond before being transferred to Wakefield prison on 2 June. The British authorities suspended Peter's brother David from duty at the post office on 30 April. A report on him, compiled by County Inspector Power, noted that David lived with his brothers, who 'hold the most advanced nationalist views'. Power accepted that David was not a member of the Irish Volunteers 'at least not openly', but observed that during the week of the Rising he 'was seen by police in company with J. J. "Ginger" O'Connell' and with other advanced nationalists. David had subscribed ten shillings towards a fund started by the *Kilkenny People* editor, E. T. Keane, for dependants of prisoners. RIC Head Constable in Kilkenny, George Frizelle, also reported that after the outbreak of the First World War he was informed that David had expressed pro-German views while under the influence of liquor in the Home Rule club. Power gave the view that he did 'not think this man ought to be retained in the government service'.[30] The suspension allowed David to look after Peter's wife and children, and to oversee work at the foundry.

The fund for prisoners mentioned by County Inspector Power collected contributions from, among others, the Dicksboro hurling club; D. W. Bollard, King Street; Rev. M. Kealy, professor, St Kieran's College; Rev. P. Holland, CC, St Canice's; and Peter's old rival on the corporation, Alderman Joseph Purcell.[31]

Another RIC report from the time records how nationalist groups in Kilkenny included many members with no interest in politics previous to the Rising. The same report states that in Kilkenny 'there was practically no sympathy with the rebels in Easter week and this condition of things might have continued were it not for … the execution of the leaders [which] completely changed the feelings of large numbers of people who, before now, looked with disfavour on the Rebellion'.[32]

Across the water the prisoners were experiencing feelings ranging from boredom to worries about how their close relatives on the outside were coping with events. A letter written by Larry, a little over two weeks after he arrived in Wakefield prison, to his sister-in law Win shows how the tedium of the cells was playing on his mind. This produced a stream of consciousness on paper that at times appears child-like. Instead of keeping the best side out, if only for Win's peace of mind, he raised the issue of iron rings bolted in his cell wall and by extension the possibility that he might be tortured:

L. DeLoughry A2/35
Wakefield Detention Brks.
C/o Chief Postal Censor,
London
28/05/16.

Dear Win,

I received your note last night and was not surprised to know that you were annoyed at my not writing but I could not help that.

I assure you I would prefer writing a letter to rubbing dust shovels, basins and lids, counting the bricks in the wall, the bolt heads on door, wondering what the iron rings in each side of cell are for and dare not ask in case they might illustrate on me and I am sure they are not for a pleasant purpose; wondering who was the prisoner that occupied this cell before me and did he think I would come after him. Washing my handkerchief twice a day to see would it dry quicker in morning or evening etc. etc. A prisoner cleaning outside my door the other day accidentally left my shutter up and when I looked out, I saw the Buster scrubbing the opposite door for all he was worth.

Tom wrote from New Ross. I will reply first opportunity. I got a book to read the other day and thinking I'd get another when finished or exchange with some other fellow. I read it in a few hours. Alas! I could not get another for a week, and the idea of exchanging was so preposterous that it stunned the warder. Nothing for it but to read it backwards and parse it and analyse it and am counting the letters now. Then you sometimes ring up your neighbour and get no answer; conclude he is lost with the very interesting occupation of trying [to] tip your ear with your tongue without touching your beard. I can tell you it requires some doing and so is very popular with prisoners.

I am looking forward to Mass today. I suppose you have received my letter by now. We find the time drags very long in cell and you would be surprised the ways we try to occupy the time.

Did I understand that Mr [E. T.] Keane is using his influence on my behalf for all the boys? Convey my very sincere gratitude for his trouble and I will always remember it to him.

In case the influence is being worked for myself, I can assure you I would leave this place with a heavy heart unless all the Kilkenny boys were with me. Anyway, I think Mr O'Brien cannot do much [more] as there are MPs (Irish) visiting prisoners here very often.

Jim Nowlan is here to the good still. We all hope (I don't know why) to be going home next week. Sorry for poor Tom Stallard – he is the only one of the crowd got victimised properly,[33]

Good bye
Best love to all
Lar.[34]

Larry and many of his fellow Kilkenny prisoners were released on 7 June 1916, having been deprived of their liberty for a little over a month. A few days previously Peter arrived in Wakefield, from where he sent the following letter to his sister, Lil. The initial rather formal tone of the letter can partly be explained by his knowledge that the postal censor would be reading it. He talks at length about how guilty he felt at having his sister visit him every day at Richmond barracks. However, later he lets down his guard, forgets that the postal censor will be reading his letter, and becomes the little brother to his big sister, demanding in an uncomfortably direct way that she send sweets to him, adding a forceful argument that he is 'in debt' to other prisoners. Lil is given the sense that she will be letting the family name down if she does not send the treats. For a brief moment, Peter loses sight of the fight for Irish freedom, to become once again the errant younger brother, who is demanding and even cunning, but, most vividly, he shows that he is human and greatly in need of his sister's love:

A 4/9 1224 Peter DeLoughry,
Irish prisoner Wakefield,
c/o Chief Postal Censor,
London

My dear Lil,

I have not yet received any letter from you. I hope you got mine alright. I posted it last Saturday. I had a letter from Win on yesterday. It was the most anxious one I have had from her. I do hope she is not fretting. I wrote to her yesterday. We can now write more than two letters per week provided we find our own stamp.

We are happy and bright here and we intend to keep so. There is nothing to be gained by worrying although we feel the injustice of keeping us here without trial or even a charge being made against us. I see in some papers how Mr Asquith stated that their guiding rule would be leniency.[35] Well this treatment may be all right for those who were actually out in the Rebellion but we see nothing lenient or even just in it. I admit we are almost as well off as we could be as prisoners, we have four hours exercise; two hours in the morning and two in the evening and visitors are allowed in and altogether the time passes quickly and pleasantly but anyone with a wife and family at home suffers enough by the thoughts of them. I suppose this is not taken into account by the people who talk of leniency. I dare say an Irishman is not supposed to have such fine feelings as love of home and family. For myself, I never had any conception what it meant. The visitors here always remind me of you and your regular visits to Richmond barracks. That was a reason for which I was glad to be sent here. It must have been very inconvenient for you to come every day as you did but it was so grand to get out to see you that in my selfishness I could not tell you not to come but I know well what a bother it should be to you but then I used say every day maybe I will be gone next visiting day. I just want to let you know that I realised fully the bother and to tell you how grateful I felt to you and Henry.

Mr Keating MP was here on Saturday. I think he was in a hurry to get off. He sent in a large parcel of fruit, cigarettes and sweets for the Kilkenny prisoners c/o me.

We had Mass here last Sunday and Rosary on Tuesday followed by a sermon but the poor little priest is not much of a preacher. We had a Father Holohan from Knocktopher here the other day and Father Warren from Kilkenny yesterday. I am sure you knew his brother, Mick, who died. He used be in the shop often.

There is a great lot gone out of this [place] today. Some say they are going to a detention camp, others that they are gone home. The only Kilkenny fellows left are Lalor, Treacy, Stephens and myself. I do hope they are gone home.

Win tells me you were starting off for Richmond barracks on Friday morning only forgetting my note and O'Connell's brother who was in to see him on Thursday promises to call out to let you know but it was only a rumour then and none of us knew whether we would be on the list or not. I believe you have a lot of sweets belonging to me. They will be most acceptable. You can send parcels direct here. I owe some to nearly every prisoner on my block. They are all very good to share any little things they get.

I must finish. There is not any chance of startling news from this place. We were treated to an aerial exhibition yesterday; a bi-plane flew over while we were out at exercises,

> Best love to all
> Yours Very Affectionately,
> Peter.[36]

Shortly after this letter was written, the British War Office put Peter on a 'Special List' which included the names of nationalist leaders deemed 'specially dangerous'. The British authorities wanted to keep these prisoners separate and so moved them to Reading jail. Peter found himself in the company of Arthur Griffith, Seán Milroy, Darrell Figgis, Pierce McCan, Dennis McCullough and P. T. Daly among others.[37] The British intention was to reduce their influence on other Irish prisoners. However, their action gave the Irish Republican leaders an opportunity to meet each other, some for the first time, to mingle, discuss strategies and plan the future for an independent Ireland. Cornelius Deere, Goolds Cross, County Tipperary, asked fellow inmates to sign an autograph book. On one page Peter signed his name simply as 'Peter DeLoughry, Kilkenny, July 23rd, '16.' Two other detainees placed their signatures below his: 'Earnán de Blagdh [Ernest Blythe] Reading Gaol, 23/7/'16' and below that 'Tomás Mac Curtáin (Corcaigh)' with the slogan in Irish 'lean ort' (carry on).[38]

6

Phoenix Flame
Rekindled, 1916–18

Peter emerged from Reading jail in August 1916 knowing fewer people in the outside world than before his imprisonment: Sir Roger Casement, Major John MacBride, Seán MacDermott, Thomas MacDonagh and Joseph Plunkett had all been executed and The O'Rahilly was killed in action.

The *Kilkenny People* reported – not for the first time – that in Wakefield prison Peter had been kept in 'solitary' in a punishment cell 'crawling with insects and other livestock'.[1] The paper also said that Peter was in 'fairly good health' and that his spirits were never better. However, his outlook had changed and, as the historian Brian Feeney explains, so had those of other Irish revolutionaries:

The returning prisoners found a country waiting for leadership and organisation. The prisoners themselves had been transformed. Internment had produced intense rage and resentment among those affected, prisoners and extended families alike. It had brought together men from all parts of the country and bonded them, even those innocent of any involvement in political conspiracy, into an organic unit. A chain of command had been established. The men learnt about ideas and policies and techniques which became common to them all, instead of innovations devised and used in one place only. Everyone knew everyone else. If they had been in different jails, they had heard on the grapevine about other men from their districts. They emerged from prison as members of an organisation with a sense of belonging and a sense of purpose.[2]

This sense of purpose was in part defined in Kilkenny by E. T. Keane, whose journalism Tom Treacy described as hard-hitting and interspersed with wit of a devastating quality:

It would be difficult to measure the tremendous importance and value of this support to the cause in Kilkenny city and county, in adjoining counties and, in fact, the whole country, as his articles were regularly quoted by the daily and provincial press of the time … Were it not for the support of the *Kilkenny People*, the work of re-organising and moulding of public opinion in favour of the cause of Irish freedom and independence would have been far more difficult.[3]

Keane singled out RIC County Inspector Power for regular attack in the newspaper, although he was unpopular for other reasons as well. During his evidence to the inquiry into the Rising, which was well publicised, Power was asked about the low level of recruits from Kilkenny and, in particular, if he attributed this to 'the men being shirkers or to their having a conscientious objection?' 'I should say shirkers,' Power replied.[4]

In his monthly reports to Dublin Castle, Power consistently cited the *Kilkenny People* as 'seditious' or 'distinctly disloyal'. He partly blamed Keane for the low level of recruitment to the British army, placing the rest of the blame on local attitudes:

There is an undercurrent of disloyalty which hampers recruiting in addition to which farmers' sons prefer self-interest and an easy life at home to the more strenuous and dangerous work in the trenches. The articles appearing from time to time in the *Kilkenny People* newspaper, largely read by people of this class, foster this spirit and encourage disaffection towards England.[5]

Another RIC report said the release of the prisoners had ended the continued references to the 'so-called cruelty of the British government' and that there was practically nothing for Irish nationalists to 'brood over now except the past'.[6]

In fact, Kilkenny nationalists had set their sights on the future. Irish Volunteer companies were reformed and expanded. Funds were set up to help families of prisoners and to lessen the effect of food shortages caused by the First World War. A branch of Cumann na mBan was established and branches of Sinn Féin mushroomed throughout the county. Count Plunkett (father of the executed Joseph Plunkett) and Countess Markievicz were given the freedom of the city.

Dublin Castle and Inspector Power sought to deprive prominent Kilkenny nationalists of their livelihoods. Power was behind the decision to temporarily suspend Peter's brother David from his duties at the post office after the Rising. When Tom Treacy returned from prison, his job as principal clerk in the city's probate office was no longer available to him.[7] The DeLoughry business was refused a permit to sell petrol. Peter complained to General Maxwell and received a letter back from Major Ivor Price, director of military intelligence, Dublin Castle, saying that the police had been asked to 'facilitate you in the matter'. Shortly afterwards, Inspector Power issued the permit.[8]

One of the first tasks undertaken by the Irish Volunteers to re-invigorate the movement after the Rising was to rename their headquarters (the Volunteer Hall) the Irish Club in August 1916 to camouflage the reorganisation.[9] Here, Edward Comerford gave Irish language and history classes,[10] Volunteers honed their shooting skills and meetings were held to spread the movement.[11] James J. Comerford described the building as weird and creepy, with an expansive cellar full of echoes and darkness, and a loft that creaked when walked on.[12] However, the renaming of the building did not fool the RIC, and Inspector Power kept the building under surveillance, having his men take notes of those who frequented it.[13]

To fund the Irish Club, the Irish Volunteers held concerts in the nearby Kilkenny cinema and theatre, the first of which drew such a large crowd that a second variety performance was held the following week. These concerts marked one of the first instances of cinema being used for revolutionary propaganda anywhere in the world. The *Kilkenny People* described the event as patriotic entertainment with 'truly Irish performances as compared with cross-Channel importations where "smut" is the predominant feature'. A recital of Pádraig Pearse's last poem was given by Miss H. M. Hoyne and the performance ended with Larry singing *The Soldier's Song*.[14]

The following week, Inspector Power had two of his men in plain clothes gain entry. They later helped him to make a comprehensive report on the event:

Photographs of all the executed rebel leaders were shown on the screen during a song which was sung by Laurence DeLoughry – the chorus of which was 'We'll chant a soldier's song' and was received with great applause. The republican flag was also shown on the screen, also a photo of Dr O'Dwyer, Bishop of Limerick[15] and altogether the performance was utterly disloyal.[16]

Power witnessed another form of disloyalty when the pipers' band of the Irish Guards arrived in Kilkenny. The *Kilkenny People* reported in a matter-of-fact manner that the citizens seemed to enjoy the music and admired its mascot, an Irish wolfhound, but that otherwise very little interest was taken in the event. Posters advertising its performance had slips pasted across them with the slogan 'Remember Easter week' and the police removed these. A fourteen-year-old schoolboy bearing what the *Kilkenny People* humorously described as the 'treasonable name of DeLoughry' was arrested on suspicion of defacing the posters but was held for only a short time.[17]

Peter and Win's fourth child, Sheila, was born in October 1916 – the others being Richard (1912), Tom (1913) and Lily (1915).[18] This increase in family commitments did not quench the couple's activities outside the family home. Win played an active role as president of the local branch of Cumann na mBan. Peter spearheaded the foundation of a branch of the Irish National Aid and Volunteer Dependants' Association in November 1916, which had been set up to help the families of those imprisoned after the Rising.[19] A year later, almost £1,500 had been subscribed.[20] Peter also helped to set up a branch of the Sinn Féin National Food Scheme in Kilkenny in November 1917, which bought and conserved food because of expected shortages due to the First World War.[21] Within four months, more than £1,100 had been donated to the fund.[22]

This burst of activity was co-ordinated by the revamped County Kilkenny Brigade of the Irish Volunteers, which held a meeting at the home of T. B. Cahill, Kilbricken, Callan, in May

1917. Among those who attended were Edward Comerford, Pat Corcoran, Leo Dardis, Peter DeLoughry, Martin Kealy, James Lalor and Tom Treacy.[23] The meeting decided to form eight battalions: Tom Treacy was elected officer commanding, Kilkenny Brigade; James Lalor was elected vice-brigade officer commanding; Edward Comerford was made quartermaster and Leo Dardis, adjutant.[24] Michael Collins had ordered the reorganisation at a meeting in Barry's Hotel in Dublin.[25]

Peter, meanwhile, maintained his position on the local authority, where his contributions to debates varied considerably. He mocked the Irish Party for supporting the introduction of British summer time,[26] complained about the decision by the Department of Agriculture and Technical Instruction not to sanction Irish language classes for teachers at various centres around the county[27] and opposed a proposal to close the public baths[28] – cleanliness was one of his obsessions.

In August 1916 E. T. Keane began a modest campaign to have Peter elected mayor at the next election, which was five months away.[29] Despite letters of strong support from Irish-Americans that were printed in the *Kilkenny People*, Peter did not put his name forward.[30] Irish Party members held a majority on the corporation and elected John Slater to succeed John Magennis as mayor.[31]

Outside local politics, Sinn Féin was beginning to score significant successes, the first of which was the election of the party candidate, Count George Noble Plunkett, in the North Roscommon by-election in February 1917. It was this victory which prompted Peter to propose at a meeting of Kilkenny Corporation, on the day the result was announced, that Plunkett be given the freedom of the city.[32] The decision prompted County Inspector Power to warn his superiors in

Dublin that if Plunkett 'is permitted to come [to Kilkenny] I fear it will have a disturbing effect and lessen the influence of Mr Redmond's [Irish Parliamentary] party'.[33]

Two months later, Sinn Féin members found themselves fighting another by-election, this time in Longford South. Peter and E. T. Keane travelled to the constituency five days before polling day to help with the campaign.[34] The constituency was flooded with Sinn Féin representatives from all over the country. The party's candidate, Joseph Magennis, defeated his Irish Party rival, Patrick McKenna, by only thirty-seven votes, a result that was greeted with jubilation in Kilkenny where tar barrels were set alight on many street corners.[35]

A big Sinn Féin convention was held in the Tholsel in Kilkenny the following month, with Arthur Griffith and John O'Mahony as the principal speakers.[36] A confidential RIC report indicates that the constabulary felt it was losing control over Sinn Féin:

> A number of young men, some of whom had been interned in connection with the Rebellion, took up a position at the door and refused to admit the police notwithstanding that they produced a written authority from the County Inspector under Sec. 51D of the Defence of the Realm regulations. Peter DeLoughry, War B list suspect, appeared to be in charge and acted as spokesman on the occasion.[37]

Two weeks later, the movement in Kilkenny organised another big meeting to set up a Sinn Féin club and close on 400 people enrolled. E. T. Keane was appointed chairman following a proposal by Peter, seconded by Alderman Purcell.[38]

The Sinn Féin political roadshow next moved to East

Clare, where its candidate, Éamon de Valera, was fighting a by-election against Patrick Lynch of the Irish Party. James Lalor recounted:

> We travelled on two motor cycles and remained for about 10 days there, i.e. until the day after the declaration of the count which resulted in a tremendous victory for de Valera and Sinn Féin … Peter DeLoughry and I assisted the Volunteers in the regulation of the crowds at meetings, escorting speakers, etc.
>
> On the way back from Clare, DeLoughry and I passed a number of men from Dublin who were halted on the road with car trouble. They were Sinn Féin supporters who were returning to Dublin after the election and whose acquaintance we had made while in Clare. After the usual salutations, one of them said: 'We will see you down in Kilkenny in about a month's time for the election there.' We then learned that Mr Patrick O'Brien, the Irish Party (Redmondite), MP for Kilkenny city, had just died.[39]

Tom Treacy said that in the latter part of 1916, the Irish Party had a powerful grip on the city and county. Since then, the tide had turned. The by-election would reveal the magnitude of this change and it attracted worldwide attention. *The Times* of London reported that two candidates were in the field for Sinn Féin: Eoin MacNeill and Peter DeLoughry.[40] Having consulted senior Sinn Féin party members, Peter stood aside to allow William T. Cosgrave to run. Having been under sentence of death for his part in the Rising, Cosgrave had the credentials that fitted the Sinn Féin mould for an election candidate.

The conferring of the freedom of Kilkenny on Countess Markievicz coincided with the announcement by E. T. Keane and Seán Milroy of Cosgrave as the Sinn Féin candidate.

Much attention was given in Milroy's speech to the decision by the British authorities to close down the *Kilkenny People*.[41] The paper was off the streets for seven weeks and deprived Cosgrave of valuable media support for his entire campaign. Inspector Power wrote that the suppression of the publication resulted in a reduction in treasonous behaviour in the city:

> This action has had a remarkably good effect and the absence of seditious articles, which had been almost a weekly feature of this paper, will have a calming effect on the people who read it. It is generally recognised even by his own friends that the editor, E. T. Keane, went far beyond reasonable criticism and, as his untrustworthy character is notorious, he has very little sympathy.[42]

Leading Sinn Féin figures converged on Kilkenny for the campaign to support Cosgrave against the Irish Party candidate, the former city mayor John Magennis. At the start of the operation, Peter annoyed Irish Party members at a meeting of the Kilkenny Board of Guardians by remarking that 'it was time to get rid of diplomacy because deep down in the hearts of everyone was the idea of independence'.[43] Dan McCarthy, who had been wounded in 1916, became Cosgrave's director of elections and members of the Kilkenny Cumann na mBan played an active part in the campaign.[44] Peter went on the hustings throughout the constituency as notable Sinn Féin representatives including Éamon de Valera, Arthur Griffith, Eoin MacNeill, Seán Milroy and Fr Michael O'Flanagan promoted their candidate. Inspector Power's forecast was that the result would be close:

> All the young people are rampant Sinn Féiners but the older and representative citizens keep aloof from it, and it is thought they

will prove their aversion to Sinn Féin by their voting at the polls. Public meetings have been held at several places and violent and seditious speeches made, notably by de Valera who seems to be reckless in his expression of his views and makes no secret of his physical force methods.[45]

Cosgrave defeated Magennis by 772 votes to 392. The result was declared amid enthusiastic scenes at the courthouse.

The defeated candidate, John Magennis, took Peter at his word and dispensed with diplomacy in a speech made immediately after the result was announced in the courthouse. Magennis said the victory for his opponent was a 'victory for intolerance, low, mean, lying and scurrilous abuse, terrorism and intimidation of the greatest type'. On the night of the Sinn Féin victory, Peter made a speech from the Victoria Hotel where he, too, left diplomacy behind:

> Kilkenny city, the cradle of Fenianism, the birth-place of James Stephens, had given its answer. (Cheers). He had listened to Mr Magennis' speech that day in the courthouse, but it was behind closed doors he made it, his audience including a few paid officials of the United Irish League and a few policemen. [Mr Magennis had] called the people of Kilkenny blackguards and intimidators. The intimidation was all on Mr Magennis' side. This fight was only the beginning and Mr Magennis and his like would be hunted out of the public positions they occupied, and in which they exercised an unhealthy influence (cheers).[46]

No sooner had the election ended than Thomas Ashe, who had taken part in the Rising, was arrested in County Longford and charged with sedition for a speech he had made. Having been sentenced to two years' hard labour, he demanded, but was refused, prisoner-of-war status. Ashe went on hunger strike on 20 September 1917 and died in the Mater hospital five days later from injuries resulting from being force-fed by the prison authorities. The jury at his inquest denounced the prison staff, saying they had performed an inhuman and dangerous operation and had been guilty of additional barbaric conduct. Accounts of his death and the outpouring of grief at his funeral made a significant impact on the strength of Sinn Féin, which did not escape the attention of Inspector Power:

A few Sinn Féin meetings were held during the month, the most important of which was at Thomastown ... at which the following prominent Sinn Féin leaders were present; Messrs. Arthur Griffith, Seán Milroy, W. T. Cosgrave, J. J. O'Mahony and Dr J. Boyd Barrett. The speeches were moderate and confined chiefly to the treatment and death of Thomas Ashe. The crowd numbered about 4,000 persons who came from this and adjoining counties and the demonstration will probably stimulate the Sinn Féin movement in the locality. About ten extreme Sinn Féiners including E. T. Keane, Peter DeLoughry, Tom Stallard went to Dublin ... to attend Ashe's funeral yesterday.[47]

Four months later, Inspector Power expressed his indignation at members of Cumann na mBan who were campaigning to raise funds:

A collection in aid of the Thomas Ashe memorial fund was made in the streets of Kilkenny on Sunday last. The collectors were mostly young girls, many of them children who acted under a Miss Hoyne who is a prominent and leading member of the

Cumann na mBan society. This woman produced a 'permit' written in Irish and signed by J. Kelly of Dublin. No permit was given by me nor was such asked![48]

Sinn Féin's run of by-election successes was interrupted by its failure in the Waterford by-election in March 1918. Peter, other Sinn Féin members from Kilkenny including Tom Treacy and party members from all over Ireland descended on the constituency. Treacy recalled that during the campaign he witnessed an exchange between Peter and an elderly man who held a prominent position in the Irish Party. He recognised Peter and shook hands with him. The Redmondite, as Treacy referred to him, introduced himself by saying he had known Peter's father, Richard, and that they had attended many cock fights together:

> Redmondite (speaking with great tenderness): Your father Peter, I knew him well. He was a good Irishman ... If he were alive today he would be on our side.
> Peter (speaking indignantly and pointing to a large Union Jack flag which hung from a top window in a nearby house): Indeed he would not. What are your party standing for only Britain and the Union Jack. That's what you stand for.[49]

The year 1918 saw the arrival of another headache for Inspector Power, when on 18 April the Military Service Bill, (in other words conscription) was extended to Ireland. While conscription was never actually introduced, the threat of it was enough to stir the Irish people into a frenzy and Inspector Power wrote that the enactment resulted in County Kilkenny being gripped by panic. A fund to resist it had already been established in the city – the National Defence Fund – and by May 1918 had ac-cumulated more than £1,000.[50]

One of the most important effects of the increased threat of conscription was how, in Kilkenny, it brought together the Irish Party, Sinn Féin and the Roman Catholic clergy. Big demonstrations against the 'conscription menace' were held. Win, as president of the local Cumann na mBan branch, signed a pledge to oppose it and to 'stand solidly behind our men during this crisis'.[51] Peter campaigned at meetings of local bodies to send letters of protest to the British government. A typical example of his approach came during a meeting of Kilkenny Corporation at which the mayor, John Slater, of the Irish Party presided:

> Mr DeLoughry, while of opinion that there was no great use in passing resolutions, said the step the mayor had taken to put forward their protest was the right one. The time had come when they should all stand together and show a bold front to the common enemy. There could be no justification for imposing conscription on Irishmen … It was up to them to show that they were not bond slaves and fight to the last. Every man should be prepared to sacrifice his life as the most effective way of defeating the object of the British government.
>
> Mr [John] Magennis [Irish Party] agreed with Councillor DeLoughry that the time for resolutions was past after the very able protests that had been made by leaders of the Irish Party members.
>
> Mr DeLoughry: I think you had better leave them out of it. They cut a sorry figure.[52]

His rhetoric became more vehement at a meeting of the Kilkenny Board of Guardians where he said that the object of conscription was 'not to provide soldiers for England but a deliberate attempt to massacre the Irish people'.[53]

Political leaders in both nationalist camps issued similar strong statements throughout Ireland. Strikes were called and the backlash intensified. The atmosphere was becoming too hot for the British government, which ordered a round-up of suspects. One man, however, was tipped off about his own imminent arrest and evaded capture. He had been responsible for the successfully managed by-election campaigns in which Peter had canvassed and they knew each other. Larry had become one of his despatch carriers after his [Larry's] release from Wakefield prison.[54]

His name was Michael Collins.

7

The Road to Lincoln, 1918

The round-up of Sinn Féin leaders proceeded throughout the country in response to what became known as the German Plot. Tom Treacy was at home in Kilkenny preparing to go out when he noticed an RIC man pacing up and down the street. He managed to make his way out and reach the Volunteer Hall without being apprehended:

> I found that the members already there had not noticed anything unusual. I related what I had seen and mentioned that I believed there was some big move on by the British ... Almost simultaneously with [three reports of military activity] came a further report that Peter DeLoughry ... was arrested. The big round-up of leaders all over the country was under way, under the British latest invention and fake excuse – the German Plot.[1]

The origin of the plot can be traced to the arrest of Joseph Dowling, a prisoner of war, who had landed from a German U-boat in County Clare with instructions to contact Sinn Féin leaders. No conclusive evidence has come to light to prove there was a plot. As Brian Feeney points out, the German Plot and conscription 'handed Sinn Féin two custom-built, gold-plated propaganda victories':

> When [the British government] did act, on the excuse of the fictitious plot, it was obviously out of simple vindictiveness, not even from a misguided belief that they could finish Sinn Féin by cutting off its head. The widespread arrests of Sinn Féin leaders had profound and long-lasting consequences, not only because of the number of victims created but also because of the men who rose to prominence in the absence of those interned.[2]

Peter was arrested as he was about to go into his house, at 11 p.m. on Friday 17 May 1918, by RIC Detective Inspector Neylon and Head Constable O'Dea. He was refused permission to see his wife and family before being removed. The two officers escorted him to the RIC barracks across the street, where Win and Larry later visited him. A party of British soldiers arrived a short time later and escorted him under fixed bayonet to the military barracks. By this time a large and excited crowd had gathered and gave him a rousing reception with wild cheers, but they were kept in check by a body of Irish Volunteers. At 1 a.m., Win, Nanny and the children were disturbed by a knock at the door, after which the authorities exhaustively searched the house but found nothing of a compromising nature.

The following morning Larry was allowed to visit Peter before he was escorted onto the train for Dublin.[3] His sister, Lil, received a telegram at 9.16 a.m.: 'Bring shirt and collar. Peter. Kingsbridge, 10.30. Lar.'[4] That day Peter was deported to England on a British destroyer with other Sinn Féin leaders. The following Thursday Win received a three-line communication from the governor of Gloucester prison stating that her husband was confined there and that he had asked 'that his bag with his clothes should be sent on'.[5]

E. T. Keane dipped his pen into more cordite than ink when writing his editorial that week. The message in it, and in future editorials, gave his newspaper the 'distinction' of again being suppressed, though not immediately. His articles also galvanised support for Sinn Féin with their stinging rhetoric and mocking tone, particularly his questioning of the source of information for the German Plot:

> Need we say that we await, and public opinion in Ireland awaits, with interest, the publication of the 'evidence' that is intended to compromise de Valera and the other Sinn Féin leaders. We cannot wholly dismiss from our minds, however, the awkward fact that whenever an unpurchaseable and incorruptible Irish leader who cannot be brought, bribed, bulldozed or bamboozled succeeds in solidly marshalling Irish public opinion in the assertion of our country's right to freedom and commands the wholehearted confidence of the Irish people, England generally lights on the discovery that he is plotting murder or treason, stratagems or spoils.
>
> It was so with Parnell.[6]

Before the British authorities decided which prisoner went where, they studied the secret service documents on each. The file on Peter showed the breadth and accuracy of the information gleaned by their espionage network:

Peter DeLoughry

Motor mechanic and part owner and manager of a foundry, Kilkenny. Took an interest in the Sinn Féin movement from the first, and became recognised leader of the Irish Volunteers in Kilkenny. Attended as delegate the annual convention of Volunteer Committee in Dublin on 31 Oct. 1916. On 26 March 1916 he attended the General Council of Volunteers in Dublin at which de Valera, Pearse, MacDonagh and all principal leaders were present. On 9 May 1916 he was arrested with other prominent suspects after the Rebellion, deported and interned having been active in organising Volunteers prior to it. On 19 April 1916 with other leading suspects he attended Count Plunkett's Sinn Féin conference in Dublin. In May 1917 took part in South Longford election. Returned to Kilkenny on 10 June 1917 accompanied by suspects Arthur Griffith and [John] O'Mahony. Took part in de Valera's election in East Clare. Attended public Volunteer funeral of Thomas Ashe in Dublin, 28 September 1917. Leading member of the Sinn Féin Food Control Committee in Kilkenny, January 1918.

Attended general council of Sinn Féin under de Valera at Mansion House, Dublin, 1918, as Kilkenny delegate.

Is secretary of the Kilkenny Sinn Féin Executive.[7]

The *Kilkenny People* became concerned about the lack of information on Peter's whereabouts. A letter dated 25 May 1918 did not reach Win for some time. It was written in a rushed fashion, but Peter still found time to include a request that would help him keep up appearances:

My dear Win,

I am writing this in train. We (de Valera, [Darrell] Figgis, [John] O'Mahony, Seán Milroy) are on our way from Gloucester – I hear to Lincoln but we would not be told. We have not been allowed to write or receive letters since I got bag but letter was found and not given to me. If you get to know where I am, send shaving outfit.

I will write the instant I am permitted,

Yours,

Peter.

We have been broken into small batches. I do not know where the others are. I heard [Arthur] Griffith to Reading.[8]

Lieutenant Jim Close of the British army was in charge of the prison guard on the train to Lincoln. He obtained each of the prisoners' signatures, some of which were written in Irish and English. It is likely that Close also posted letters for the prisoners, as the one sent by Peter did not go through the postal censor.[9]

Peter was one of thirteen prisoners taken to Lincoln, the others being P. F. de Búrca, Seán Corcoran, Paul Dawson Cusack, Éamon de Valera, Seamus Ua Duibne (James J. Dobbyn), Seán Etchingham, Michael J. Lennon, Seán McGarry, John O'Mahony, Seán Milroy, Philip Monahan and Thomas Ruane.[10] They would be joined later by seven other prisoners: Michael Colivet, Éamon Corbett, Seamus Cotter, Laurence Lardner, Alasdair McCabe, Terence MacSwiney and Samuel O'Flaherty.

Back in Kilkenny city, the urban district council was unanimous in passing a resolution condemning the arrests, denouncing the German Plot and affirming that the British government's action 'was directed to blackening the name of Ireland'. One member asked if the authorities had resurrected Richard Pigott, the man who had attempted to blacken Parnell's name by forging letters.[11]

County Inspector Power reported that the arrests had had a 'restraining and deterrent effect on Sinn Féin here notwithstanding that there is still a certain amount of "bluffing" going on'. He said that while nationalists and Sinn Féin were attempting to discredit the legitimacy of the German Plot, 'thinking people are satisfied of the complicity by Sinn Féin [in] German intrigue'. He said these thinking people were sceptical of their repudiations, having frequently heard 'up Germany' and 'up the Kaiser' being proclaimed at Sinn Féin meetings and gatherings. However, Power had to admit that because of the anti-conscription campaign there was a very bitter feeling against the police, which made it impossible for them to obtain any information of what might be going on.[12]

E. T. Keane made much propaganda out of any crumb of information that came his way about the prisoners. He told readers on 1 June 1918 that Win had not received any communication since the letter from the governor of Gloucester prison and that it was stated that prisoners would not be allowed to write or receive letters or to receive parcels of food or cigarettes.[13] But this was not true. Peter had been allowed to write a letter home on 24 May, in which he transcribed the order of the Defence of the Realm Act under which he was being detained. By 3 June restrictions on sending or receiving letters were eased as indicated in a letter from Peter to his sister, Lil.[14]

The delay in letters reaching their destination allowed E. T. Keane to instil a sense of panic in his next report, where he told readers that Win had not received a single line from her husband since his incarceration and that as a result she had no idea of his location, how he was being treated or the condition of his health. 'It is like the silence of the grave,' he wrote, before telling readers that families of other prisoners were being put through the same ordeal. Keane underlined the fact that those arrested did not have time to make arrangements to provide for their families, and women and children were feeling the brunt of unnecessary financial loss.[15]

The Kilkenny Board of Guardians met shortly after County Inspector Power asserted that 'thinking people' were sceptical of Sinn Féin's assertion that the German Plot was a fiction. This meeting, attended by John Magennis and other Irish Party stalwarts, unanimously agreed to elect Peter chairman of the Board of Guardians.[16] The Irish Party, the party of 'thinking people', was now falling into line with Sinn Féin policies. This was a case of the Irish Party playing a reluctant game of catch-up to survive, but political events and the feeling of the people also drove them to this agenda.

A further headache for Power was announced by Keane at the formal opening of a Sinn Féin club at 19 Parliament Street, which was attended by Eoin MacNeill. Members heard that a demonstration would be held against the arrests at the parade in Kilkenny city at the end of June.[17] The *Kilkenny People* described it as one of the largest protest gatherings ever held in the city. County Inspector Power reckoned that upwards of 6,000 people turned up. Despite this, he reported that the Sinn Féin organisation had not shown much activity during the month, the protest was orderly and the speeches were of the usual character but rather wild in language:

> This meeting will probably give a fillip to the movement which was inclined to decline since the arrest of the leaders … If the people were let alone and not stirred up by agitators and sedition mongers, I believe the disloyal movement would soon die down. I know many so-called Sinn Féiners are in reality against the movement but owing to fear have to protest to endorse it.[18]

In his speech to the gathering, Keane spoke of Shane O'Neill, Parnell and de Valera, linking past Irish heroes with present ones, which was typical of his rhetoric and appealed to his audience. Tradition and a sense of place were some elements used to stir up the spirit of nationalism that kept the Sinn Féin flame burning:

> We have also lost – temporarily lost – the able and honoured services of one of our most respected citizens, Peter DeLoughry (cheers). We know him, many of us, from his childhood, and we know that he is incapable of being guilty of any action except such as conduces to the honour and freedom of Ireland. (Cheers, and a voice: 'Like his father before him.') And as my friend in the crowd says, his father before him was the same (cheers).[19]

8

Life in Lincoln, 1918

Shortly after arriving at Gloucester prison, Peter and his fellow inmates had been removed from their cells and put on a train, but they were not told its destination. In the prison a number of them had been held in constricted space and for an indefinite period which, as Darrell Figgis explained, was 'certain to waste the mind as well as the body, and so, with frayed nerves, [prisoners] are given an opportunity of torturing one another'.[1] He also said that, early in the journey, a guard told them that they were being brought to Lincoln,[2] but at Derby they learned that one of them was for Durham jail:

> Our thoughts at once turned to de Valera, and we began commiserating with him. But he defied them … The thought that we were still further to be broken, and that he would probably be taken to solitary confinement, threw a shadow over us for the rest of the journey.[3]

Each prisoner on the train had been arrested on suspicion of being complicit in the German Plot and, under regulations laid out in the Defence of the Realm Act, a sentence of death could be imposed on any person proven to have conspired with the enemy. It was late when they reached Lincoln train station, where they were transferred to a bus to take them to their destination:

> When we started our journey we began singing the *Soldier's Song*. We continued singing all the way to the jail, one song after another. As we passed within the jail gates our chorus was 'Dear old Ireland! Brave old Ireland! Ireland, boys, Hurrah!' De Valera turned and said as we entered: 'Isn't it fine, when you come to think of it, the generations of Irishmen who have gone into prison singing as we are now.'[4]

On arrival, they were immediately locked in cells. Before falling asleep that night, Figgis heard the captain of the guard outside saying that one of the prisoners was to be taken to Durham the following day: 'I have his papers here. His name is, yes, Figgis.'[5]

The conditions at Lincoln were less rigorous than in other prisons in which the Sinn Féin leaders had been incarcerated.[6] Figgis said the cells were also different, having a large window with clear glass which came so low that by standing on the floor he could look out onto the grounds laid out with fruit trees, flowers and vegetables.[7] In fact the two-storey annexe was normally used as a borstal but was empty because the First World War had absorbed the boys who had been housed there.[8] James J. Dobbyn said the prison guards 'sat on them' and treated them as 'arch enemies', believing them to be in league with Germany.[9]

Prisoners were confined to single cells, the doors of which were open from 6 a.m. to 9 p.m. They were allowed to exercise from 9.30 a.m. to 11.45 a.m. and from 2.30 p.m. to 4.30 p.m. in a large enclosed area beside the prison building. Seán Etchingham lamented that they had no water closets. When asked about the food, he said he liked live horses but dead ones did not appeal to him. What told on the prisoners most were the indefiniteness of their incarceration and disappointments caused by the periodical unfounded rumours of release.[10]

Within three weeks of their arrival, the prisoners had organised a 'Lincoln jail GAA athletic sports' competition which gave Seán Milroy, a talented cartoonist, much ammunition to caricature his fellow inmates. Most were subjected to Milroy's caustic crayons in one of two sketch-books known to have survived. In one of his drawings, the portly John O'Mahony is sketched and recorded as the winner of the 'Half-hour-go-as-you-please' race. Another illustration is of a tug-of-war between the married and single men. De Valera is listed as winning the half-mile flat.[11] Peter is portrayed crossing the Alps announcing that he would now have 'some great yarns to tell the boys', a reference to his once having been to Rome. Seán McGarry, general secretary of the Irish Volunteers and head of the supreme council of the IRB, is ribbed over his fondness for alcohol. Much is made of de Valera having obtained a typewriter and a gramophone for his cell.

Peter's testiness did not escape Milroy's attention. He depicts himself in the process of drawing with a dialogue bubble saying, 'Now please, try to look pleasant DeLoughry.'[12]

As Etchingham pointed out, the Irish prisoners had to deal with the annoyance and, in some cases, the fear of not knowing their fate. They were worried about their families at home. The sense of injustice at having their liberty taken away from them without a valid reason preyed on their sensitivities and they had to deal with the tedium of prison life and with being deprived of the company of women. They survived these ordeals by throwing themselves into a range of activities. Classes in

Irish, given by de Valera and Lennon, were held daily in the borstal classroom, situated close to the prisoners' cell-block. Peter's student exercise book includes examples of verb forms, exercises and corrections made by the two teachers.[13] De Valera also gave lessons in Spanish.[14] Dobbyn recalls that lessons were also given in Greek and other subjects.[15] (Samuel O'Flaherty held a BA degree from University College Dublin, in Latin and Greek.) Dobbyn gave singing lessons and Etchingham recalled that the prisoners had a 'very decent Church choir, Paul Dawson Cusack acting as organist'.[16] These activities were designed to show the prison guards that they were not dealing with ordinary criminals. This view is supported by one of the first decisions taken by the prisoners – not to accept food parcels. The reason they gave was that, in their minds, it was the duty of the British government to feed them properly.[17] As the months wore on, this self-imposed restriction was eased.

The authorities also eased restrictions on the prisoners' post, although letters continued to be censored. In a letter Peter sent to his sister, the influence which the Irish-Ireland colony in Lincoln was having on him is apparent. By this time he was known by his fellow inmates as Peadar and had also acquired a thirst for knowledge as he felt that he knew less about Irish history than the other prisoners. His request for books reflects his interest in this subject. The claustrophobia of prison life was preying on him and was not helped by the way in which food parcels were being rifled by those no doubt angry at the treats the Irish prisoners were getting while strict rationing was in force in Britain. There is an air of child-like resentment in the way he responded to his parcels being opened by the prison authorities:

Peter DeLoughry,
Lincoln Prison,
Aug. 14, 1918.

My dear Lil,

Your letter dated Aug. 6, I received on Monday last. I received your parcel on Friday last but the jam had completely disappeared except for what was smeared about the cakes and paper. I got an empty pot. There was a hole in parcel where the other was taken out. This is a common thing with parcels coming here. There is no doubt they are pilfered in P.O. The two cakes and tart arrived all right and were very nice but it is too bad to lose 4 lbs jam. So better not send jam again. This is the second time it has happened to yours and twice from home also …

I got Henry's [Mangan, Lil's husband] papers all right on the 8th inst. and they were a great treat. Everyone here thought poem very good. I only got a look through it as there is such a demand for it. I prefer to wait until they all have contents devoured. I have just got it left into my cell this moment.

I also got the three copies of *Treann na Gaeilge* and the balls (four, three solid and one tennis) safely today. Don't forget to let me know price of balls. We are very glad to get them as it is very difficult to get them here and it is the only kind of exercise we have.

I want to study Irish history while I am here so I want a book or two. Has Henry *Mitchel's History of Ireland* and Mrs Green's *Making and Undoing*?[18] I believe the latter is at home or ask him are these the best to begin with. He will understand I want what I will get the most profit out of and I intend reading and re-reading and checking my knowledge so I don't care whether they are written in an attractive form or not. Tell him not to attempt to buy any book if he hasn't it himself. If he lets me know title some of the men here will probably have them at home or here. There is no great hurry, just I would like to get them sometime.

I hope Win & Co. are having good weather in Tramore.[19] It is beautiful here for some days past – a bit too hot. Hoping yourself and all the family are well,

Yours V. Affectionately,

Peter.[20]

The civil servants who worked in the office of the postal censor were assiduous in their task of combing through letters sent and received by all the Irish internees, not just those in Lincoln. Between 14 July 1918 and 15 March 1919, the office examined 25,000 letters, 745 telegrams and 1,585 newspapers and printed documents: 393 letters were referred to other departments. The censor retained 484 communications because they were deemed to contain secondary meaning, were seditious and abusive, referred to political matters or contravened other prison regulations. Despite this, the final report submitted by the censor admitted that the results had been practically valueless owing to the fact that the internees in all the prisons devised one means or another to evade censorship either by entrusting letters to prisoners released on parole or by some unknown method.[21]

To help with decrypting the suspected secondary meanings, the censor included a six-and-a-half page addendum to his fourth report listing the terms and words used and their decoded meanings. 'Bloodhounds' stood for police, 'carnival' indicated a general election, 'huns' referred to the English, Ireland was camouflaged as 'invalid' and 'notice of eviction' was used for conscription. Attempts were also made to blur references to individuals: Professor Eoin MacNeill was 'Eoin the Uncertain', Lord French varied between 'St Patrick II' and the 'primitive man', while Sir Edward Carson was referred to as the 'white chief of bigotry'. This dictionary, however, proved useless when the censor's readers came across impregnable correspondence such as this from Seán Corcoran to his sister, Maggie:

> Tell Tom that the three sacks did after all set fire to the 'dung hill'. The time he used jibe me over this a heavy shower might indeed quench the little fire for generations.[22]

Staff at the censor's office had their task made more difficult by streams of mundane messages into which they tried to inveigle a hidden and treacherous meaning. To add to their bafflement, one prisoner requested books on yachting; another wanted news on what form the new government had taken in Russia and on the politics of Poland; and there was a flood of letters from Alasdair McCabe demanding publications from relatives and friends to help him write a book on the economy of Ireland.

A consistent complaint by the postal censor was the claim that prisoners deliberately back-dated letters and then complained of the inordinate amount of time it took to process their correspondence:

> Open complaints with regard to the treatment or of the prison food are few: the prisoners, however, adopt indirect methods of insinuating that they are subjected to discomforts and minor annoyances, e.g.
>
> The deliberate mis-statement of the dates of letters received to enlarge upon delays of censorship. J. [Seamus] Cotter complains

of the delay of a letter which he states was written on 6 Oct.: Note was kept of this letter which was dated 8 Oct.

J. [John] O'Mahony's custom of suggesting that he has lost 33 lbs. in weight omitting to relate that he still scales close on fifteen stone.[23]

Other aspects of prison life also emerged in the correspondence, ranging from suspected codes to the harmful effects of prison life on the mind. For example:

Directorate of Military Intelligence
Postal censorship (extracts)

Paul Dawson Cusack (Granard, County Longford)

He has been the recipient of specially made 'sweets' from 'John Cowley's factory' similar to those sent to Dr Bryan Cusack of Birmingham prison. There is a strong suspicion that these sweets, at one time, contained messages, but since the matter has been referred to the governor for examination no further mention or hint has been noted.

F. (Proinsias) de Búrca (Carrickmacross, County Monaghan)

This prisoner is apparently a medical student of advanced years with a wife and young family dependent upon him. The worry of his internment which nullified his past steps towards his degrees and made future qualification impossible caused a bad nervous breakdown, so severe that his release is believed to be imminent. His correspondence before his illness was hostile and full of complaints against the restrictions of his position but in subject of no interest, dealing almost entirely with medical matters.

[He corresponds with:–]

R. Johnson, 8 Rosemount Terrace, Booterstown, deals with medical and examination matters.

Note. [Alasdair] McCabe has written in de Búrca's name to R. Johnson of Booterstown announcing his imminent release and asking that either he (Johnson) or someone from 'No. 6' [Harcourt Street, Dublin, Sinn Féin headquarters] should meet him at Kingstown.[24]

John O'Mahony (Dublin, born in Kilkenny)

He is in communication with:–

Messrs. Champion Davies & Co. Ltd., a British firm with whom O'Mahony did a good deal of business. They have repudiated all connection with his company since his imprisonment and after writing recriminations to him have circularised the trade to the effect that communication with an adherent of Sinn Féin is incompatible with loyalty.

Messrs. Thorne, Cocoa works, Leeds, who have followed the action of Messrs. Champion Davies mentioned above.

The correspondence of this prisoner has been chiefly in reference to the alleged detention of his business and home communications. The tone of his remarks is abusive, his chief object being apparently to impress upon all sympathisers the suspicion that he is the victim of a government plot to ruin his business connection.[25]

Another form of writing preoccupied the prisoners from September 1918: contributions to a bi-monthly journal called

The Insect, which was edited by Milroy, with McGarry as his 'printer's devil'. The editor informed readers that poetry was not inadmissible, but warned intending contributors that *The Insect* was not started as 'a nursery for long-haired lunatics. There must be reason if not rhyme in the effusions sent in.' Readers were also advised where to send their contributions:

> We call attention to the fact that the address of *The Insect* is C 2.15 [Milroy's cell]. Our reason for so doing is that a contributor, who had a funny story for our paper the other day, passed our office and went on to Peadar DeLoughry's cell. That was carrying the joke too far.[26]

The election manifestos of James J. Dobbyn and Peter for the position of quartermaster for the prisoners gave them the opportunity to poke fun at one another and at the predicament in which they found themselves. The elections for this rank appeared to have been contrived more to provide amusement than to select leaders. Dobbyn opened his manifesto by calling on all 'free and independent electors of Lincoln jail' and confiding that he was surprised and dejected that he was not being unanimously re-elected. In his election address, Peter said he believed that his candidature should deter any 'foul-mouthed, muddle-headed, base-hearted factionist' from entering the list against him. He asked his fellow prisoners: 'Have I not kept up an abundant supply of handballs with which to stir the athletic spirit of my comrades? … Have I not, during my term of office, regaled the hours of our exile with anecdote and narrative of my wondrous exploits during my pilgrimage in Rome?' He issued a word of warning about his rival: 'Beware of a man with a beard, especially a Belfast man. You have had dire experience of two quartermasters with beards and you are not likely to be cajoled again by such disreputable devices.'[27]

The result of the election is not known. However, the good humour evident in the manifestos can be contrasted with other contributions to the journal indicating that Peter had not lost his argumentative streak:

In the hottest discussion, Peadar won't fail
To break the thread by some awful tale,
Usually concerning the Board at home,
Or the queer things that happened to him in Rome.

The third edition of *The Insect* included a review of a musical evening held by the internees. Peter was complimented for giving 'some charming selections from that charming opera, *Tales of Hoffman*. His second item, a recitation of *Truthful James* tickled his audience immensely.'[28]

To celebrate de Valera's birthday on 14 October 1918, the prisoners staged a 'grand opera in three acts' entitled 'Paula, the linking girl' (a play on the word Lincoln) by Paul Dawson Cusack. Milroy produced the programme, which had sketches of the main players. Peter was able to call on his acting experience in his role as 'Orlando, le Diablo'. Other cast members included 'Signor Dobbiano' and 'M. Michael D'Olivette', with 'Signor Cottero' listed as producer.[29]

Milroy continued caricaturing his fellow inmates. A sketch of de Valera depicts him with his gramophone and Blick typewriter. The page beside the sketch is signed by de Valera on 11 November 1918, the day that all guns ceased firing on the Western Front.[30]

The end of the First World War was soon followed by the 1918 general election in which Sinn Féin became the dominant nationalist party in Ireland. Several prisoners in Lincoln stood in the election. John O'Mahony announced the results from a balcony in the prison having secured a copy of a Sunday newspaper. Sinn Féin had won seventy-three seats, the Irish Party secured only six and unionists obtained twenty-six. The internees received the announcement with 'colossal enthusiasm'.[31] Colivet, de Valera, Etchingham, McCabe, Mac-Swiney and O'Mahony had all been elected. O'Flaherty and Milroy had entered their names in constituencies in Ulster. However, Sinn Féin had decided reluctantly that it was better not to split the nationalist vote, so an agreement was reached to 'cede' to the Irish Party candidates in four Ulster constituencies.[32]

The election results uncovered a hidden talent among the Lincoln prisoners. Etchingham recalled that a competition was set up among them to see who would forecast the results most accurately:

> Phil Monahan proved himself a political prophet. Not alone did he give the exact returns, but he explained why certain seats would be lost and how other doubtful ones would be won and said that the Louth majority would be the smallest. Three prizes had been decided on but Mr Monahan's forecast was so accurate that the prisoners unanimously agreed that he should be awarded the lot – 1s. per prisoner, making 18s. in all.[33]

As the significance of the results sank into their minds, resentment of their incarceration grew. The postal censor commented on a letter Peter sent on 30 December to Win, describing the extract quoted as 'typical of the more outspoken of the inter-nees since the election results became known':

> [The results make for] a peculiar situation as we are the strongest party outside the government and it raises a nice point by the fact that the government have the leader and most of the members of the 'Opposition' in jail without charge or trial. I do not imagine it will disturb their consciences but at the same time an important constitutional situation is created.[34]

In Kilkenny North, W. T. Cosgrave was elected unopposed for Sinn Féin. In Kilkenny South, James O'Mara, Sinn Féin, defeated Matthew Keating of the Irish Party, despite Bishop Brownrigg's pledging his support for Keating in letters to local newspapers, arguing that support for 'the other side' would 'seriously jeopardise the most vital interests of the country'.[35]

Even after the general election, electioneering in Kilkenny didn't stop. E. T. Keane launched a campaign to have Peter voted in as mayor, telling readers that Councillor DeLoughry had been marked out for special victimisation by the British government.[36]

Prisoners who thought that the end of the First World War would bring their release were disappointed; they remained locked up without trial. Despite this, they made the best of Christmas celebrations. They produced a Christmas day menu for the 'Royal Lincoln Hotel' which tempted diners with sumptuous courses including dessert 'plum pudding (brandy sauce not arrived)'.[37]

Peter received a handball and Christmas postcard from his niece, Lelia, with the greeting 'love and best wishes to Uncle Peter, de Valera and all the rest, from Lelia Ní Mongáin'. Peter referred to the present in a letter to his sister, sent in the new year, in which he complained that de Valera had put them [the handball and postcard] into his pocket without so much as a by your leave.[38]

Prison life appeared by this point to be taking its toll on Peter, as did the rifling of food parcels:

> Peter DeLoughry
> Lincoln prison
> 8 January 1918

My dear Lil,

Your letter of 5th inst. just received, also your box, which I have just opened. Everything all right except the jam about half of which is lost by the covering of pot getting broken. Our parcels seem to get very rough handling but matters might be worse. As it was, the cigarettes escaped. Lots of cigs have been destroyed coming here by jam getting mixed up with them. Tell Dalton how thankful I am and I am sure he had a bit of a job getting them. I have enough cigarettes now to last me some time and I cannot smoke at all these days. I have a slight cold and they irritate my throat.

I am sure mince pies will be nice. I will try and heat them. Win told me she had some from you and that they were lovely …

No danger of getting 'swelled head' over *People* reports as I should be very dull if I did not realise that personal merit is not put forward as any claim but it is simply as a protest against our unjust arrest and imprisonment. I suppose I better write no more as I had a letter sent back from censor last week for either referring to mayoralty or election. I do not know which,

Yrs.

Peter[39]

Back in Kilkenny, E. T. Keane and other Sinn Féin members found strong opposition to their campaign to have Peter elected as first citizen of their city. The remnants of the Irish Party wanted at first to co-opt a member for St John's Ward and had fixed ideas about rotating the mayoralty amongst themselves. On top of this, the RIC threatened Keane against holding public meetings in support of the campaign. At a rally in the Parade, Keane answered these threats with a defiant logic that was cheered by the crowd:

> I want to state at the outset that this peaceable meeting we are holding tonight is, in the eyes of the British law in this country, an illegal meeting. Today the responsible heads of the police authorities in this town called at my house and at the houses of some of my friends and warned us that this meeting was an illegal meeting. The message, I ought to say, was courteously delivered and I have no fault to find with the manner of its delivery at all. They told me that they would not interfere with the meeting, but that if we held it we would do so at our own risk. Well, we accept that risk, my friends and I, but if any representatives of the police authorities be present here, I want to send this word back to them: that whether it be a legal or an illegal meeting in their eyes, the object of the meeting is to demand that effect be given to an Act of the British parliament in connection with the election now pending in Kilkenny (cheers). On this occasion, at all events, we are not out to obstruct British law but to demand that British law be carried into effect.[40]

Pat Corcoran stood in Peter's place for the seat in St John's Ward and won easily. This allowed Peter to be co-opted when Corcoran resigned and at a meeting of Kilkenny Corporation on Thursday 23 January, Peter was elected mayor. Members then went to the DeLoughry family home and delivered the sword and mace and the chain of office to Win. That night thousands turned out for a procession through the city led by St Patrick's brass band. Keane and Larry made speeches. As these were being delivered, a telegram was sent to Lincoln prison to tell Peter that the corporation had given him the highest honour it was in their power to bestow; he was now mayor of the city, the vote had been unanimous.[41]

9

Escape from Lincoln – Thoughts Emerge, 1918–19

Fenner Brockway had nothing to do with the escape from Lincoln prison, but the success of the Irish internees in subverting prison security to help him, illustrated the breadth of their canniness that would be later used for the escape.[1] He was an Englishman of high honour and principle. A dedicated pacifist, he opposed conscription and consequently was the recipient of white feathers from women whose boyfriends or relatives had enlisted to fight in the First World War. He was not moved by this, remarking, after a while, that he had accumulated enough white feathers to construct a fan. He was imprisoned for his beliefs and for eight months up to April 1919, was placed in solitary confinement for twenty-three hours a day. No other prisoner was allowed into the exercise yard while he was taking his one hour of fresh air. He was subjected to one month of 'bread and water treatment' until a doctor would not allow any more. He made friends with a robin which, as he recalled, flew into his cell one 'wonderful day!' to feed from crumbs from his punishment rations.

It was during this time at Lincoln prison that he first made contact with the Irish internees. A prisoner who worked as a handyman and therefore could wander about the complex doing odd jobs appeared at his window one day. His name was 'Trusty'. He was a remarkable-looking man: tall, broad and straight, with a leonine head of waving grey hair and a flowing beard.

The following day Trusty delivered a little brown packet in which Brockway found a note, a pencil and a sheet of paper on which to reply. The note read: 'Dear Brockway – Just heard you are here. What can we do for you? De Valera, Milroy and sixteen other Irish rebels are interned. We are Irishmen and can do anything you want – except get you out. Have your reply ready for "Trusty" when he calls tomorrow. Cheerio! Alastar Macaba.'

When a number of Irish prisoners were released, one of them delivered a letter from Brockway to his wife, Lilla, who was looking after their two young daughters and living in hardship in a caravan. It was the only communication she received from her husband during his imprisonment.

Brockway also made out a list of newspapers he wanted; the *Manchester Guardian*, *Labour Leader*, *New Statesman*, *Economist* and *Observer*.[2] Three days later, the deliveries began. Brockway lowered twine from his cell window, waited and hauled up the papers. Following a bout of illness, he was moved to a first floor cell where he worried that the paper round would end. When he went to the toilet the following day, he found a note projecting from a crevice between two bricks which instructed him to lift the cover from a drain-pipe. There he found an edition of the *Manchester Guardian*. Cleaning the lavatories was one of Trusty's duties and he always timed this task to ensure he could leave a newspaper for Brockway. This continued until Brockway's term in prison ended.[3]

Michael J. Lennon described Brockway as 'a goodly man' and dared not say how they had communicated with him. However, communicate with him they did. Lennon wrote a letter to Brockway when their prison ordeal was over saying, 'Probably, you don't remember me but I was in C14 [Cell 14] in Lincoln with you and read your weekly notes to A. McCabe'.[4] Indeed, Brockway did remember, recounting thirty-five years later, 'It is true to say that [the Irish prisoners] saved my mind.'[5] This episode illustrates the gulf that existed, not between Brockway and the Irish prisoners, but between all of them and the barbarity of the prison regime that was honed and kept inhumane by the British government.

The Irish prisoners advanced their skill at subverting the prison system, identified its weaknesses and exploited them. James J. Dobbyn said that the warders treated the Irish internees as 'arch enemies' when they first arrived, believing that they were in league with Germany. Dobbyn recalled that, as time went by and the prisoners were refused a public trial, the prison guards came to the conclusion that there was no German Plot and 'turned the other way'.[6] The warders on patrol through the corridors of Lincoln prison at the time would have witnessed Seán Milroy puffing a cigarette and sketching in his cell; the flamboyant Paul Dawson Cusack, who on occasion cooked for the prisoners, complaining about the quality of vegetables; Samuel O'Flaherty explaining the synthetic inflectional forms of Greek verbs; Michael J. Lennon calling 'students' to their Irish or Spanish classes; preparations for a musical evening with the performers rehearsing their recitations; Seán Etchingham elaborating on the finer points of horse-racing or yachting; Alasdair McCabe deep in thought while attempting to finish a chapter of his book on the economy of Ireland; de Valera standing beside his gramophone and typewriter showing his profound knowledge of mathematics by studying quaternions – a number system that extends to complex numbers; and Laurence Lardner arguing with Thomas Ruane about a controversial point in Irish history in between games of handball. John O'Mahony was inclined to invite the warders into his cell to give them a quick 'snifter' of one of the many bottles of whiskey he had squirrelled into the prison, while recounting a humorous yarn about his work as a travelling salesman and hotelier. The warders now had six MPs and a mayor under their charge. They could have been forgiven for thinking that planning a premature exit was not one of the prisoners' preoccupations. They were wrong.

There were many factors against the success of an escape as any plan would be heavily reliant on help from the outside. Communication was limited. The postal censor was aware from an early stage of codes or hidden messages used in letters to and from the internees and despite the large volume of post which the staff at the censor's office had to comb through, their observations were keen:

> [Thomas] Ruane has been suspected of using a pre-arranged stamp code in communicating with his brother, but since the end of August the practice has ceased – possibly owing to the fact that the irregular position of the stamps was altered in the censorship.[7]

The censor made a correct observation about de Valera's correspondence, which illustrates another limiting factor for the potential escapers. De Valera knew or strongly suspected that his letters would be read with great care and so he used other prisoners to send out his messages in their letters. As a result of this, information from de Valera arrived at its source later than expected and reached its correspondent second-hand:

> The correspondence of this internee is generally harmless to a most marked degree and suggests a deliberate and premeditated abstention from matters of political interest. Instructions and enquiries emanating from de Valera have been issued through the medium of fellow prisoners (*vide* Corcoran, Dobbyn, Etchingham).[8]

The postal censor had another string to his bow – his staff knew or had employed someone with a knowledge of Irish and of the corrupt forms of Irish place-names in English:

10.12.18 [Seán Corcoran] to Joe Sheehy.
Extract:–

> The counting I notice won't take place till a week or so later. Watch Moclair.
> (Moclair – possibly deliberate corruption of Gaelic for 'My Clare,' The connection between E. Mayo and E. Clare in the common candidature of de Valera is possibly worthy of note.)[9]

In a letter from Nelly O'Ryan to Etchingham, the censor picked out the name 'William McAlla', interpreting it as a reference to William Sears, editor of the *Enniscorthy Echo* (McAlla = Echo in Gaelic).[10]

There was the added possibility of coded messages being misunderstood and the difficulty posed by not being able to conduct a simultaneous discussion between those inside and outside where suggestions and possible complications could be dealt with immediately rather than having to wait until the next message. The prisoners also needed to be sure that those bringing the messages in and out could be trusted and that their nerves would not become frayed.

The physical problems of escape also had to be considered. The locked cell doors were the immediate obstacles, but the prison was also greatly secured by high walls that were fortified some distance away at the back (north) by a barbed wire fence. The thick wall had a door on the prison side and a five-bar gate layered with corrugated iron on the outside: the same key opened them both. A military guard assisted the warders in watching the prison. Britain remained a militarised country despite the fact that the First World War had ended. Despite the communications problem, breaking through the security cordon remained the greatest challenge.

Other factors magnified the difficulty of executing an escape. People 'on the run' were restricted in their travel by petrol rationing. De Valera's height and imposing appearance were likely to attract attention. For an escape to succeed, the plan had to ensure that the alert would not be raised too soon. The elements, too, had a part to play. The winter raised the prospect of snow where tracks could be easily identified. An escape during the full moon would restrict their movements. Finally, an escape by other Irish prisoners in the lead-up to the Lincoln escape would be likely to lead to increased security and the plan having to be abandoned or altered.

The plan needed to appeal to the right side of the brain as well as to the left. Art and engineering had to become constant companions.

First attempt: November 1918–January 1919

When the First World War ended, the prisoners were disappointed that they were not released and became irritable, which manifested itself in concrete thoughts of escape. Michael J. Lennon was the first to make Peter seriously consider its feasibility, but Peter rejected several proposals put to him. Finally, Lennon managed to secure a promise from Peter that he would assess the options open to them and choose the best one. After careful consideration, Peter decided that 'there was only one way of escaping and that was probably the very easiest way – to open the door and walk out'. He noticed that there was a door in the prison wall of the exercise yard:

> I discovered that all the locks in the prison with the exception of the cell door lock were the same. I therefore discovered that to open the locks, after they were closed for the night by the governor's representative, one required a master key. The key usually held by the warder simply opened the door when it was, what I might call, half-locked. In the evenings, the governor's representative on making his inspection gives the lock bolt a second shot and, when thus locked, the ordinary warder's key would not open it.

Peter spoke to Seán McGarry and they agreed that if anyone was to escape, de Valera should be the one, so they approached him with the idea:

> [De Valera] seemed at first to think the matter of escape was impossible but when we convinced him that there was a reasonable chance of success, he not only became enthusiastic but, as far as I

remember, he wanted to know if there was any chance of getting out next day. The enthusiasm of de Valera was a bit of a handicap, to me at least, because once he got the idea of escape fixed in his head he was very impatient.[11]

According to the historian Diarmaid Ferriter, de Valera's mind wandered in many directions while he was in Lincoln. The idea of escape appeared to be just the trigger to set off his creative juices which, according to Peter, could be a difficult characteristic for other prisoners to deal with, particularly when such limited resources were to hand to help make escape a reality.[12]

De Valera and McGarry next approached James J. Dobbyn in his cell and asked him if he would be willing to become an assistant altar server to stand in for de Valera who had been acting as a *de facto* sacristan during masses for the prisoners. The plan was to take an impression of the key which the chaplain regularly left in the sacristy before celebrating mass. Dobbyn agreed to cover for de Valera while he took an impression.[13] A Capstan tobacco tin was secured from one of the prisoners and a large nick was made on one side to allow the shank of the key to sink into it. The tin was filled with the melted or softened wax from candle butts taken from a drawer in the sacristy.[14] Peter tutored de Valera on how the shape of the key should be recorded; impressions were to be made in the wax of the key's side, back and point.

For three Sundays, de Valera trained Dobbyn in the task of serving mass, teaching him the Latin responses. The chaplain's keys were deliberately moved to see if he would notice but he did not.[15] Finally, they decided to put their plan into action. De Valera deliberately left the wine or water cruet in the sacristy, which gave him an excuse to leave the altar. He had kept the tin of wax close to his skin so that his body heat would soften it, but it remained too hard and the impression could not be made.[16] Dobbyn recalled the cat and mouse game he had to play with the unsuspecting chaplain as another attempt got under way:

> [De Valera] was in a hurry and possibly a wee bit nervous. He was not going to be shot for doing it, but he was nervous of failing.
>
> During it – this was the final attempt – I had to cover up. If the priest moved in Dev's direction, I had been instructed to get between them and draw his attention or push him if necessary to ask about that thing, what is that there and so on, not during mass, during mass the crowd was there – warders and all.
>
> This took place in the wee anteroom just beside the altar. I was carrying the stuff out and in. [The chaplain] was vesting and I was helping him and literally standing in his way – settling things. Dev was sitting on a wee gallery – two or three steps and he had the keys in a cloth. The cloth was to deaden the sound – somewhere in the middle of it. I heard a clink – it was like your bell ringing – it was only a tiny clink but it seemed like a hammer. It took me all my time not to look back.
>
> Afterwards, Dev asked me had I noticed it and I told him it sounded like Big Ben. Well, he said, the priest did not look round. You see, I could not look at the priest.[17]

De Valera said it was 'delightful' to feel the key shank sinking into the wax to its full depth. With the plan and elevation of the key acquired, the keys were returned and the chaplain was none the wiser.

De Valera described the second phase of the escape plan:

> The first step was complete – the next was to contrive to get the impression out so that a key could be made.

> I had once been at a 'show' in the old Empire – where the Olympia now is in Dame Street [Dublin]. A tipsy comedian was trying to enter his house late at night. He was unable to get the latch key into the lock. Meantime, somebody else sang, 'I couldn't get that latch key in, upon my word, I couldn't.' This gave me an idea.[18]

At this point Seán Milroy's talent as a cartoonist was called upon. On de Valera's instructions, Milroy drew a picture postcard showing McGarry with trembling legs (more tipsy than cold) attempting to insert an enormous key into his own front door. A dialogue bubble had McGarry saying, 'Blasted keyhole seems to have shrunk' with a caption, 'Xmas 1917 can't get in'. A holly branch lies in the snow above the greeting 'Happy Xmas'. In the bottom right-hand corner of the cartoon is a smaller and separate image of McGarry sitting disconsolately in his cell facing a giant keyhole with the caption, 'Xmas 1918 can't get out'. The representations were topped and tailed by the captions: 'Sean's troubles' and 'Christmas tragedies'. De Valera had traced the outline of the impression the key made in the wax onto paper, the dimensions of which he had asked Milroy to incorporate into the sketch.[19] In other words, the humorous illustrations contained the exact sizes of the master key in the main cartoon and of the keyhole in the smaller sketch. The next step was to get the postcard out and to explain its hidden significance so that a key might be made and smuggled in.[20]

The prisoners, warders and prison authorities were aware that John O'Mahony was partial to whiskey and that, on occasion, he received a bottle from friends. The escape committee felt it was just possible that one of the warders would be prepared to forward a letter – circumventing the postal censor – from O'Mahony to a friend asking for a bottle of whiskey. They needed to make a daring statement in a mundane manner so that the warder would be fooled. Nothing could be left to chance. Four elements were employed to make the communication credible and insignificant, and the first was to use O'Mahony, or rather his reputation. De Valera felt that 'a humorous letter coming from him would be taken as a matter of course'. Second, the use of humour in the postcard illustrations was intended to make the warder smile or chuckle and thus smother suspicion rising in his mind. Third, de Valera believed that any hint of danger in the communication could be reduced or eradicated if it were addressed to a priest. John O'Mahony, who knew England well, having worked there as a travelling salesman, selected as the recipient, Fr James Kavanagh, a native of Mullinavat, County Kilkenny, now a curate at Leeds cathedral. Two enclosures were now needed; a letter to Fr Kavanagh asking him to pass on to a friend of O'Mahony's an enclosed postcard which had the McGarry cartoon and a short message on it. The letter to Fr Kavanagh opened with 'My dear Father'. The prisoners had to decide what fictional name to use in the postcard message to be written to O'Mahony's whiskey-buying fictional friend. They decided on one that resonated with informality and that was cheerily and inherently English. This was the fourth element aimed at making the communication appear insignificant. The postcard message opened with 'My dear Tommie'. The illusion of harmlessness was now complete. The prisoners believed that the postcard to 'Tommie' and the letter, even though it was addressed to Fr Kavanagh, would reach their accomplices on the outside.

The greatest difficulty lay ahead. The postcard and the letter had to explain – without the warder knowing – that the prisoners were planning an escape and that the representations in the sketches were to be used to make a key which they wanted smuggled in. The messages also had to give an idea of when the escape was to take place. How could this be achieved? Portions of the postcard message were written in English, Irish and Latin, and the letter was written in English and Latin. This linguistic camouflage allowed the prisoners to insert other details about where the postcard and letter should be sent on to, a code that could be used to denote the date of the escape, descriptions about the lay-out of the prison that Proinsias de Búrca (who had been released) could fill in, and that a rope ladder should be brought along by those outside as a back-up in case the key did not work.

Samuel O'Flaherty, a classics scholar, composed the Latin passages. De Valera was as familiar with the Irish language as he was with English and had a thorough knowledge of Latin. The non-English language sections were inserted under the pretence that they were quotations, extending good wishes and asking for a bottle of whiskey. The prisoners thought, correctly, that the warder would know neither Irish nor Latin and that the ruses employed would be enough to convince him of the innocence of the text.

The postcard message to 'Tommie' opened with an introductory sentence in English in O'Mahony's hand explaining that the best wishes he could send were those which de Valera had written in his (O'Mahony's) autograph book. There followed a short but loaded sentence, again in English and written by O'Mahony, 'Field will translate'. Field was the code name used for Michael Collins. The message continued with quotation marks indicating that the following passages were a transcription of de Valera's good wishes. These paragraphs take up the remainder of the communication and were written by de Valera in Irish script. This allowed him not only to conceal his message in a language that was outside the warder's knowledge, but also to insert English words into his text disguised by the Irish script.[21] It is a mark of de Valera's intense attention to detail that when writing under cover of the Irish script he still kept referring to himself in the third person, keeping to the essence of the communication (that someone else was writing it). He became the actor continuing to play in character even though he had walked off the stage.

One of the more important hidden messages contained in the Irish script was the direction to those outside to decide on a date and to send in a letter about an ill relative who was recuperating, using the phrase, 'Billie got up the –th of last month.' This would signify the date of the escape.

The second enclosure – the letter addressed to Fr Kavanagh – was written in English by O'Mahony but was sandwiched by two Latin phrases composed by O'Flaherty:

Lincoln Dec 24th 1918.

My dear Father,

We all greet you. In the words of the old Roman … [illegible] epistolam [illegible] ut, per nuntium fidelem <u>statim</u> mittas ad illam mulierem, cujus domicilium notavi, rogat et orat dux noster Hibernicus. [Our Irish leader asks and requests that, by a faithful[22] messenger, you immediately send [illegible] letter [illegible] to that woman, whose home I have indicated.][23]

The letter ended with the second Latin inscription:

Hanc <u>quoque</u> epistolam mitte cum altera inclusa ad dublien(sis).
[Send this letter <u>also</u> along with the other enclosure to Dublin.]
　　SOM.[24]

Between the two Latin phrases was O'Mahony's English language text in which he incorporated at least half a dozen coded devices. He opened with a bold statement that the letter was not going through the usual channels, so that receipt of it should be acknowledged only by a Christmas card. Here, he partially implicated the warder who was to deliver the message, but was careful not to identify the channel of communication. This impressed on the warder the authenticity of the letter and also showed that O'Mahony could be trusted to protect the warder's identity.

O'Mahony employed a form of allegory throughout the text. He described the prisoners' feelings of claustrophobia and their keen sense of longing for freedom:

We inhabit the most easterly wing of the building – the hall running north and south – and spend most of our time in our cells or moping around the small garden within the walls. Outside the wall to the north is a much bigger space but we are not allowed into it. It is a pity … it is surrounded by barbed wire paling six feet high and the nearest road [Wragby Road] is nearly a half a mile beyond it … It is tantalising for in a big field of which the enclosure is a part, goal posts have been erected and we are too far away to see the matches played from the window. The ground belongs to the military hospital. I believe we see it about six in the evening brilliantly lighted up on our left as we look out the window.[25]

While O'Mahony appears to be using descriptions of the prison surrounds to confirm his argument about loss of freedom, he is actually imparting vital details that would be indispensable to those outside co-operating in an escape.

References to light, illumination and brightness pervade the letter. These he uses in conjunction with a play on words. The word 'matches' (in a sporting sense) is linked with the word 'window' but the connotation of its other meaning is pressed home; two other references are made to 'light' and 'window':

Standing at this window I smoke a cigar and de Valera watches the Plough revolve round the Polar Star – He studies the stars. I watch the lights on earth, the motor and cycle lights coming along the road from the east or perhaps north-east towards the town and blinking as the objects get between them and us – my cigar must look like an evolving star, if it can be seen as far as the road perched up in the sky as we are in this window.[26]

Anyone reading the letter, knowing that it refers to an escape, would be unlikely to miss the repeated reference suggesting that light could be used to give a signal from the window. The way in which most of the letter was written – as a stream of consciousness – was aimed at giving it an 'airiness' or abstract quality, far removed from a studied form that would be more likely to convey sinister information. The Irish prisoners counted on the warder holding the generally accepted view that anything appearing foolish or bizarre was unlikely to be dangerous. Included in this strange way of writing were references to de Valera's interest in astronomy, his love of dark nights and how the next new moon (when it is dark unlike a full moon) or the one after it should satisfy him.

The quirky nature of the writing continues to the very end where an important reference is made:

> Dev last night told me a story of a famous Xmas in Irish history – there was snow on the ground as usual of course, I said, I thought that [was] a bad thing and he nearly hit me when he saw the kind of interest I was taking in it. Even the mention of Dublin Castle in the story didn't win my attention. This story would give you an idea of the line in which our thoughts are turning.[27]

This was a reference to the escape of Hugh Roe O'Donnell and two companions from Dublin Castle on Christmas Eve, 1592, a reference that would have been well-known to most schoolchildren in Ireland but not to an English prison warder. However, the plan 'was so clever it almost didn't work'.[28]

The postcard and letter were sent and received by Fr Kavanagh, and while he must have known that there were hidden messages in them he is unlikely to have understood their significance. Both communications appear to have raised more curiosity than suspicion and so he brought them to the honorary secretary of Sinn Féin in England, Liam McMahon, who asked one of his employees, Patrick O'Donoghue, a founder member of the Sinn Féin branch in Manchester, to deliver them:[29]

> I crossed to Dublin that evening and contacted Martin Conlan, who, in turn, made an appointment with Michael Collins. I saw Collins that night in Mrs McGarry's house and I showed him the postcard. Both Collins and myself decided that the postcard was a code relating to the proposed escape of prisoners from Lincoln. However, we had not enough information to formulate

any definite plans although the full significance of the drawing of the key was now understood by all of us.[30]

The message was more welcome than the prisoners might have thought. Collins and Harry Boland 'had been racking their brains for a means to get in touch with the [prisoners] to try to get their co-operation for an escape'.[31] Collins was director of intelligence of the Irish Volunteers and distractions for the Sinn Féin leadership in Dublin at this time were great, as the first sitting of Dáil Éireann on 21 January 1919 was being planned.[32] But a deadline loomed over the escape; it was imperative that de Valera be freed in time to attend the post-war Paris peace conference. Other 'small nations' of Europe were busy preparing to put their cases at this conference, but nationalist Ireland was severely hampered because so many of its leaders, elected and unelected, were in prison.

The prisoners' careful planning and attention to detail were mirrored by the manner in which Boland and Collins set about organising a scheme on the outside. Collins' notes included hand-drawn maps of the Lincoln area, details of distances from Lincoln to other towns and cities, an audit of items needed, a proposed relay of how the prisoners would be transported after the escape (including the names of drivers) and details of which banks in England should be used to transfer and withdraw money to meet expenses. All the resources of the Sinn Féin headquarters were mobilised for the operation, including the most important element, the vast network of its Irish contacts in Britain.[33]

A member of staff at Sinn Féin headquarters, Frank Kelly, was sent to Lincoln to send word home at once if de Valera was suddenly released and to examine factors that might help the escape plan. Kelly had spent his early youth in England which had given him an accent that he was able to turn to good account on his mission. He sought out the pubs frequented by the Lincoln prison guards and infiltrated their company. Having consumed copious amounts of 'bad war beer' he abandoned this line of espionage; the warders were near retirement age and unlikely to jeopardise their pension to help free Irish prisoners.

The tendency of nationalists, both inside and outside the prison, to be over-cautious proved to be an initial obstacle. Posing as a visitor to Lincoln, Kelly asked the Catholic prisoners' chaplain to smuggle in an 'innocent' letter to John O'Mahony. The letter was received and an equally innocent reply was sent out: but there was no follow-up. Kelly later heard that the prisoners 'didn't bite as they thought it was a trap'.[34]

Back in Dublin, Fintan Murphy was detailed by Richard Mulcahy to have a key made by Harry Boland's brother Gerald, who was the resident engineer at Crooksling sanatorium. Gerald Boland recalled Murphy's visit:

He had a sketch (postcard) showing Seán McGarry with a large key in his hand. It was made exactly to show the works of the key. Also there was a note in [de Valera's] handwriting telling whoever made the key to make sure it was thin enough to enter the key-hole which was supposed to be exactly reproducing the prison lock. I told Fintan that if a key was made that then it would break even if made of steel not to mention the soft iron blank he had with him. He insisted on me cutting it which I reluctantly did and, as I had told him, it broke.[35]

Murphy and Gerald Boland went to an iron moulder, Sem Russell in Christchurch Place, Dublin, who cut a key. The two returned to McGarry's house where his wife was making a circular cake in which the key would be hidden. They discussed the best area to place it and decided to put it close to the edge. While the cake was being baked, Murphy sought further instruction from Mulcahy, who told him to travel to Lincoln and deliver it. During the crossing, Murphy had a chance encounter with another Sinn Féin activist, Tom Cullen:

> He was probably no less surprised to see me than I was to see him but such was the code existing that neither of us enquired of the other … We just accepted the fact that we were both bound for England on business – no doubt of 'national importance' but to enquire what? No! Unless one of us should volunteer the information.
>
> He joined me in a meal and we chatted of passing events and presently retired, to part eventually at Holyhead, I for Sheffield and Lincoln, and Tom for I know not where.[36]

Again, over-cautious natures conspired to threaten Murphy's task. Cullen was on his way to try to free Irish prisoners from Usk, a mission that had the potential to lead to heightened security and possibly scupper the Lincoln escape plan.

The prisoners sent out at least two communications after the humorous postcard. One was sent to Seán McGarry's wife and written in Irish by de Valera. The forthright message opened with a question as to whether or not she had received the postcard and did she not understand it: the escape plans set out in the postcard were repeated. There is a note written in English and in another hand at the bottom of the letter, 'See

Field [Collins] at once about this. If he is not available, get someone as good.'[37]

John O'Mahony wrote another letter, dated 10 January 1919, to Fr Kavanagh saying that he was aware he had received the humorous postcard but was afraid that it had not been sent to its ultimate destination. O'Mahony apologised for his poor Latin in the previous correspondence, a reference that allowed him to veer back into Latin again to explain that they needed to be careful not to alert the warder who was 'posting' the letter:

> *Timeo ne nuntius qui hanc espistolam*[38] *portat eam intelligat,*[39] *quam ob rem cautum esse me oportel.*[40] [I fear that the messenger who carries this letter does not understand it, and that is why I have to be cautious.][41]

O'Mahony reverted to English and underlined the importance of the previous communication. As the postcard had been sent almost three weeks previously, the sense of frustration is evident. The internees had endured the ordeal of spending Christmas and New Year away from their families. Every letter or parcel was greeted with an expectation that was only matched by the disappointment when no key arrived. On top of this they questioned whether the humorous postcard had been too clever. De Valera's own impatience and the 'silence' from the outside world added to a difficult end to 1918 and an uncomfortable beginning to 1919 for the prisoners. However, the incessant finger-tapping was about to stop.

Fintan Murphy reached Lincoln at around nine o'clock on a January morning:

It was somewhat early to make a call at the jail and I went into a small restaurant and took a leisurely breakfast … My sole object was to get the cake safely inside the prison and satisfy myself that it would be delivered to the 'consignee'. I considered what would be a plausible story. It would hardly do to be a visitor direct from Dublin and an Irishman at that. Having been born in London and having no difficulty in reverting to an English accent, I [decided to pretend to be] a commercial traveller, and, whilst in Manchester, I had met an acquaintance from Dublin who had asked me, when she learned I was passing through Lincoln, if I would oblige her by leaving a parcel at the jail for a friend of hers who was there as an Irish political prisoner. This was a safe enough reason for my action …

In a strange town it is difficult enough, I thought, in the ordinary way to enquire the way to and show an interest in the jail. I, with my parcel, found it more difficult still, but I boldly took the plunge and, to my surprise, found it simple. Nobody took any particular interest in my enquiries and, with little trouble, I soon found myself before the jail gates [that were] more or less exactly like the numerous other jails which I had seen from the outside or inside.

I knocked at the wicket gate in the main door and presently it was opened to me by the warder on duty. He enquired my business and I readily repeated my story handing him at the same time my parcel. He made no move to take it and I was somewhat taken aback. He muttered something about the chief warder which I did not understand and I again tendered him the parcel. He then told me forcibly that I must see the chief warder and that I should come inside for that purpose. This was an unexpected development but I had to make up my mind quickly to take the chance. I stepped inside the gate which he immediately closed and locked behind me and led me into what I well knew was the reception office and he then left me with my parcel to fetch the chief. I knew the procedure; questions, opening of the parcel, if a cake, cutting or prodding it with a knife. I was undoubtedly in a quandary. If he cut the cake, what were the chances of missing the key? I knew its appropriate length but where it lay in the cake exactly I did not know. If he came across it I was undoubtedly 'for it'.[42] I could hardly expect anything less than to join my comrades inside. Well, I had to stand up to it now and hope for the best.

Presently, the chief came in, a gruff individual of the usual prison type obviously more used to dealing with persons convicted of small and big crimes. I greeted him civilly and, on his demand as to my business, I repeated to him my carefully rehearsed story as to how I came to be there. He grunted disagreeably and commented on how these 'so-and-so' Irish prisoners were able to get butter, bacon and all other good things whilst decent English people were on rations and had to do with margarine, etc. I inclined to agree with him but once again explained I was only obliging an acquaintance in Manchester. Meanwhile, I watched the parcel being slowly opened and waited for the climax. At last the cake lay exposed on the table and whilst we continued our conversation he produced a long knife. I assumed that it was hardly possible for him to miss the key but I observed that instead of cutting it in four quarters, as I expected he would do, he merely stabbed it through and through and, with further sundry grumblings at luxuries for the rebel prisoners, he escorted me to the gate and let me out. I was immensely relieved both that I was outside and the cake inside the jail and I strolled down to the railway station to depart from the town of Lincoln to which I have never since returned.[43]

The cake was delivered and the key extracted. De Valera was overjoyed. He examined it and checked its size with a copy of the drawing that had been sent out. It was exact. McGarry tried the key in a barred door in one of the corridors. It broke.

Disappointment engulfed the prisoners. De Valera had suspected that the key was too small despite its size conforming to the copy of the measurement. His theory for the bad fit was that the wax in which the impression had been made had shrunk when it cooled, resulting in the wrong dimensions being transferred to the postcard image.[44] When McGarry reported that the key had broken in the corridor door, de Valera chastised him, 'If you want to test a key again, there are plenty of vacant cell doors to do it in!'[45] Peter extracted the broken part from the lock using a wire.[46]

The work would have to be done all over again.

10

Escape from Lincoln – Peter's Key Turns, 1919

'I am quite satisfied now that it is possible to be miserable in jail.'[1] So wrote Seán Milroy in the opening of his book on prisons in Ireland. Despite all the planning, his cleverly drawn cartoon of McGarry had come to naught. He tried again, this time sketching the required dimensions of the key camouflaged to some degree by an elaborate Celtic design with the caption *Eochar na Saoirse* – the Key to Freedom.

In the cells, the tick of a metaphoric clock grew louder and more harrowing as the days passed. The pendulum moved against the prisoners with increasing momentum, since the Paris peace conference that de Valera hoped to attend was imminent. There were three other potential hindrances to the escape: the prisoners believed that using Fr Kavanagh would quicken communication; Seán Etchingham suffered a near fatal illness; and an escape from Usk prison raised the prospect of increased security at Lincoln.

Second attempt

McGarry's second postcard reached Liam McMahon and Paddy O'Donoghue via Fr Kavanagh, but without an accompanying explanatory letter. Harry Boland, who was in Manchester, was present when Fr Kavanagh arrived to explain what had happened. Liam McMahon recorded the exchange:

> [Fr Kavanagh] said he was watched all the time since he left his house in Leeds. He suspected something was happening while he was in the train. He said he feigned sleep and felt someone searching his pockets which was all rot. He did not bring the message but said he had given it to a teacher; she was to be in the Midland Hotel and was to bring the correspondence at six o'clock. Miss [Kathleen] Talty was Captain of Cumann na mBan [in Manchester] at the time and Fr Kavanagh asked her to go to the hotel to contact this lady. Of course, Miss Talty could not contact her because the lady was not there. She came back and reported it. I never saw Harry Boland in a temper before that. Harry Boland ordered Paddy O'Donoghue to go back with Fr Kavanagh to Leeds and contact this girl. When they got to Leeds Fr Kavanagh would not take Paddy to the address. He said he would go himself and when he came back he said she had accidentally thrown it in the fire. It is my belief that he burned it himself because he was a nervous little man. This caused further delay as word had to be sent to the prisoners that their last communication had been destroyed before its contents were noted.[2]

Those planning the escape had not so much inveigled the priest into their scheme as duped him. Whether Fr Kavanagh had an inkling of the escape or knew the import of the messages, his view had changed radically by the time he met Boland.

When Seán Etchingham fell critically ill, the prisoners felt his impending death and the distraction caused by it would slow things down, but it did not, because he was eventually released. The seriousness of Etchingham's illness was outlined in a letter written by Nan MacSwiney to her brother Terence, and the points she makes might have been intended more for the postal censor's attention than for her brother:

> I was in Dublin last week and saw Etchingham. He was practically dying. He was gasping and just said between his gasps that they had let him out so that he should not die on their hands. He said you were 'good' to him – you all need to be good to one another in that vile place. He said you were losing your vitality. I sometimes wonder how God lets such incarnate devils pollute the earth. But every death they bring about, directly or indirectly, is sharpening their own difficulties. Sharpening the sword that will cut the cable once and for all. It occurs to me now that one's views of them are censored. They like to do their dirty work in secret and always cut out the Truth; and the Truth shines all the more glaringly because of their fear of it.[3]

One day after his release, on his arrival in Ireland, Etchingham gave an interview to the *Irish Independent* which explained how it had come about:

> Asked how Mr de Valera was, he replied, 'As usual, unbending and unbreakable.' He went on to say that his own health began to fail about September and from that time he was gradually losing weight. While at Mass on New Year's Eve he had a seizure and was removed to his cell by two of his comrades and attended to by a priest and doctor. Since then he was somewhat better but for two months past was unable to partake of solid food.
>
> On 31 December, de Valera, who took a paternal interest in him, went to the governor and said that things were nearing a

breaking point. 'If anything happens Etchingham,' he said, 'you will get the trouble you are looking for.' The doctor then came to him and said that he had been telling them of his condition, and made an examination of him. The following day, however, two rolls of butter, which were brought to the prison for him were handed back to the donor, butter being rationed.

Afterwards he had two slight seizures and on Monday last he was brought to the hospital. Then he felt the loss of the attention he had been receiving from his comrades, de Valera himself having been in the habit of making toast and Bovril drinks for him. His hospital fare for the night was three-quarters of a pint of cold milk, a lump of bread and half an ounce of margarine. De Valera came to see him on Tuesday morning and at midday, the governor and doctor informed him that an order had come for his immediate release. He believed it was from Dublin Castle. He asked one of the warders to be allowed to see his comrades and the reply was that he should see the chief warder. The latter said he should see the governor, and the governor refused the request …

Then he refused to go without seeing them and the governor brought de Valera, saying [to him], 'That should satisfy you.' He still refused to leave, remarking that they would have to drag him from the prison if he was not permitted to say farewell to his comrades. In this, he was supported by de Valera and eventually the governor said he would bring the men to the prison gate, where they could shake hands with him. This was done, and he left, accompanied by the hospital attendant … He concluded by saying that de Valera was full of hope for the future.[4]

As a result of his intransigence, Etchingham was able to secretly bring out a letter from Fenner Brockway to his wife, Lilla, and, more important for the Irish prisoners, clarifications of the escape plan. Piaras Béaslaí recounted the reaction of Michael Collins when he heard of Etchingham's arrival in Dublin:

> Collins got word that Etchingham had a message for him and hurried back to Dublin from England. I remember well his sudden arrival, bursting travel-stained and worn into a room in Harcourt Street where Con Collins and I were working, with the cry, 'Where's Etchingham?' We were unable to tell him. He stormed at Con Collins for not having located him. He must have succeeded in finding him, for he returned to England that night.[5]

Their meeting must have taken place on 22 January 1919, a day after the Dáil had convened for its first session, during which de Valera, Arthur Griffith, Seán T. Ó Ceallaigh and Count Plunkett were nominated to represent Ireland at the Paris peace conference. Both Harry Boland and Michael Collins were recorded as having been present during the roll-call for the first Dáil session, but they were, in fact, in England preparing for the escape. The decision to have it appear that they were in Dublin was made so that the British authorities would not become suspicious about their absence at such an important event.

Boland, who was staying at the Waverly Hotel in Lincoln, attempted to clear up the confusion by writing a letter to Seán Milroy explaining that a previous communication from the prisoner (via Fr Kavanagh) had been lost. He also let the prisoners know that they had understood the letter accompanying the McGarry postcard where de Valera had suggested using the code of sending in a letter about an ill relative who was recuperating to signify the date of the escape. Boland chose Milroy's wife (Milroy was a bachelor) as the ill relative:

64, Mid Abbey St
Waverley Hotel,
Lincoln,

Seán, a chara dílis [my good friend],

I have come to Lincoln at Billie's request. Your wife has again been stricken down with the flu. I do not wish to alarm you but I am afraid she is in a bad way. Ní dóigh liom [I don't think so]. Billie was bad last month and he got such a fright that he is very uneasy about the Mrs. He thinks you should ask parole to see your wife. Billie got up on the 24th of last month. He is not quite well. He asked me to come to Lincoln and send this appeal to you to apply for a week's parole as he thinks you would listen to me and bend your proud spirit to ask this favour of the government. I do not wish to alarm you. We were all delighted with your Xmas card and he hopes you got parcel and map key. I will be glad to know that goods were delivered in good condition as the letter of acknowledgement was lost. The post officials are very careless. Everything is A-1 in Ireland and I hope to sail away le Debh amháin sé a chlog Dé hAoine. An bhfuil aon sgeul agat orm? Freagra leis on sagairt. Táim anseo. [with Dev only (or alone) at six o'clock on Friday. Do you have any story for me? Answer with the priest. I am here.][6]

In Boland's recollections, he mentioned having dealings with the chaplain to the prisoners, Canon Scott, and it is likely, but not certain, that this man was used to get messages into the jail.[7]

The postal censor noticed communications referring in code to the fact that Boland and Collins were in England, which should have raised an alarm. The first was sent to Seán Milroy, the second to Seán Corcoran:

Directorate of Military Intelligence
Postal censorship (extracts)

21.1.19 Miss R. Green, Sr Mary's, Wellington Road, Ashton-under-Lyne, refers to the visit of Harry Boland to Manchester. Extract:–

I suppose you've heard of all the great happenings in Manchester. At least if not passed by censor some record was given in the *Manchester Guardian*. We had a distinguished visitor in Manchester yesterday, H.B.

27.1.19. From Maggie Corcoran.
Extract:–

Sunny Jordan and Sunny Mooney went to England last week working. There are not many Volunteers now in the town.[8]

The final problem for the escape planners was the escape of four Irish prisoners, George Geraghty, Joe McGrath, Barney Mellows and Frank Shouldice, from Usk prison on the evening of 21 January. The alarm was not raised until the following day. However, the regaining of those men's liberty raised fears that the British authorities would impose stricter security measures in other prisons where Irish people were being held. This might have been averted had Fintan Murphy or Tom Cullen informed each other of their respective missions when they had met on a crossing from Ireland to England earlier that month. Murphy had been detailed to deliver the first cake to Lincoln prison while Cullen was on his way to help with plans for the escape from Usk.

On hearing of the Usk escape, Boland and Collins rushed to Lincoln and discovered that the closer watch they feared had not been put in force.[9] In a letter dated 23 January and smuggled into the prisoners, Collins moved to clarify several points. His impatience, however, is apparent:

Dublin
23.1.19

A Sheáin, a chara,

We fear here that the previous note sent you was not fully understood. It is essential that you send a pretty complete answer as bearer is coming back to Dublin at once. A dtuigeann tú leat mé? [Do you understand me?]

The letter informed the detainees that he had spoken with Etchingham and de Búrca and that they (the prisoners to whom the letter was addressed) ought to 'understand Billie's position in the scheme of things'. He told them that Billie got up on 28 December – code that the planned date of the escape had been changed to 28 January. This of course shattered all hopes of de Valera attending the opening of the Paris peace conference on 18 January. Collins then veered into Irish, asking if prison security had been strengthened and at what time they reckoned the prison guards would notice their absence. He also told them to direct future correspondence to Paddy O'Donoghue before concluding that 'for your wife's sake attend to these things at once as word must go back to her at once'.[10]

The fact that Collins used code and wrote some of it in Irish indicated either that the bearer was not fully trusted or that it was a safety net used in case the letter fell into the wrong hands.

A day after the letter was sent, Frank Kelly delivered a cake to the prison. He was spared the ordeal that Fintan Murphy had to endure as the gate-keeper took it from him at the door.[11] Inside were two keys that had been made by a locksmith in Manchester on Harry Boland's orders. The cake was baked by Liam McMahon's housekeeper, Mrs O'Sullivan, and brought to Lincoln by Boland, who handed it over to Kelly.[12] Having tested the keys, John O'Mahony and de Valera sent word out that they did not work.

Third attempt

The prisoners were not yet aware that Fr Kavanagh was less than enthusiastic about receiving and delivering their messages and a communication was again sent to him pleading that he ensure that this and the previous letters reached their 'final destination'. O'Mahony asked the priest to let them know that this had been done by sending a message of congratulations to Peter DeLoughry on his election (the previous day) as mayor of Kilkenny. He also suggested that 'the customary present [a cake with key] should come next time to the above mayor. Seán [McGarry] has already got two [and] it is as well let them go round'. Attached to this letter was one written by de Valera in Irish in which he explained that the first key broke and that the 'thing ye sent today [the key delivered by Frank Kelly] is too small'. At the bottom of the letter he drew a sketch of a keyhole and asked that a blank be sent in that would match the dimension of his drawing. He also said that two prisoners would be smoking at a window at the back of the prison at a quarter to seven on the planned evening of the escape, 28 January, before concluding with a caution, 'It is necessary to be careful.'[13]

Harry Boland involved himself directly in the third attempt by delivering another cake, this time with blank keys, to the prison governor. A written record of Boland's account explains how Boland went to the prison and asked to see some of the prisoners but was refused:

> He finally talked to the chaplain and wanted to present the cake but the chaplain was not inclined to let it go through and finally Boland saw the governor of Lincoln prison and told him that there had been a lot of talk by the friends of the prisoners about the way in which the goods which were sent into the prisoners were broken up and spoiled. Boland said: 'I told them I had no interest in the prisoner as I was simply a travelling man for an ironmonger's house in Dublin and I showed him my card, and the owner of the firm was a friend … Of course all this time they were looking for me themselves and at that time I wore a moustache and a pair of glasses. The governor agreed with me that the cake should go in untouched and it was sent in and the keys reached de Valera.'[14]

A letter from Boland reached the prisoners in which three coded phrases were explained. Each phrase included the word 'parole' and was to be used in the next letter from the prisoners depending on their readiness to go through with the plan. 'I have applied for parole' meant the prisoners could reach the back wall at 6 p.m. on Tuesday 28 January, 'I have not applied for parole' meant they could not reach the back wall on that date, and 'I will not apply for parole' was code for the escape plan being postponed.[15]

The blanks got through to the prisoners on the day of the planned escape, Tuesday 28 January. Having tested them, de Valera sent out a letter in Irish to their fellow conspirators on the outside. The tone of disappointment is mixed with typical de Valera focus on detail and a schoolmasterish repetition of important points:

Tuesday night[16]

My dearest Mic[hael],

We received parcel today. Sadly, we are in bad luck. In the 'blanks' that ye sent to us there is a groove [hole or slot] right in its middle – the place where there should not be any groove at all.

They are no good like that. If it were not for the holes in them we would have done the business beautifully and we would have been out of here as soon as ye were ready. Now ye will have to send a few others to us that do not have any groove in them, and another 'file' as well …

If we are not ready to do the deed on Saturday, half past seven on Sunday evening will be the time, the new moon will be above that evening, ye know.

If we fail on Sunday, we will have to wait until a quarter past eight on Monday night and after that it will not be possible to do the deed at all because the suitable moon will not be there for another fortnight …[17]

Put on the parcel 'Mayor DeLoughry. With congratulations and best wishes from a few Kilkenny exiles – J. Dardis.' …

This hole is the actual size of the key hole into which the key fits tightly.[18]

Fourth attempt

A fourth cake was taken to the prison by Kathleen Talty, who gave this account of the preparations:

> The cake was baked by my sister, Mrs Liam McMahon, with her house-keeper, Mrs O'Sullivan. I saw my sister put the key at one end and files at the other end of the cake. It was oblong.
>
> We packed it with other things in an attaché case which I took on the 7.30 a.m. train to Lincoln. It was snowing heavily. The carriage, in which I was alone, had no heating and was very cold. When I arrived at Lincoln station I was met by Michael Collins and Frank Kelly. We went to Kelly's Hotel where I had a meal. I took a taxi to the jail, and on arrival, asked the door-keeper if I could see Mr DeLoughry, who, a short time before had been elected mayor of Kilkenny.
>
> I told him that I had just returned from Ireland where some friends of Mr DeLoughry's had met me and asked me to bring a parcel to him. The door-keeper then asked me to write my name and address on a plain postcard. This I did. I was living in Manchester. I asked if I could see any of the prisoners but he refused this request. He then told me to put the parcel on the floor. I did so and then took up my empty case. He opened the door and let me go.
>
> On my way back to Lincoln town, I met a warder who said to me, 'Ah, they will soon be out.' Little did he know, Michael Collins was waiting at the hotel for me and we both returned that same evening. He had a dreadful cold and his shoes were in a very bad condition with the soles nearly worn away. I tried to get him a pair but the good shops were closed. After a meal at Liam Mc-Mahon's, he and Michael Collins went to Paddy O'Donoghue's house to make further arrangements for the escape.[19]

When the cake arrived, the prisoners asked the governor not to cut it but to allow Peter the honour of doing so. The governor agreed. A blank key and two small files were extracted and Peter set to work.[20] He had to be careful. Dobbyn said that during a previous attempt to fashion a key it got stuck in a lock, '[The prisoners] could not get it out and the warder walked past it … there it was sticking out of the lock and he did not see it.'[21]

Peter described the task as 'trying and at times exasperating. I had to be as noiseless as I could … With the files and two stout pen-knives I made a key. It wasn't exactly artistic.'[22]

At lunch-time each day [Peter] took twenty minutes in removing the lock on the door upstairs, taking it to his cell, working on the key, and replacing the lock. He was ably assisted by one of his fellow prisoners, I think [Seán] Corcoran was his name[23] … who used to do sentry while Peter was working on the lock and key.[24]

Eventually Peter completed his work and knew that it had 'to open three colossal doors' by giving their locks the second shot needed to open them.[25] The time had come for the key to be tested.

On Friday 31 January, de Valera sent the following letter out to Boland in which he expressed a fear that letters sent through the postal censor might have raised suspicions:

Friday night

Dear Michael,
    The things came. We are sure that they will do the business

beautifully. We will be ready on the day that ye have now chosen, at a quarter to seven. We are hoping that it will be completely dark. Tonight it is so bright, with the snow, that you could see everything almost as far as the road. If it were to be like that when ye are coming, it would be better to proceed close to the shrubbery (it is dark there) until ye come as far as the wire. Ye can show the sign to us when ye are half of the way from the road after ye have seen our sign. That will be [there] to be seen at forty minutes after six exactly.

*There is no need for a message to be brought to ye to be very careful. Two letters came here (through the censor) one from M and one from L saying that your comrade is in M and he is going to Dublin and returning again to M. The girls for certain with the letters. It will not do if they have laid out a trap for us.

We are not too sure if there is a soldier walking outside the wall. There is often a fire in the garden opposite the big door at the back of the prison – weeds of course by the gardener. Do not let it worry ye.

Do your own business, Mic[hael] do not heed my Irish or me. Seán.

* P.S. We made references to the story above because H. is in M. Perhaps ye might wish to make some alteration because of that knowledge being with the censor.[26]

Following the four weeks of coded, fractious and exasperating communications, with as many attempts to craft a key compatible with the locks, the date and time of the escape were finally decided upon. Boland, Collins and their allies on the outside sprang into action once they had received the green light from de Valera. Contingency plans were their priority. An IRA lieutenant, James Fitzgerald, was detailed to secure a rope ladder in case the key did not work:

[It] was given to me in Mrs Pearse's house at Oakley Road, Ranelagh. It was to be used in the Lincoln prison escape and I got it from Colonel Joe O'Reilly. My duty was to take it to London and the parcel, containing the rope ladder had all the appearance of a drum wrapped up. I was armed at the same time with a revolver.

When I got to Dún Laoghaire with my parcel, intending to take the mail boat, Black and Tans were at the gang-way, but they did not interfere with me.[27] When I got on board I resolved to put the rope ladder downstairs for greater safety but when I reached a likely spot for the parcel there were four coffins there containing dead Black and Tans, and I was ordered to go upstairs.[28]

Fitzgerald got the package safely to London and handed it over to Fintan Murphy:

I was in some doubts as to how I should carry the ladder. To cover it or parcel it would make it a very bulky and perhaps suspicious bundle. I decided therefore that boldness was the best policy, and, as has often occurred before with me, the best way to get away with it. I merely rolled up the ladder and tied it thus and carried it for all the world to see. As I suspected no one gave it more than a passing glance and I booked my train seat for Manchester, putting the bundle in the rack above my head. Unadventurously I reached Manchester in the evening and was met at the train by Mick Collins and Harry Boland who smiled broadly when I told them how I had travelled with the exposed bundle.[29]

Paddy O'Donoghue began putting in place plans for a relay of taxis to ferry the prisoners away from Lincoln once they were out. O'Donoghue used a friend of his, the manager of

Beecham's Opera House, to secure tickets for a performance for himself, Boland and Collins:

> After the opera we were invited to supper by Sir Thomas Beecham in the Midland Hotel. We were all naturally in very good form. I introduced Collins and Boland to Sir Thomas Beecham under their proper names and he expressed his delight at meeting prominent people interested in the Irish independence movement.[30]

The following afternoon, Saturday, Boland, Collins, Murphy and O'Donoghue went to Lincoln.[31] O'Donoghue explained the preparations:

> We left Fintan Murphy at Worksop with instructions to have a car at his disposal about the time we would arrive there. Petrol restrictions were very severe at the time and we could not extend beyond Worksop on the first stage. Leaving Murphy behind, the three of us went to Lincoln and I engaged a car there. I had used the driver of this car on several occasions before and had become very friendly with him.[32]

Inside the prison, Dobbyn had for some days been fixed to the window of his cell taking notes of the times of patrol changes. He stood on a stool for three hours gauging the shift patterns. His observations were keen and he was able to tell that a soldier was going on leave if he was 'sprucely dressed' and unarmed. Fourteen soldiers would be going on leave.[33]

Michael Lennon said that as the day of the planned escape drew nearer, prisoners who were not aware of the scheme were called together in the common room by de Valera:

He drew us around him and in a low voice told us that an escape was in contemplation and that he would be accompanied by Seán Milroy and Seán McGarry, each of whom had served in the GPO.[34]

He said that on the night of the escape a task would be assigned to each of us and that after the escape we were to insist on such rights as we had been enjoying in the prison and not allow the British to curtail them. He said that [John] O'Mahony would be camp commandant after the escape. After this announcement, President de Valera led us in night prayers in Irish as usual, adding a special prayer for the success of the escape. From memory the prayer was St Bernard's *Memorare* which he read from the Catholic Truth Society prayer book.[35]

Zero hour – the day of the escape

Monday 3 February arrived. Fenner Brockway spotted a note being slipped under his door. He picked it up and opened it:

One morning, Alastar Mac's note (we wrote to each other every day) advised me in careful language that I might expect something exciting. I spent that day on the tip-toe of expectation, half-expecting release, straining my ears to interpret distant sounds.[36]

On Peter's instruction, de Valera attached the key to his braces with a bootlace.[37] He checked its effectiveness in the locks of cell doors when he was not being observed. He also practised lighting matches from the window at the exact time agreed on the days running up to 3 February. Lennon recalled that on the evening of the planned escape, de Valera, McGarry and Milroy were 'provided with a meal of fried eggs, bacon and fried bread cooked by Paul Dawson Cusack'.[38]

De Valera had instructed Boland and Collins to be outside the prison at 6.40 p.m. However, all accounts, including one given by Michael Lennon, say the escape was planned for an hour later. It is likely that Boland conveyed last minute refinements through the prison chaplain to McGarry explaining this change. Boland, Collins and O'Donoghue arrived by taxi in the vicinity of the prison, heavily armed. O'Donoghue 'instructed the driver to remain with his car at a certain hotel on the verge of the town. I stayed with the driver and Collins and Boland left me and went to the gates of the jail which was about a quarter of a mile distant.'[39] There they met Frank Kelly, who handed them the rope ladder they had given him earlier that evening. Kelly then set about his next task, keeping watch on Wragby Road (to the north of the prison). Boland and Collins cut through the barbed wire fence enclosing the grounds at the back of the prison and got through. They had to be careful because of the nearby military hospital.[40]

Inside, the prisoners were making final preparations:

After their meal, the three men left the room, Milroy returning soon after to say with a grin, 'We're off.' He was wearing an overcoat and, over his boots wore a number of prison socks, which were to serve as muffs as he crept over the gravel of the prison yard, which he would have to cross.[41] It was 18.48 when Milroy left the room. We finished our meal and said night prayers.[42]

One of the last conversations between de Valera and Peter in prison concerned the key. Peter made de Valera promise he would return it to him on the outside, to which he agreed.[43]

Neither knew for certain whether the latest engineered key, which had a peculiar variance to shoot the second bolt, would work.

At 7.40 p.m. Boland flashed his torch at the appointed window, but was unable to turn it off as the catch stuck. 'It was like a searchlight,' de Valera said afterwards, 'I clutched my hair with apprehension.' Boland quickly put the torch in his coat pocket and managed to extinguish the light. De Valera lit several matches and allowed them to blaze for a few seconds before blowing them out.[44]

Collins and Boland stole to the gate of the prison wall and waited, during which time one of them tried to open the gate from their side with a key which Boland may have had fashioned by a locksmith in Manchester.[45]

De Valera recounted the journey from the prison building during which he was careful to lock each door behind him:

> The key opened the doors beautifully and I got from cell to corridor out into the enclosure and to the gate in the prison wall through which we intended to escape. Harry Boland was outside. There were answering calls. Then Harry said they had tried to open the [gate] from the outside with a key which they had made and that the key had broken in the lock.[46]

For a few heart-breaking moments all seemed lost and their thoughts turned to an alternative means of escape. De Valera asked if they had brought the rope ladder. They had. He then breathed a prayer and inserted his own key in the lock with the hope of pushing out the broken stub. It tinkled to the ground outside.[47] He turned the key and the bolt released. The final obstacle had been breached.

Peter DeLoughry, top left, with his mother, Bridget, and brothers John, top right, David and Larry.
(Courtesy of Aedine Mangan)

Peter DeLoughry's father, Richard.
(Courtesy of Brenda Clausard)

Larry DeLoughry in Irish costume.
(Courtesy of Brenda Clausard)

John DeLoughry.
(Courtesy of Brenda Clausard)

Lil Mangan.
(Courtesy of Brenda Clausard)

Peter DeLoughry *circa* 1900.
(Courtesy of Brenda Clausard)

Win and Peter DeLoughry.
(Courtesy of Brenda Clausard)

Front page of Irish Volunteers (Kilkenny) subscription book. *(Courtesy of Pádraigín Ní Dhubhluachra)*

Peter DeLoughry's signature in Tomás Mac Curtáin's notebook from Reading jail. *(By kind permission of Fionnuala Mac Curtain)*

Postcard drawing by Seán Milroy in which the proportions of the key and lock are camouflaged in a comic postcard.
(*By kind permission of UCD-OFM Partnership*)

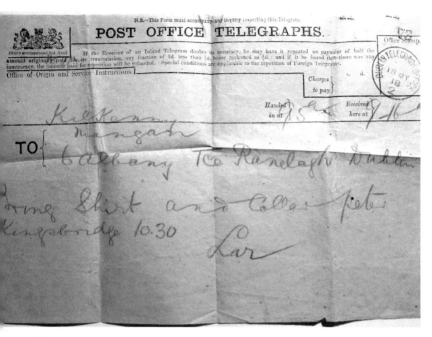

Telegram from Peter DeLoughry's brother Larry to their sister, Lil,
following the round-up of German plot suspects.
(*Courtesy of Brenda Clausard*)

Cheque written by Peter DeLoughry to Michael Collins.
(*Courtesy of Pádraigín Ní Dhubhluachra*)

Peter DeLoughry as mayor of Kilkenny.
(*Courtesy of Brenda Clausard*)

Peter DeLoughry's wife, Win, and four of their children, Dick, Tom, Lily and Sheila. (*Courtesy of Brenda Clausard*)

Win and Peter DeLoughry with their children Tom, Dick, Sheila, Peadar, Nessa and Lily. (*Courtesy of Pádraigín Ní Dhubhluachra*)

The Minister for Local Government, Tom Derrig, and Éamon de Valera at DeLoughry's funeral. (*Courtesy of Brenda Clausard*)

Peter DeLoughry's eldest son, Richard, his wife Anna T. (Cissie) De Loughry and de Valera holding Peter's key during a visit to Rothe House, Kilkenny, in 1966. (*Courtesy of Tom Brett Photography, Kilkenny*)

The three stepped into the outside world. De Valera wanted to close and lock the gate behind him, but was dissuaded from doing so because of the noise it would make. He immediately assumed command, reproaching Boland and Collins for having come themselves. He took the former's gun, fearing his impetuosity would get the better of him. They dumped the rope ladder in a nearby trench.

> We had only got a few feet outside the gate when we saw three soldiers and three girls coming along the field towards the prison and de Valera said, 'It is all up with us now' and wanted to run. I [Boland] told him that the men were busy with what they were doing and that it would take very little to get by them.[48]

They had a hard time finding the place where the wire had been cut but finally got through. As they neared Wragby Road, they could see that the men were wounded British soldiers from the military hospital lingering with their wives or girlfriends. However, Boland's impetuosity came to the rescue – he gave his heavy fur-lined coat to de Valera who put it on. 'I'll be your WAAC,' he said.[49] 'Link me.' De Valera did.[50]

> ... then we walked towards the soldiers and the three girls, and as they came near us, I started to joke with one of the girls about the kind of a night [it was] and her soldier boy, and as I went by, I jogged her in a jocular way and all of them laughing passed us. I pretended to be drunk myself.[51]

The prisoners and their accomplices then walked to the taxi in which Paddy O'Donoghue was waiting. De Valera, McGarry and Milroy got in. The taxi drove off. Collins and Boland disappeared on foot into the darkness and cold of that February night. The three men had escaped from jail, but now they had to escape from England. All would depend on the plan devised by Boland and Collins and indeed its execution.

Michael Lennon said that after de Valera, McGarry and Milroy had left, the remaining Irish internees tried to act normally:

> Those who played bridge went to Cusack's cell, the others walked up and down the hall or read in their cells. I remained in the common room for a nightly game of solo. From memory, Alec McCabe, Seán Corcoran, Tommy Ruane (killed in the Civil War) and Jim Dobbyn participated in the game. We played dealer out and never played for stakes.
>
> Some time during the game, someone came in and told us that the trio had got away all right. During the night, Jim Dobbyn, I think it was, said, 'When the warder comes ask him for a few minutes longer. Tell him there's a competition and that we are playing a rubber.' Someone said something about competition and rubber and he left, returning after about ten minutes.[52]

John O'Mahony waylaid a warder who was beginning to lock the cells doors by inviting him into his cell to share a whiskey with him.[53] The prisoners had two other tricks up their sleeve as Dobbyn explained:

> Now it came to closing time – nine o'clock. At that time a bell went. We were supposed to have the Rosary and all said – you had to go quietly to your cell but there was always a bit of a delay. You had to empty your basin. You had to get the water in for the night. A wee tin of water – you had to get your pipe filled to get it

lit because of the shortage of matches … That delayed everything. We got away with twenty minutes doing that. It reached the stage where apparently they smelt a rat.[54]

Meanwhile, Brockway was becoming depressed, as the expected surprise promised in McCabe's note had not happened:

> I got down my board and made my bed. I stood on my stool at the window for a long time and looked at the stars. A feeling of great depression came over me. Alastair's note had tuned me up to thrilled expectation; now I went down to the depth of reaction. How like a tomb this cell was! Perhaps I was already dead; perhaps all this thinking I was alive was sheer delusion; perhaps this was really a coffin. Then suddenly, I was sitting up straight, my heart bumping with excitement. Whistles were blowing, voices shouting, doors banging. I listened intently. More warders were being marched into the prison. They were being paraded at the centre and instructions given to them. I could hear steps in the yard outside. I jumped up, dragged the stool to the window and looked into the night. Lights were flashing here and there, into odd corners. There could be only one explanation. There had been an escape.[55]

The prisoners played their last delaying card when one of them feigned illness, which turned out to be a trump as Dobbyn recalled:

> [The call came] 'Get them in quick.' The next thing they all scurried to lock us in. I heard a call for me … 'You're wanted down here – [Seán Corcoran] has fainted.'
> He was a strong country chap from Mayo and I raced down and turned him over where he had fallen at his own door … It

would hold them up a while; they would have to go to get the hospital orderly for we would not let them shut the door on this man – they wanted to lock him into his cell.

We said, 'No, you can't do that with a sick man, he might be dead before anyone comes.' They had to go and get the hospital orderly. That delayed them about twenty minutes at least.[56]

Lennon described the sounds he heard from his cell:

I heard the voices of the guard, the fixing of bayonets and the clatter of the rifles. Someone shouted: 'Search the grounds.' Shortly afterwards I heard cell doors being opened seemingly upstairs.

Then my own cell door was opened. I turned my face to the wall. Someone in heavy boots and dragging a rifle entered and with what I accurately sensed was an old-style stable lantern lit up the cell and then lowered the lantern and looked under the bed.[57]

Brockway, too, was still trying to make sense of the noise:

I was as excited as though it had been myself. I put my mouth to the open pane and jeered at the warders outside. 'You won't find him,' I shouted. 'You won't find him. We'll all escape and you won't find any of us.' A warder lifted his light to my window for a moment and then went on with his task, walking gingerly, throwing his light from side to side. I stood at the window and jeered until the search of the yard had concluded and the lights had gone. Then I listened at the door, trying to appraise the various sounds until they had ceased. I was fairly confident that the escaped prisoners had not been recaptured. The warders would have shouted the news to each other if they had caught them.[58]

The alarm had been raised at 10.40 p.m., meaning that by the time search parties were despatched and the hue and cry uttered, the escaped prisoners had a three-and-a-half-hour start.

11

Escape from Lincoln – Aftermath, 1919

As the remaining prisoners settled down for the night, the plan to escort de Valera, McGarry and Milroy to safe houses continued apace. The proposal was to ferry them from Lincoln to Worksop where they would transfer to another car, from there to Sheffield where a similar change would take place, and thence to Manchester.

Lincoln →(26 miles) Worksop →(18 miles) Sheffield →(40 miles) Manchester

(*Estimates of distances noted by Michael Collins along the escape route*)

Paddy O'Donoghue was in charge of getting them from Lincoln to Worksop. The second leg would be managed by Fintan Murphy, whose account of the preparations for this shows that he met with an extraordinary number of petty and unexpected difficulties:

I [had] left Manchester for Worksop during [the] week to make the appropriate arrangements at my 'control'. Once again I had to think up some more 'plausible stories' to avert any possible attention being attracted by what would undoubtedly be suspicious and curious requests and movements. I decided to wait until I reached Worksop and had an opportunity of inspecting the lay-out of the town.

I found it much the same as any other English county town of that time, with its narrow Main Street (Bridge Street), its inn-like public houses and its roads leading out into the country itself. It was more important, however, that I should examine it as to its relation on the one hand to Lincoln and the other to Sheffield and then to consider how best to arrange for the transfer from one car to another. In this matter, Worksop was made for the plan. The road leading out to Sheffield ran straight through the town – the road to Lincoln led off this at right angles and joined it actually before it reached Worksop. This was admirable as it did away with the necessity of passing through the town at all. This was not all, however, as at the opposite side of the road where Lincoln Road led in was an old English inn with, in front of it, a deep bay-like yard open to the road.

My plan began to form in my mind. The car from Lincoln should drive into this yard; my charges should dismount as if they were coming in with me for a late dinner. I should dismiss the car and, when it was out of sight, I would bring my men along the Sheffield Road and pick up my car to send them on their way. So far, so good. I had next to arrange for my car.

Here my difficulties really began. It was only three months since the war had stopped. War conditions still prevailed; there was a shortage of petrol; a regulation existed that where travel could be made by any other means, such as the railway, motors could not be hired. I therefore decided to consult the railway time-table so that I might study the connections at Sheffield and so have my story rehearsed before attempting to hire a car.

By extraordinary coincidence the time-table played into my hands. I found that a train left Sheffield at 9.20 p.m. on Sunday.

I also found that a train left Worksop which was timed to arrive in Sheffield at 9.25 p.m. My story was made up instantly. I could not get away from Worksop except by train arriving at Sheffield at 9.25 p.m. and I must catch the connection leaving Sheffield at 9.20 p.m.

What to do? I must engage a taxi to take me from Worksop to Sheffield to make it. Armed with my story, I walked along Sheffield Road until I found a garage where I asked the clerk for a taxi the following Sunday evening to take me to Sheffield. At first, of course, I was met with a refusal, my attention being drawn to the regulations. I then, however, explained my dilemma about catching my Sheffield connection and after some demur, I succeeded in hiring it. Things seemed to be working out perfectly and having arranged to pick up the taxi on Sunday evening, I returned to Manchester and reported my success. Similar arrangements were made at Sheffield although, strange to say, I neither remember who was there nor how the details were worked out.

We had nothing to do for the remaining days and we just waited expectantly. I proposed to go to Worksop on the Saturday afternoon and billet myself in a hotel there, and in due course, I bade goodbye and good luck to Mick, Harry, Liam McMahon and Paddy O'Donoghue and went on my way.

When I arrived back in Worksop I selected a hotel in Bridge Street which, luck would have it, I found was right opposite the police station. I booked a room and found it also was in the front and actually overlooked the station. Looking out and noticing how quiet and peaceful everything was, I thought amusedly what consternation there would be if the object of my presence there were known.

The Sunday passed quietly for me as I wandered around in the bright February sunlight. I was glad it was dry and bright as I would probably have to hang around a good deal before the day was over. I now began to feel a certain amount of anxiety as I was, of course, completely out of touch with all my colleagues and I began to wonder what would happen if anything went wrong. I should myself probably have no difficulty in getting away safely but what of Harry and Mick at Lincoln? They would find it hard to escape if suspicions were aroused or if their plans went wrong. With these thoughts in my mind, I passed the afternoon with a stroll towards my 'contact' point and, as evening fell, I began to get ready for the great event.

Towards eight o'clock I called at the garage to pick up my taxi. Once again, I had to think up a story to explain to the driver why he should wait in a rather indefinite way, more or less on the side of the road, instead of picking me up at a hotel. Naturally, I must have him far enough away from the inn where I proposed receiving my guests so that he would not observe their arrival. Again, I would not be travelling with them and any suspicion on that score required to be dissipated. I told him I was dining with friends that evening and I would call for him when I was ready for him. I felt myself that my story was weak but I had to take my chance on it. To my relief he took no more than the usual notice of my instructions and I wandered back to my post.

By my watch, I was approaching 'zero hour', but of course there would bound to be some delay and I reckoned that the limit of my wait should be 8.30 p.m. That would still leave plenty of time to make Sheffield according to plan. The minutes crept on and I gazed down the Lincoln Road in the dusk. Not a sign of a vehicle, not a movement on that quiet Sunday evening. I glanced at my watch again and found it was a quarter of an hour after the scheduled time. Not much, I agree but in the circumstances enough to begin to make me anxious.

I decided to walk down the Lincoln Road a bit and see would I meet the car. I was now also beginning to get worried about my driver. He would wonder why I was delaying so long. My trip down the road yielded no result and I decided to go and interview the driver. As I expected, he was beginning to get uneasy and informed me that I would never make Sheffield in time for my train. This was a contingency which I had not taken into account. I endeavoured, as best I could, to allay his doubts and reassured him that we would make it in time. Once again, I returned to my post getting more worried each moment and almost coming to a conclusion that our efforts, after so much good organisation, had gone awry. Apart from the satisfaction of achieving the escape in the face of all the difficulties, I realised what a setback it would probably be to our whole movement if we failed to get out de Valera, who was our chief in more ways than one.

Presently, I saw lights approaching down the Lincoln Road and my heart gave a turn. At last they were coming! As it slowed at the turn I advanced towards it to see its occupants when, to my disappointment, I saw it contained only one occupant and it turned in towards Worksop. I now felt sure that it had all been in vain and there would be nothing for me to do but take my taxi and proceed to Sheffield and try and establish communication again with the others. Still, I waited.

Three-quarters of an hour or more later, a car hove into sight on the Lincoln Road once again, and I prayed fervently that they had at last arrived. My prayer was answered. I went forward to meet the car and saw the figures of de Valera, Seán Milroy and Seán McGarry.[1] I saluted them casually and told the driver to go up to the inn where they got out. Then in the presence of the driver, I told them that dinner had been waiting for them for some time and that due to their lateness I feared it would be spoiled. I pride myself that I carried off the matter casually enough and then, having dismissed the driver and made a feint of going towards the inn as if to enter I hurriedly explained to them the plan for their next stages and took them as rapidly as possible up the Sheffield Road to my taxi.

Arrived there, I anticipated trouble with my driver and I was not disappointed. He protested strenuously that it was impossible to make my connection at Sheffield and that it was useless trying. I urged him, however, that he must do it and my charges got into the car and having bade them God speed, and amidst much grumbling from the driver, I breathed a sigh of relief as I saw them disappear down the road.

I strolled back to the main street and scarcely failed to suppress my chuckles on the success, so far at any rate. They were out and that was the most important point.

I entered my hotel and felt I was entitled to a drink with myself after my anxious hours. How calm and unexcited the crowd in that bar were; the typical English crowd which you would expect to see in such a place on a Sunday evening, some playing darts, others chatting at the bar, the bored barmaid. I ordered my glass of war near-beer and lingered over it as I observed my companions and wondered how the travellers were progressing.

I turned in early and slept soundly and on Monday morning awaking early, I wondered whether the escape had yet created a stir. I looked out of the window and glanced across at the police station to see how the land lay there. Not a stir. Obviously this town had not learned of it yet. I got the morning paper when I went down to my breakfast. Not a word in it. Good! No hue and cry had yet been raised, and there was no necessity to make a hurried exit.

I took the next train to London and when I arrived at St Pancras, there, in large letters on the evening paper placards were the words 'De Valera escapes from Lincoln.'[2]

By the time the prisoners in Lincoln were beginning their daily routine, de Valera, McGarry and Milroy had completed their journey; the last leg, from Sheffield to Manchester, having been organised by Liam McMahon. The plan by Boland and Collins estimated their arrival in Manchester at midnight. The freed prisoners arrived in the city at five past midnight when each was squirrelled away to safe houses in the sleeping city.

The governor of Lincoln prison had much to contend with on the day the escape became known. He did not need any more trouble, but the prisoners decided to give him an extra helping in any case. Michael J. Lennon's account of this incident gives an insight into his frustration: an exasperation that also exploded in a cloud over Westminster:

> Peter DeLoughry asked to be allowed to see the governor as he had not been brought to the bath-house for his daily bath – he had a bath each morning at around 7 a.m. DeLoughry was then mayor of Kilkenny and had been some fourteen years in public life. 'You don't expect everything to be normal after what has happened?' protested the governor, a retired army captain.[3]
>
> DeLoughry protested that the escape had nothing to do with him and that he had not had his bath. 'I did all in my power for you and now you do the dirty on me,' complained the governor.
>
> 'We had it hot and heavy,' reported DeLoughry, but in the end, the governor said: 'Oh well, I suppose it was your job to escape and mine to keep you in!'

Next morning, DeLoughry had his bath as usual.[4]

Reports of the escape were telegraphed across the world. *The Sydney Morning Herald* announced: 'The Sinn Féin leaders, de Valera, Milroy and McGarry have escaped from Lincoln prison.'[5] *The New York Times* was unrestrained in its assessment of security at Lincoln prison: 'It was an easy matter for the trio to walk out to a waiting automobile which took them toward the coast.'[6] Press reports of the escape, theories on how it was executed and sightings of de Valera filled newspaper columns from Rio de Janeiro to Moscow, from Beijing to Ottawa and from Delhi to Paris.

The *Star*, a London evening newspaper, told readers that the escape had created 'quite a stir in the House of Commons' and there were fears that the three escaped prisoners would make a scene before the election of the Speaker of the House.[7] The escape was the subject of debate at Westminster throughout February 1919 and regained global prominence the following month with the publication of an interview given by Seán T. Ó Ceallaigh at the Paris peace conference to the Associated Press. Ó Ceallaigh gave a fanciful account of how the escape was planned, saying that a Sinn Féin member began working on a garden plot near the prison and sang a song in Irish informing de Valera, who was in earshot, that an attempt would be made to free him. As Ó Ceallaigh continued his explanation he warmed to the embellishments: after women from Lincoln had failed to attract the attention of soldiers and sentries, 'a telegram was sent to Dublin for two handsome young women, both highly cultured university graduates who arrayed themselves as shop girls and crossed the Channel'. According to Ó Ceallaigh, the women succeeded in flirting with the prison guards, distracting them from observing messages being sent in and out.[8]

The article was the source of much amusement, particularly among the remaining Irish prisoners. Paul Dawson Cusack wrote a letter describing Ó Ceallaigh's account as 'absurd and more like a cinema plot from Mexico than anything else. If de Valera sees it he will be amused, particularly about the singing part, as, poor man, he doesn't know one note from another.'[9]

The British home secretary, Edward Shortt, was asked in the House of Commons if there was any truth in the statement that the escape was facilitated by 'women inveigling the sentries from their posts?' Mr Shortt replied: 'None of the sentries has any knowledge of any ladies. (Laughter).'[10]

Peter and his fellow inmates found much-needed entertainment in the continuing press reports that were at times bizarre, at times funny. The historian David Fitzpatrick says that de Valera's escape and disappearance 'became a matter of worldwide speculation, and 568 readers of one illustrated magazine entered a competition to "find de Valera" somewhere among squiggles on a sketch map of Ireland, Britain and France'.[11]

A reward of £5 was offered for information that would lead to the capture of de Valera, McGarry and Milroy.[12] The *Sunday Independent* listed the sightings of de Valera that had been printed in British newspapers. He had been spotted in more than a dozen locations including Gravesend, Paris, Modane in south-east France, Glasgow, in a small boat and on the lonely east coast. The same report, which likened him to the Scarlet Pimpernel, also gave a list of the latest rumours: he was in New York; he got there by balloon or aeroplane; he flew to France by seaplane; he was dressed as a priest; he was dressed as a lady; he was not alive at all.[13]

'Ireland,' said the *Daily Express*, 'is full of stories of banshees, leprechauns and quaint spirits, and de Valera is just a distillation of all these mystic things. The funny part of it is that he is not even an Irishman. In our view, the government are quite right in not taking him at the valuation which the Irish people have placed on him.'[14]

De Valera arrived in Dublin on 20 February, having been smuggled onto a ship.[15] His fellow escapers also made their way to Ireland. Seán McGarry took advantage of the Waterloo Cup being run and dressed as a bookie and had a bag with the name 'Billy Ellsworth' printed on it. Seán Milroy was dressed as a strolling musician. He dyed his grey hair brown and carried a violin case.[16]

Back in Lincoln prison, the Irish prisoners who remained experienced the evaporation of exhilaration as time passed from the day of the escape. The censor noticed from their letters a 'certain apathy'.[17] Peter, in a letter to his sister, two weeks after the escape, appeared maudlin, a mood strengthened by his recollection of the stricken Seán Etchingham, who had been allowed home because of his poor health:

Number: 391
Name: Peter DeLoughry,
Lincoln prison.
Feb. 13, 1919.

My dear Lil,

Your letter of the 9th received yesterday and despite your 'fears' I was here when it arrived. Certainly all the reports about release were very annoying to us and must be equally so to our friends at home. We are getting used to it all now.

I am indeed sorry to hear that Etchingham is still so ill, we were in hopes that he would pull round rapidly with good food and nursing in his native air. I greatly fear he was too far gone …

Nothing exciting here. Much more lonely since DeV & Co. went for those of us who decided to remain. Elaborate precautions to secure that no more take French leave.

Very hard frost lately but days fine.
Hope all are well.
Love to all
Yours Affectionately
Peter.[18]

The inquiry into the Lincoln prison escape failed to establish how it was done. The prison authorities sniped at the War Office for not having provided extra security. Irish officials in Dublin Castle lobbied privately and publicly for the release of the 'German Plot' prisoners. Morale among prison staff nosedived. Every time a prisoner fell ill, the authorities were blamed. An influenza pandemic raging at the time forced up the number of prisoners whose health declined. The deaths of Richard Coleman in Usk prison and Pierce McCan in Gloucester prison gave Sinn Féin opportunities to show its muscle by mounting monster gatherings at their funerals. The Lincoln prison escape continued to pervade newspaper columns in Britain, Ireland and elsewhere.

The start of the Irish War of Independence in January 1919 placed another burden on the British government and in March 1919 a general release of prisoners was ordered, but even this was not free from controversy. The release was staggered to avert a single demonstration for the homecoming of the prisoners, but this resulted in several rallies throughout Ireland as each prisoner returned. No opportunity was lost to embarrass the British government. Michael Colivet complained in an interview with the *Irish Independent* of his treatment immediately after being released:

When leaving Lincoln we asked if the tickets given us would

entitle us to travel saloon, the chief warder of the prison said they would. Everything was all right until we got to Holyhead. It was about 2 a.m. – wild, cold and miserable. We presented our tickets but the checker refused to allow us on board the steamer. Our tickets were marked 'via Holyhead' but as the name 'Kingstown' was not added we could not travel, he said, unless we paid the excess of 7/6.

Of course, we refused to pay this, especially as we got only 10/- each to cover our expenses from the prison authorities. We were compelled to wait there at the pier, and it was a great hardship, particularly on a few who were quite weak. Ultimately, but not until every place on board was occupied and when no places were left for us to rest ourselves, they let us through. I don't know who is responsible for this; but, in the interest of those of our fellows who are recovering from the influenza epidemic, and who are greatly weakened, I protest as strongly as I can. It is a scandalous bit of business.[19]

Peter was among the Irish prisoners released (10 March) and on his arrival in Dublin he stayed with his sister, Lil, and her husband, Henry Mangan. One of his first moves to readjust himself to family life was to invite their nine-year-old daughter Lelia for tea in Bewley's restaurant. The little girl dressed herself in an Irish costume, used by one of her brothers in a stage play, but had to explain her attire to her dismayed mother:

I came down and my mother gave one horrified look at me. I said, 'I put on my socks' and she said, 'So I see but what is that you have on you?' I said that this was my Irish costume. She said that it hadn't been ironed and it hadn't been washed and my uncle said, 'Let her. It's an Irish costume and if she thinks that's the appropriate thing for escorting me to town, out we go.' So my mother couldn't say any more and my heroic uncle took me down Grafton Street, into Bewley's, sat feeding me with cream buns and brought me home in the most disreputable-looking Irish costume that ever was. I consider that he was a greater hero in escorting such a child into town and back than he was in putting up with the exigencies of life in Lincoln jail or even in making the key with which the 'chief' escaped.[20]

After this, following ten months in prison, Peter was on his way home to his wife, Win, their children (Dick, who was seven, Tom, six, Lily, four, Sheila, three), and Nanny. Peter and W. T. Cosgrave, who had won in the Kilkenny North constituency while in prison, arrived to a triumphant reception which was held at the Parade.[21] Peter was greeted by Win at the local train station. Understandably she had not wanted him to be part of any escape from Lincoln prison because she believed his liberty was close.[22] Alderman James Nowlan, who had been standing in for Peter as mayor, announced to the cheering crowd: 'I have the greatest possible pleasure in putting on DeLoughry, the felon, the mayoral chain of the city of Kilkenny.' In a speech delivered in Irish and English, Peter said the British government must realise that it was not dealing with a rebel party but with a rebel people. In his address, E. T. Keane joked that he could name the first four in the Lincoln handicap, de Valera, McGarry and Milroy. 'There was a fourth in the race,' he said, 'and her name was Dora [acronym for Defence of the Realm Act] but she got so badly mauled at the barbed wire fence that she was unable to continue the course.'[23]

The *Kilkenny Moderator*, which generally supported the

British Conservative Party, deviated from its straight report of the event, giving this view of Peter's character:

> It [the welcoming] was a spontaneous manifestation of respect and admiration for one who, no matter what his politics may be, has always shown himself to be consistent. He is one of those who does not blow hot and cold to suit exigencies, whether in private or public life. He says exactly what he means, not what he thinks will suit others, and for this characteristic he is admired even by those who might differ acutely from him.[24]

This bluntness was apparent in the speech Peter delivered at his homecoming. His audience knew that he had spent many months in jail with de Valera and probably expected Peter to speak of hope and unity. This he did, but he also told the crowd: 'we should not hesitate to criticise our leaders'.[25]

Daniel J. Stapleton, lieutenant, No. 1 Company, 1st Battalion, Kilkenny Brigade, said news of the escape 'spread through the country and it would appear that this was a signal for intensive activity on the part of all our [IRA][26] units throughout the land'.[27] For Tom Treacy, brigade commandant, Kilkenny, the release of the 'German Plot' prisoners allowed him to return to normal life, having been on the run since escaping arrest at the time of the round-up ten months earlier.

Violence escalated in Ireland throughout 1919. In Kilkenny, the IRA arranged lines of communication, noted the strength of RIC and British army forces, and the oath of allegiance to the Dáil was administered.[28] (The oath caused difficulties in Kilkenny as elsewhere. Ned Comerford raised strong objections and demanded to know what the position would be in the event of Dáil Éireann ever letting down or betraying the Republic. The chief of staff, Richard Mulcahy, had to visit the city to reassure the Kilkenny Volunteers. Comerford then withdrew his objection.)[29] Arms were seized. A disloyal British soldier obliged the Kilkenny Republicans by selling rifles to them before he was found out.[30] Brigade and battalion meetings were held at the Sinn Féin office in Parliament Street, beside Peter's home and business, although on occasion the Tholsel was used. Shortly after his return, Peter attended one of these meetings and was described by E. T. Keane as the accredited leader of the Sinn Féin movement in Kilkenny.[31]

Not long after his release, Peter, along with Win, who was president of Kilkenny Cumann na mBan, were surprise guests of honour at a Cumann na mBan event in Rothe House. The couple were presented with an inscribed silver loving-cup that Peter said he hoped, for the sake of the givers, would be cherished by those who came after them. Peter had been given the impression that the function was to be a celebration of Irish-Ireland and told the assembly, 'This secret has been well kept. I never believed or thought much of the old hackneyed tag about women being unable to keep a secret.'[32]

The Irish-Ireland element in Kilkenny continued to make its presence felt. Sinn Féin announced in April 1919 that an Irish class was 'in full swing' and that new members were cordially invited.[33] Peter's brother, Larry, continued to perform on stage. On St Patrick's Day 1919, he had appeared in another performance of *The Memory of the Dead* written by Count Markievicz.[34]

Indeed, Peter's return allowed Larry more freedom to indulge in leisure pursuits. Larry recorded his activities during Peter's time in Lincoln as follows:

1 April 1918 to 31 March 1919

> I was working in my brother's shop about this time and hand
> grenade cases were being made at his foundry. The RIC barracks
> was at the other side of the street and it was my duty to keep
> watch on the barracks while the work was in progress. The
> shop was used as a depot for delivering despatches and parcels
> from different [IRA] branches and it was I who delivered these
> messages.[35]

Aside from taking up the reins of the family business once
again and carrying out his duties as mayor, Peter also found
himself at the centre of an industrial dispute between Statham's
motor garage and its workers, after management refused to
recognise their union. The mechanics downed tools in early
March and were supported by the firm's clerical workers.
Mass demonstrations were organised. The *Kilkenny People* was
seen as unsympathetic to the strikers, whose leaders described
a notice in that paper seeking clerical workers as a 'scab
advertisement'.[36] Peter wrote letters to both parties offering
himself as a mediator and a conference was held in early
April, after which they accepted Peter's recommendations and
the strike ended.

The resolution added another string to Peter's bow, that
of industrial relations mediator. The strike at Statham's was
one of a number of instances of unrest among workers in the
county during 1919 and marked the emergence of the fight for
workers' rights in Kilkenny. However, Peter's relationship with
the labour movement was not all clear sailing and he went
against workers who objected to a take-over of Sullivan's brewery by Smithwick's brewery. Peter's stance may be explained

by the fact that the local Sinn Féin treasurer, W. F. O'Meara, was manager of Smithwick's brewery. The RIC noted that because of Peter's stance, the Labour Party was planning to oust Sinn Féin members from the corporation at the next municipal elections.[37] This deterioration in the relationship between Sinn Féin and the Labour Party contrasted strongly with that enjoyed by the two organisations in the run-up to the 1918 general election when the Labour Party had allowed Sinn Féin a clear run by not putting forward a candidate.

Despite this row, Sinn Féin's prominence continued to grow in Kilkenny, helped not least by the conferring of the freedom of the city on W. T. Cosgrave. Peter played an integral part in the planning of this event which was attended by his former prison colleague Seán Milroy, Countess Markievicz and Fr Michael O'Flanagan.[38]

Peter also devoted a large part of his time to lobbying for improvements to the city's public services. He led a petition against the imposition of a motor permit which was brought in under the Defence of the Realm Act. However, issues such as public lighting, the city's sewers and even political differences with the Labour Party had to be put into second place on Peter's list of priorities four months after his release from Lincoln prison:

> The British government began to turn its attention to Ireland on 4 July 1919 a week after the Versailles Treaty was signed. Sinn Féin, the Irish Volunteers, Cumann na mBan and the Gaelic League were proclaimed illegal in various counties.[39]

The impact was felt keenly by two of Kilkenny's leading citizens, E. T. Keane and Alderman James Nowlan. Their houses and those of Tom Treacy, James Lalor and others were raided. The Sinn Féin office in Parliament Street was ransacked by British soldiers with fixed bayonets on Saturday 12 September 1919.

In late September Keane and Nowlan, who was national president of the GAA, were arrested for possession of arms and brought to Cork jail. They were convicted and sentenced to twenty-eight days' imprisonment. In his monthly report, RIC County Inspector Power said that 'E. T. Keane, who was president of the Sinn Féin club here, is utterly discredited since he recognised the court martial at which he was tried and convicted'.[40] As Keane had refused to recognise British authority in Ireland for a long time, his recognition of the court martial showed up an inconsistency in his political stance. Keane was released a few days early:

> Mr Keane was receiving hospital treatment and, on Friday and Saturday morning, was submitted to a special examination by the medical officer of the prison who on Sunday morning informed Mr Keane that he had on the previous day recommended his discharge as he believed his continued confinement would seriously affect his health … Mr Keane is in a weak condition and has lost weight considerably during his incarceration.[41]

12

War of Independence, 1920

Throughout 1920 Peter built on his political base, strengthened his oratory and moved his vehemence against the RIC, the British army and the British government into fifth gear.

His brother Larry, who was still living at the family home and business in Parliament Street, remained equally committed to the armed struggle. Their brother David was setting up a hotel on the other side of the city and the British authorities kept a very close eye on him. The family business was opposite the RIC barracks in Parliament Street and David's hotel was beside the other RIC barracks in the city on John Street.

Peter won his second consecutive term of office as mayor of Kilkenny in January 1920 and used his victory to revive the mayoral banquet. This was a politically canny move, bringing together the clergy, his political opponents, captains of industry and the press, though E. T. Keane was absent because of the illness that had befallen him in Cork jail. The friction that existed between Sinn Féin and the Labour Party was, for the moment at least, ended and Peter was re-elected mayor without opposition. County Inspector Power noted in his monthly report that 'Sinn Féin and Labour have a majority at present and appear to have reconciled some differences which had existed and which may again recur'.[1]

Apart from his re-election, Peter and Win had another reason to celebrate in early January, with the birth of another daughter.[2] As was usual at the time, babies were born in the family home, but the couple's fifth child, Nessa, was born in a family home that doubled as a bomb factory. Thomas Murphy, her maternal uncle, was one of many involved in the production of ordnance at the foundry and one of the most colourful of these explosives engineers was Joe McMahon from County Clare, who had arrived in Kilkenny in the middle of 1918. Martin Cassidy, officer commanding, 'A' Company, 1st Battalion, Kilkenny Brigade (1917–1921) described McMahon as a 'real live-wire'.[3] James Lalor gave an account that explained how justified Cassidy's description of McMahon was:

> On one occasion while grenades were being made, we received a quantity of gelignite to be used in their manufacture from the 3rd battalion (Castlecomer) area. This particular lot had been taken from the coal mines near Castlecomer and was frozen when we got it. To thaw it out, Joe put it into the stove of a gas oven in DeLoughry's workshop and lit the gas full on. Missing the gelignite, I asked him where he had put it and when he told me, I went to the stove and I was shaking as I turned the gas off. Poor Joe! He was subsequently killed when giving a demonstration of these same grenades in Cavan.[4]

How these grenades were to be used became clear in early January 1920 when Tom Treacy travelled to Dublin to meet the IRA chief of staff, Richard Mulcahy, and was ordered to take an RIC barracks 'either by strategy or attack'.[5]

Detailed knowledge of Peter's activities on behalf of the Republican movement at this time was uncovered following a raid by the British authorities on the Sinn Féin headquarters in Dublin. Letters were found which showed that Peter was involved in raising subscriptions for the Dáil loan set up by Michael Collins to fund the establishment of an Irish Republic:

Dáil loan – Co. Kilkenny

Correspondence 24.2.20 to 7.5.20. between M. Collins, James Lalor, Friary Street, Kilkenny, and P. DeLoughrey [*sic*], mayor of Kilkenny, reference organisation and collection of subscriptions. A letter dated 11.3.20, Lalor to M.C. states that no more letters are to be sent through Miss Buggy, but to the manager, the cinema, Kilkenny.[6]

Peter wrote cheques for sizeable amounts from bank accounts where subscriptions had been deposited. The cheques were made out to William T. Cosgrave, Arthur Griffith, Michael Collins and W. F. O'Meara. The amounts ranged from £10 to O'Meara to £453 to Collins.[7]

Deaths both natural and violent pervaded Peter's life throughout the year. The lord mayor of Cork, Tomás Mac Curtáin (with whom Peter had been imprisoned in Reading after 1916) was shot dead by British forces at his home in front of his family. Peter, Tom Stallard and E. T. Keane attended the funeral and were received at City Hall in Cork by Terence MacSwiney, with whom Peter had been lodged in Lincoln prison.[8]

The laying of a foundation stone for a memorial to Archbishop Croke in Thurles afforded Peter a platform outside his electoral patch to bang the Republican drum. He made a speech guaranteed to touch the raw nerve of Republicans by mentioning Pierce McCan, a Tipperary man, who died in a British prison at around the same time that Peter was released from Lincoln:

> The last time I stood in this square of Thurles, since fittingly christened Liberty Square, was barely over twelve months ago. I had come with many others of my fellow countrymen straight from an English prison. But the joy of our home-coming was turned to tears and our hearts were filled with grief for the death of one of the best beloved of our comrades. Pierce McCan did not live to receive the welcome that Tipperary had prepared for him. Like the Spartan warrior of old he came back to Tipperary 'not with his shield but on it' and he rendered up to Tipperary the shield he had received, stainless as when he got it and untarnished as his own pure and noble life.[9]

Back in Kilkenny, Tom Treacy was completing plans for an attack on an RIC barracks following the orders he had been given in January by Richard Mulcahy. Having consulted the Kilkenny officers, Treacy decided eventually to attack Hugginstown RIC barracks and detailed preparations were made. Telephone and telegraph wires were cut, bombs were transported to the area and the men involved were told of their specific tasks. The attack was set for the night of 8 March 1920. The barracks was riddled by fire and Joe McMahon managed to get onto the roof and drop bombs into the building. The RIC officers inside returned fire as their wives and children took cover. (Treacy had opened the engagement by telling those inside that the women and children would be allowed out without being harmed. However, the women and children remained in the barracks.) The RIC officers surrendered after forty-five minutes and arms were brought out and laid on the ground outside. However, a Constable Thomas Ryan, who was thirty-eight and a married man with three children, had been seriously wounded and died shortly afterwards.[10] Peter had been involved in the planning of this attack and had allowed his foundry to be used to make bombs for the assault. His brother-in-law Thomas Murphy took part in the attack.

Shortly after the attack, the RIC called to Peter's business where he also had motor cars for hire, and took impressions of tyres. Several people were arrested but no one was charged. Hugginstown RIC barracks was the third in Ireland to be captured. Afterwards, many RIC barracks in rural areas were closed and the constables moved to larger urban centres. The Kilkenny IRA burned down more than a dozen abandoned barracks in April and May of 1920. Tom Treacy and James Lalor were arrested in early April but released several weeks later and Peter welcomed them back at public ceremonies.

Peter put in an impressive performance in the county council elections in May and topped the poll in the Kilkenny electoral area securing 1,179 first preference votes, 560 votes ahead of his nearest rival. One of the first decisions taken by the new county council was to pledge allegiance to Dáil Éireann.[11]

The Kilkenny Brigade acted on Dáil decrees for the setting up of a police force and a court system. Peter sat as a judge in Kilkenny. Tom Treacy, who acted as clerk to the court, recalled that those who sought justice from these courts were not all rabid Republicans:

Some of the first cases to be dealt with related to the larceny of jewellery, plate and other valuables from the residences of Major Humphrey, Talbotsinch, and Major Joyce of Sion House, Kilkenny, both ex-British army officers. Another early case related to the stealing of cattle from the lands of Sir Wheeler Cuffe, Leyrath. These people had reported their losses to the RIC at the time of the occurrences but without result. They then reported them to someone whom they knew to be connected with Sinn Féin or the [IRA]. The Republican Police quickly discovered the culprits, and traced and restored the missing property and cattle to the rightful owners without undue delay. The owners expressed their grateful thanks to the Republican Police and their appreciation of the magnificent police and detective work. All these people were unionists, and I just mention these few cases as a sample of how justice and fair play was administered under the Republic regardless of political or religious affiliations.

One of the ex-British majors referred to in the preceding paragraph, on the day following that on which his property was restored to him, called to the RIC barracks and created a scene. He cursed and thundered at the RIC shouting that they were not worth a curse as police to protect or recover people's property, that he had recovered his property in a twinkling, not thanks to them, and that it was a blessing that there was someone in the country to protect him and people like him from thieves who were prowling around and whom they (the RIC) made no attempt to bring to justice.[12]

In June the committee of the Gowran Park races asked Peter to supply Republican Police to preserve order and regulate traffic. During the day, the Volunteers took three pickpockets into custody and stolen money was restored to its owners.[13]

Two months later, Volunteers in Graiguenamanagh arrested an ex-British soldier named William Kenny, who had reported their activities to the RIC. Kenny was allowed to see a local priest following his conviction. John Walsh, commandant, IRA, Kilkenny, said that as the British army might hear gunfire, it was decided to execute Kenny by drowning:

> We gagged and blindfolded him and, having bound his arms and legs, we dropped him into the River Barrow at a point just a few yards from [Blanchfield's] eel house. The water at this point would be eight or ten feet deep and, as an additional precaution, we tied a 56 lb weight to his body before dropping him into the river. As far as I can now recollect, the date of Kenny's execution was 31 August 1920. About two months later, his decomposed body was washed ashore about three miles further down the river and, with two other volunteers, I had the gruesome task of again tying weights and heavy stones to the body and dropping it into the river for a second time.[14]

Peter's fellow Sinn Féin stalwart in Kilkenny, Pat Corcoran, died from natural causes in August 1920 and this hit Peter very hard, as their friendship went back a long way. A wooden overmantel in the DeLoughry house at 18 Parliament Street had been designed and made by Corcoran as a wedding present for Peter and Win in 1911.[15] He had been one of the first Kilkenny men to be arrested after the 1916 Rising; 250 British soldiers surrounded his house before his arrest. In paying tribute to him at a meeting of Kilkenny Corporation, Peter said he felt the utmost difficulty in giving expression to the loss he, Kilkenny and Ireland had sustained.[16]

At a meeting of the Association of Irish Municipal Authorities in September, Peter proposed that Terence Mac-Swiney, who was then lord mayor of Cork and on hunger strike in Brixton prison, be elected president of the association. The motion was passed. MacSwiney died the following month having been on hunger strike for seventy-four days. A few days later, word came through that Kevin Barry had been executed by hanging in Mountjoy prison. Kilkenny Corporation adjourned in sympathy with Barry's family, at Peter's request. Auxiliaries raided Peter's home that same week.[17]

Around this time, the Black and Tans, British military and RIC raided the Sinn Féin office beside Peter's home and business while he was making grenade casings. Peter's bomb factory was turning out a lot of explosives, some of which were demanded by general headquarters in Dublin. GHQ had also asked Peter to use his influence to get other foundry owners around the country to follow his lead and turn their skills to producing ordnance. Tom Treacy recalled that Peter 'subsequently told me that he had approached all those he knew and tried his very best, but his efforts were fruitless as those whom he approached were afraid to engage in this dangerous work'.[18]

This military innovation in Kilkenny, recognised by GHQ, was not the first to be noticed by those outside the county. The strategy employed for the attack on Hugginstown barracks was copied and used by other battalions throughout Ireland. In the south of the county, the RIC recorded the use of flash-lamp signalling.[19] Patrick Dunphy of Castlecomer, captain, 'B' Company, 3rd Battalion, Kilkenny Brigade, recalled another form of signalling: 'It was the use as horns of bottles from which the bottoms had been removed, the sound of which could be heard for a distance of up to two miles.'[20] The Kilkenny battalions had also aided officers of the Tipperary brigade in their attack on Drangan barracks in June 1920.

Brigadier General F. P. Crozier, commandant, Auxiliary Division, RIC, wrote that in mid-October 1920 he sent out companies (strength 100 men each with motor tenders) to nine counties which he described as 'hot spots'.[21] When his commander in Kilkenny, Colonel John Kirkwood, who had commanded a regular battalion of the Royal Irish Rifles during the First World War, asked to be relieved of his post, Crozier summoned him to Dublin and was horrified by his appearance: 'wan, haggard, restless, I put him on the mail-boat and, wishing him God's speed, attributed his condition to "nerves"'.[22] By December, the RIC reported that the 'situation in the county [Kilkenny] remains on the whole unsatisfactory'.[23]

It was with some surprise, therefore, that Tom Treacy and James Lalor learned that GHQ was not happy with the Kilkenny Brigade. Lalor and Treacy were called to Dublin by the chief of staff, Richard Mulcahy, for separate meetings in November in which Mulcahy raised the prospect of an attack on Woodstock House where the Auxiliaries had set up their headquarters. Both gave replies that the Kilkenny Brigade was making arrangements for such an attack along with other particulars about the fortification. Mulcahy announced he knew exactly how many Auxiliaries were camped there and their addresses in England. Present at both meetings was Ernie O'Malley, an officer attached to GHQ of the IRA, who acted as a training officer for rural units, and Mulcahy told Lalor and Treacy that O'Malley would be going down to Kilkenny to plan and execute an attack on Woodstock House. O'Malley said little at both meetings other than to ask Lalor for directions so he would find his way to the cinema in Parliament Street when he arrived in Kilkenny.

O'Malley was twenty-three years old at this time. He had

been in Dublin during the 1916 Rising and, although not a Volunteer at the time, had been involved in a skirmish with the British forces. His biographer, Richard English, describes him as 'a revolutionary Irish Republican, an exponent of that physical force tradition which has formed so significant a part of Irish and Anglo-Irish history in the modern period'. English observes that O'Malley was an 'important practitioner' and 'shrewd chronicler' of 'this aggressive version of Irish nationalism'.[24]

The Kilkenny Brigade knew about O'Malley's abilities and outstanding courage, not least because some of them had fought alongside him in the attack on Drangan RIC barracks in County Tipperary. In February 1920, four months before the Drangan attack, O'Malley and Eoin O'Duffy had led the capture of the RIC barracks in Ballytrain in County Monaghan. In September 1920 he and Liam Lynch organised the capture of a British army barracks in Mallow in County Cork, the only such capture by Republicans during the War of Independence. Aside from his obvious talent as a military tactician and courageous fighter, O'Malley was aware of the harm spies could do to Irish Republicanism. As early as 1917, O'Malley was taking precautions to guard against infiltration. When writing to Volunteers at this time, he used the Sinn Féin post, which involved the purchase of special stamps from trusted newsagents in whose shops letters could be left and quickly delivered. 'The British opened mail and it was no use leaving anything to chance,' he wrote.[25]

Shortly before his journey to Kilkenny, O'Malley was again reminded of the danger of confidential material falling into the wrong hands. In his book *On Another Man's Wound*, O'Malley wrote that during two raids, British forces had seized papers belonging to Richard Mulcahy, which he said were the most reliable insight the British secret service could get into the Republican movement. These papers, he explained, included plans for a systematic destruction of docks, warehouses and technical plants in England.[26] O'Malley took precautions before undertaking his journey by leaving his own papers in a concealed cupboard, adding that 'there was no sense in risking my notes and papers in a county like Kilkenny'.[27]

Armed with this wariness, military skill and courage, O'Malley arranged to travel by train to Kilkenny on a Saturday in November arriving at 9.20 at night. He gave instructions not to be met at the railway station, saying that he would make his way to the cinema in Parliament Street, which was jointly owned and managed by Tom Stallard and Peter. However, O'Malley did not arrive at the appointed time and Lalor and Treacy were still waiting for him weeks later when they were both arrested on 23 November 1920 by British forces.[28]

According to James J. Comerford, O'Malley did not arrive in Kilkenny until 29 November. Three days later he visited the Coon Company and called a meeting which was attended by, among others, Comerford, George O'Dwyer, Robert Shore and Frank Clear:

> He warned us to avoid arrest. 'A man in jail,' he said, 'is a total loss to the cause.' He cautioned us not to carry any names of [IRA] men or any other [IRA] papers in our pockets, to prevent them from falling into the hands of the Crown forces. He really gave us a long pep talk like a 'fire and brimstone' sermon. To know more about us before placing us in a 'flying column' and to send us training notes on guerrilla war, he wrote down names and address of officers and some men.[29]

On Saturday 4 December 1920, members of the Kilkenny Brigade held a meeting in the Gaelic rooms of Rothe House to establish the number of arms available and the number of men fit for action. Brigade members were also planning to elect officers to replace their imprisoned leaders, Lalor and Treacy. However, before the meeting started, word came to them that Ernie O'Malley had arrived at Tom Stallard's house so James Roughan, who was acquainted with O'Malley, left the Gaelic rooms and brought O'Malley to the meeting. O'Malley wrote down in his notebook particulars for each battalion area regarding men and arms. Before the meeting ended he demanded a gun and was provided with one. The meeting adjourned to Tom Stallard's house the following afternoon.[30]

James J. Comerford said that at this second meeting, O'Malley spoke 'forcefully, bluntly, emphatically and at times rather surly as he rapped the table with his knuckles. He showed impatience'.[31] Peter was elected Kilkenny Brigade commandant to fill the vacancy caused by the arrest of Commandant Tom Treacy. Two other officers were re-elected to positions they already held, Edward Comerford as brigade quartermaster and Seán Byrne as brigade adjutant. O'Malley wrote their names in his notebook.[32] He said that the new brigadier, Peter, did not impress him by any show of energy or resolution. He judged Peter to be more of a steady businessman, stout, easy spoken, the mayor of the city and observed that he (Peter) did not refuse to accept responsibility. He assumed that the 'attempted capture of the Auxiliary headquarters [at Woodstock] would be outside his [Peter's] life'. O'Malley described the Kilkenny Brigade members as slack, poor material with 'no direction from above and no drive'. He believed that 'they had not tried to solve the problems of their commands'.[33]

At this meeting, the possibilities of attacking Woodstock were explored. A suggestion by O'Malley that he inspect Woodstock and that he stay with James Hanrahan, who lived in Cappagh, raised alarm among members of the Kilkenny Brigade. They warned O'Malley that Hanrahan's house was under constant observation and subject to frequent raids by the Auxiliaries. However, three days later, O'Malley informed Tom Stallard, with whom he was staying, that he was going to Inistioge. Stallard again warned him of the threat posed by staying at Hanrahan's home:

> Stallard said to him: 'You have that book in your pocket with the names of the officers.' O'Malley said: 'I have.' Stallard said: 'Can't you leave me that book; you might meet those fellows [Auxiliaries] on the road; it is dangerous to be carrying it about. Any time you want it you can have it.' O'Malley said: 'No, I will keep it myself.' O'Malley took the book with him. He had maps with him.[34]

James Hanrahan and Edward Holland brought O'Malley by pony and trap to Hanrahan's house. They arrived at around 5.30 in the evening. Having had tea, O'Malley started to read a book entitled *Mr Britling Sees It Through*.[35] He remained at the fire reading until ten o'clock in the evening, when a local Volunteer arrived to warn him that the Auxiliaries were busy in the village holding up and searching people. O'Malley showed little interest in a suggestion by Hanrahan to send scouts into the village. The following morning, Thomas and Andrew Hanrahan reported that the Auxiliaries were coming in the direction of the Hanrahans' house. James Hanrahan reported this to O'Malley, who was in bed:

He asked Hanrahan how many and was told about a dozen. 'A nice bag,' said O'Malley, and settled down again in the bed. The Auxiliaries passed by the house shortly after … Before breakfast, Hanrahan's sister told O'Malley that Rev. Father J. Kearns was coming that morning to anoint her mother who was very ill in the house. Breakfast was then ready … While O'Malley was at breakfast, Hanrahan's sister reported that the Auxiliaries were raiding Cappagh farmyard (half a mile away by road, a quarter mile across the fields). O'Malley said nothing to this … A few minutes after the warning about Cappagh farmyard and while O'Malley and Holland were still at breakfast, an Auxiliary came into the room and others were seen outside and a rush of feet upstairs was heard. Without any speech the Auxiliary who came in proceeded to search a china cabinet. Hanrahan was in the room at the time … More Auxiliaries then entered.[36]

O'Malley's own account of what happened that morning was that his maps were on the window and his notebook was open on the table. He closed it and pushed it to one side. An order to search O'Malley prompted him to jump up and attempt to draw his gun out of his pocket, but it became stuck in the lining.[37]

Fr Kearns arrived at Hanrahan's house to anoint Mrs Hanrahan at the same time as the Auxiliary officer and O'Malley were locked in combat but, as he was carrying the Blessed Sacrament he went straight up the stairs to Mrs Hanrahan. When he got there he found Auxiliaries searching her room but he told them to clear out as he wished to attend to the sick. They went without a word.[38]

In the front room below, an Auxiliary saw O'Malley's notebook, took it up and examined the notes which showed that the Kilkenny Republicans had four brigades of eight battalions with 103 rifles, 4,900 rounds of rifle ammunition, 471 shot guns and 3,490 rounds of shot-gun ammunition. It also listed the names of the Kilkenny Brigade.[39] The Auxiliary announced to his comrades: 'We have the lot' and jumped with delight:

> The Auxiliaries were so pleased with what they found in the book that they ran to tell each other the news and decided to burn the premises. They set fire to hay, straw and outhouses and sent a Crossley tender to Woodstock for petrol to burn the dwelling house. In the meantime, Fr Kearns, who had arrived after the Auxiliaries, had been administering the Last Sacraments to Mrs Hanrahan. The Auxiliaries then carried her out of the house on a mattress and left her in the yard in the frost from which plight she was rescued by Mrs Newport [and her husband, Protestant neighbours, who were landed gentry][40] … The other occupants of the house were compelled to leave and, the supply of petrol having arrived, the Auxiliaries spilled it over bedding, furniture, floors, etc. They broke windows to ensure a draught and, having set the house on fire, remained for some time watching the flames.[41]

As the outhouses were burning, the Auxiliaries acceded to a plea from Thomas Hanrahan to allow him to release the animals locked within.

In the days that followed, the Auxiliaries used the notebook to seek out and arrest most of the leaders of the Kilkenny Brigade, including Peter.

13

Fire Turns Inwards, 1920–21

While in captivity, Ernie O'Malley met two other prisoners from Thomastown and they told him that the Black and Tans had arrested 'the whole countryside' and that, 'mad with rage, they were half murdering anyone they took'.[1] The *Kilkenny People* reported that after the burning of the Hanrahan home, British forces searched almost every farmhouse within a two mile radius of Inistioge. Six other people, including James Hanrahan, had been arrested at the same time or shortly after O'Malley's arrest. Further arrests followed. James Roughan, the 7th Battalion commander who had conveyed O'Malley to the Rothe House meeting the previous Saturday, was removed to Dublin Castle where he endured a severe beating at the hands of the Auxiliaries in a vain attempt to extract information from him. Edward Holland, who had accompanied O'Malley with pony and cart from Kilkenny city to Inistioge, was later tried in Waterford and sentenced to ten years' penal servitude.[2] Edward Aylward, commandant, 7th Battalion, was arrested, but escaped from custody.[3]

Edward Comerford, the quartermaster of Kilkenny Brigade, and Peter were detained the day after O'Malley's notebook was seized. Peter was arrested at his home in the afternoon and brought to Kilkenny military barracks in a lorry. The following day he was handed over to the Auxiliaries and taken by lorry to Woodstock. At the gates of the avenue he was blindfolded, and later kept in a wine cellar with John Carroll, assistant surveyor, Thomastown, and Jack Kelly, New Ross. Both Peter and Carroll were then used as 'human shields' by the Auxiliaries as they carried out searches in Thomastown and Graiguenamanagh. It was usual for the Black and Tans to hold a gun to the back of the hostage's head in full view of passers-by during these outings. Reports of this reached O'Malley, who heard in prison about Peter being brought around by the Auxiliaries and told that if there was an attack on the convoy they would 'blow his head off'.[4]

The *Kilkenny People* would later re-publish an account of Peter's experiences which he described in an interview with the *Irish Independent*:

On Monday [13 December] he was again blindfolded and informed that he was being brought for a short drive. He was placed in a lorry and, going down the avenue, he was asked did he know what he was there for. Replying that he did not, one of the party said that in case of an ambush they had instructions to shoot him. He was brought to Thomastown. In the evening Mr Kelly was taken on a similar drive. Next day, Mr Carroll and [Peter] were taken to Graiguenamanagh and for three or four hours were kept standing one at each end of the road in full view of the public while guards were doing their business.

They were then brought to the hotel and, as some tea and eggs were just ready for them, they were ordered out without getting them. He was subsequently brought to Kilkenny military barracks after spending a whole day in Thomastown workhouse without any food, arriving in Kilkenny at 8.15 p.m.[5]

The *Manchester Guardian* published this account by its correspondent in Dublin:

> The practice began immediately after the establishment of martial law in four counties of the south and west on 10 December, and the first recorded instance was that in which the hostage was the Mayor of Kilkenny, a town which did not at that time fall within the martial law area but has since been included in it.[6]

Peter kept notes using a pencil and small sheets of paper, which have survived. On one sheet is a hand-drawn calendar month of December 1921, beginning on 10 December, the day of his arrest. His outings as a hostage are also detailed along with a complaint he made about such treatment:

> Saw commanding officer after asking for him three times. Protested against being used as hostage.

> Wed 15th – Taken blindfolded to Thomastown Union thence to Kilkenny military barracks.
> Thurs 16 – By lorry to Dublin (eight-and-a-half-hours). Freezing all day.[7]

Before Peter was transported to Dublin along with five other prisoners, they were handcuffed in pairs. No provision was made for feeding them, but they were able to buy some food at Castledermott in County Kildare.[8] Among the prisoners being transferred to the capital with Peter were O'Malley and

Holland. Members of the Kilkenny Brigade recounted what happened during their transportation:

> There were numerous stoppages and there was talk among the Auxiliaries of shooting O'Malley and Holland.
>
> Peter DeLoughry, on one of the stoppages, asked one of the Auxiliaries to tell the officer [who was] in charge of O'Malley and Holland that he wished to speak to him. The message was conveyed and the officer, having spoken to DeLoughry, took precautions against the shooting. The convoy consisted of fourteen tenders with six prisoners and about 100 military and Auxiliaries, and O'Malley and Holland were near the leading tender.
>
> On leaving Kilcullen one of the tenders from the rear shot out and rushed the hill past the other tenders towards the front. There was an immediate halt of the convoy by the officer in charge of O'Malley and Holland.
>
> Revolvers were drawn and the tender was compelled to go back to its original position.[9]

Peter's notes while in captivity describe his next movements:

> Ned Comerford, Holland, Steward,[10] Joe Rice, Jim Rowan [Roughan] with me.
>
> Spent night in Beggars Bush [barracks] by myself. Next day, Friday 17th taken to guard room, Dublin Castle where I rejoined Comerford & co.
>
> Wed 22nd – Taken to Arbour Hill barracks.
>
> Dec 31 – Wrote commandant re rug.[11]

Peter asked for a rug because he was in poor health at the time. Larry sent a letter of protest about his brother's treatment to Commander Kenworthy and Arthur Henderson MP. The letter was reprinted in the local Kilkenny press and in it Larry explained that his brother had been arrested without notice and had no time to bring sufficient clothing with him. He warned that because Peter's health was not strong, long journeys on motor lorries would endanger his life and argued that because no charge had been preferred against Peter, the only reason he could see for his continued detention was to use him as a hostage during searches by the Auxiliaries. Larry also made it clear that the letter was not a plea for mercy, as neither he nor Peter would ever be party to any sort of appeal either for justice or mercy to the British government.[12]

For the third time and for the second Christmas, Peter's wife, Win, and his children were left without his company because of his being imprisoned. Peter's brother David did not escape difficulty either. His Temperance Hotel in John Street, Kilkenny, was commandeered by British forces during the latter part of December 1920.[13] It was left to their sister, Lil, and her husband, Henry Mangan, city accountant, Dublin Corporation, to look after Peter's needs as best they could. Lil secured permission from Dublin Castle on 29 December to visit Peter. Again, his notes throw light on how well they looked after him by listing the supplies they furnished him with:

Dec. 26 – Recd. Henry – (2 bx cigs)
1 tin milk, 1 cocoa, 2 sandwiches
Lil – thermos flask with tea, sandwiches
2 cakes, slab toffee

Dec 28th – Lil 6 apples, box dates, 6 scones

30th – Lil brown and white cake

4 mince pies, Piece rich cake

30th – Lil Bovril 2 pkts biscuits, chocolate milk, jam

31st – 2 parcels (reg.) Win. Clothes etc.[14]

A little over five weeks into his detention, his captors made a request to Peter:

On Tuesday last [18 January 1921] the commandant informed him that he had orders for his release but he was to sign a document which contained questions to this effect: 'Do you belong to the [IRA] and, if so, are you prepared to resign?' Also an undertaking to carry out the laws and regulations at present in force and to give his address where he was to be found day and night.

Ald. DeLoughry refused to sign the document and said he would only take an unconditional release.

Yesterday [21 January] the commandant told him, while his sister was visiting him, that he had orders to release him without signing the document.

Several congratulatory wires from friends in Kilkenny, including one from the town clerk, were sent to the mayor.[15]

No reason was given for his release.

The following month Peter was re-elected mayor of Kilkenny for a third successive term. In his acceptance speech he said he realised that the position of an Irish mayor was not at all an enviable one. With reference to Mac Curtáin and MacSwiney, he said that 'a special set seems to be made against the heads of Irish municipalities who have given their allegiance to the principles of freedom'. His closing remarks give an insight into his state of mind at this most turbulent time:

I never desired any other end than one which would guarantee to the people of this country, no matter at what altar they kneel or what politics they profess, the enjoyment of those rights and privileges which have been defined in the American Declaration of Independence as 'life, liberty and the pursuit of happiness'.[16]

Two weeks after the election, liberty and happiness for the DeLoughry family became as elusive as ever. The centre of Kilkenny city was cordoned off by the British military, RIC and Auxiliary forces, who said the manoeuvre was to ensure that people were complying with an order to post the names of inhabitants of each house on their front door and to locate a man prominently associated with the IRA who was believed to be in the area. The DeLoughry home in Parliament Street was raided on Saturday evening, 12 February, but neither Peter nor his brother Larry could be found and the house was occupied by the Black and Tans for three days. Nanny, Win and her five children were locked in the cellar and were not allowed to leave the house. Win had concealed a gun under her skirt before the occupation.[17]

Searches were made for Peter in the Capuchin friary, the adjoining convent and the District Lunatic Asylum. On Sunday, an empty coffin being conveyed to the country was taken out of the hearse and opened by the military.[18] Later that day, Larry and three brothers from Kieran Street – James, Michael and Thomas Bateman – were arrested.[19] The air was charged with cordite. Fingers caressed triggers. Sudden noises sent bolts of panic through the streets. The Auxiliaries detained three men who called to see Peter. A fourteen-year-old boy, John DeLoughry, Peter's nephew and godson, stopped outside the well-guarded DeLoughry house, went up to the sentry and announced that he was there to deliver milk to the household. He was allowed in each morning and was the only civilian to enter and exit the premises during the three-day occupation.[20]

The Black and Tans ended their occupation of the De-Loughry home on Tuesday evening. Aside from enduring long absences from her imprisoned husband, Win now had another burden, enunciated in an editorial in the *Kilkenny People*:

> The circumstances of [Peter's] recent imprisonment are aggravated by the fact that his business has also been made to suffer severely by the withdrawal of permits entitling him to use his three motor cars for hiring purposes. The result of this is to involve him in heavy financial loss because the forced sale of motor cars during the present slump in the trade means, in addition to the paralysis of his business, the sale of valuable stock at a big sacrifice.[21]

The departure of the Black and Tans from the family home was some comfort to Nanny, Win and the five children, but then Larry was arrested and Peter was now in hiding. Larry was lodged in Woodstock and, as Peter had been, was used as a hostage during raids by the Auxiliaries:

> I was locked up with two others who, posing as [IRA] prisoners, tried to get information out of me. I knew from their questions that they were spies.[22]

Larry was brought before a military court a little over two weeks after his arrest, where he faced charges of making a statement 'likely to cause disaffection to His Majesty' and withholding information from an officer of the crown:

When the charges had been read, Mr DeLoughry in a firm voice exclaimed: I may say that I refuse to recognise the authority of this court to try me.

President – That does not make any difference.

A member of the Auxiliary police force stated that on the morning of 18 February, he arrived at the house where the accused sleeps at about 7.30. He asked him where he had been the previous night and he refused to state. He then arrested him.

President – Anything else?
Witness – No.

Another Auxiliary policeman stated he was at Woodstock on a day subsequent to the accused's arrest. He had the accused brought up to a room there and asked him where he had been the night previous to his arrest and he refused to state. He then asked him was he a loyal subject of the king and he said he was not. He [witness] then told him that he had committed an offence under the martial law proclamations …

President (to Mr DeLoughry) – Have you anything to say?

Mr DeLoughry – No; I refuse to recognise this court.

President – Fined £20 …

Mr DeLoughry – £20! I have not twenty pence.

President – You can have till next Saturday.

Mr DeLoughry – You will get no twenty pounds from me because I haven't it; and if I had it I would not give it.

President – We can take something else.

At the conclusion of the court, Mr DeLoughry was released having been in custody since the 13th inst.[23]

Larry was re-arrested a week later and convicted of not having paid the fine. He was removed to Bere Island internment camp where he was imprisoned for the following five months.[24] During this time, he learned how to play chess and became a competent player.

Peter, too, remained out of sight for the following five months. He is believed to have divided his time between his own and Tom Stallard's house. With little to do at home except hide in an upstairs locker when someone called to the front door, he installed a system of bells in the house. These had a dual function of averting unnecessary journeys in the sprawling premises and as a warning sign in case the Black and Tans swooped again.[25] It is also likely that he spent some time outside Kilkenny, where he had less prospect of being recognised. Mrs Marie Johnson, wife of the first Irish Labour Party leader, Thomas Johnson, recalled an incident when Peter made 'a daring jump from a moving train in which he had been cornered and captured'. He rolled down an embankment, under fire, and got away to his sister's house in Ranelagh, from which he was transferred to Mrs Johnson's care.[26] Peter's colleague on Kilkenny Corporation, John McKenna, stated at a meeting that during this period in hiding, Peter 'carried out hazardous duties he was called on to perform faithfully and well'.[27]

Throughout the War of Independence, but particularly at this time of Peter's enforced hiding, Win and Nanny carried messages to other members of the Kilkenny Brigade. They were aware of the dangers of doing this, but most likely felt comforted that the British forces would not suspect women of carrying such correspondence. However, from an RIC report written in Kilkenny in March 1921, the opposite appears to have been the case:

> The Cumann na mBan are active recently in the circulation of seditious literature and no doubt in carrying arms and despatches.[28]

The previous December, the British military, the RIC and the Auxiliaries had rounded up most leaders of the Kilkenny Brigade and, at that time, it looked as if the Republican movement in the city and county had been dealt a severe blow. However, among the individuals whose names were written in O'Malley's notebook was one who had evaded capture and made his mark. He had been a member of the Dublin Metropolitan Police and had served for a time with the New Zealand Mounted Police and the Sydney Police before returning to Ireland in 1916 and he took over the reins when the others were captured. Within a month of George O'Dwyer assuming his new command, the British military, the RIC and the Auxiliaries began to face a different kind of warfare, one that built up into a relentless and powerful bombardment that was only halted when a Truce was agreed in July, after which O'Dwyer oversaw their departure from the city and the county.[29]

O'Dwyer's military strategy was to make each of the battalions semi-autonomous, which strengthened confidentiality, a policy being employed in other counties. Previously, local commands were subject to orders from the brigade council, but now they could make up their own minds about what to do or not to do in their own terrain. This semi-autonomy was the source of much bewilderment among the Kilkenny

Republicans, as they had been used to seeking and accepting direction. However, O'Dwyer visited them as much as he could, given that he was on the run. This effective mode of command was the basis for criticism from Ernie O'Malley, who had escaped from Kilmainham jail on 21 February 1921 and who had been appointed by the IRA Council as commandant general over the 2nd Southern Division, which took in, among others, the Kilkenny Brigade. O'Malley said that on inspecting the Kilkenny Brigade in the summer of 1921, he found that the brigade staff had seldom sent orders to battalions; they had never been on inspection. He also claimed that on the western Kilkenny boundary, enemy patrols were numerous.[30]

This renewed criticism of the Kilkenny Brigade, published in O'Malley's book in 1936, was replied to by surviving Kilkenny Republicans in a series of articles in the *Irish Press*:

> George O'Dwyer, the brigade commandant, while 'on the run' started to reorganise the brigade immediately after O'Malley's arrest [December 1920]. He visited all the battalions, often accompanied by the adjutant, J. J. Byrne, and reorganised them. O'Malley's 'inspection' consisted of a flying rush through a small portion of the brigade area and out again, without summoning officers to meet him; he did not look up any officers in Kilkenny city. He then reported unfavourably to GHQ. Eoin O'Duffy sent a communication to George O'Dwyer who replied that O'Malley's report 'came very well from an officer who, through his own carelessness in allowing notes to be captured, broke up the organisation which we had to piece together and did piece [together] successfully'.[31]

Members of Kilkenny Brigade were part-time soldiers fighting a part-time war and O'Malley was a full-time military leader hell-bent on fighting a full-time war. These two roads were never going to meet. An assessment of the merits and demerits of the arguments put forward by O'Malley and by members of the Kilkenny Brigade against each other can be helped in part by considering the view taken of the Kilkenny Brigade by the local police force. The monthly RIC reports help to plot the progression of the Kilkenny Brigade from December 1920 – the month most of the Kilkenny leaders and O'Malley had been arrested – through to June 1921. These reports recorded what the enemy was saying about the Republican onslaught; they were not inclined to offer compliments to Republicans.

A month after O'Dwyer's stewardship began, the RIC was describing the Kilkenny IRA as 'extremely well-organised' and 'widely active'. In February the local police despatch noted that the county was 'unsettled and disturbed' by the appearance of flying columns. During the same month the RIC reported that the local battalions were operating in the 'utmost secrecy' and that 'clever and elaborate precautions were being taken to prevent information reaching the police'. These RIC reports support the view of the historian Jim Maher that by March 1921, 'the 7th battalion, Kilkenny Brigade flying column was reaching maturity and displaying the toughness and the aggressiveness of a first class active service unit'.[32]

Posters were put up in Kilmanagh declaring the district a Republican military area and threatening death to all its opponents. In June the local police chief inspector sent a despatch to Dublin Castle admitting, for the first time, that strong patrols could not be sent out in the west of the county. Telegraph and telephone communications were cut, roads were dug up, ambushes of British military carried out, Auxiliaries abducted or shot dead and information came through of arms being smuggled from England. Such was the expertise and effectiveness of O'Dwyer's command that he confounded a greater army at every turn. The result of his bombardment – both mental and physical – of British forces compares favourably with that of Republican successes elsewhere in Ireland at the time.[33] By July the British government felt it wise to agree to a Truce.

The fact that a cessation of fighting had to be negotiated at all showed the growing strength of the IRA, which was bolstered in Kilkenny by the local battalions and, elsewhere, by commanders such as O'Malley, whose campaigns outside his Kilkenny blind spot did much to strengthen the hand of Republicans.[34]

14

Treaty and Civil War, 1921–22

The most important effect of the Truce for Peter was that he could resume his duties as mayor. Peter's first appearance at an urban district council meeting following his period in hiding was welcomed by Councillor John McKenna, who raised the hope that Peter would be allowed to do his work undisturbed now that the 'stormy days are over'. Peter echoed the sentiment that the city and country were now 'at the beginning of peace and prosperity'.[1]

Nothing could have been further from reality. As conversations and then talks got under way between Republican and British leaders on a treaty, tensions in Ireland abounded. British forces fired a shot at the tricolour flying over the Tholsel and the British commander in the district wrote a letter to the corporation asking members to lower the flag, describing its presence as provocative. Corporation members referred the matter to the chief liaison officer, who was mediating on thorny issues both great and small between the British and Republican powers. *The Freeman's Journal* said he would have plenty to occupy him if reports from around the country were to be believed.[2]

The Kilkenny Board of Guardians objected to the British

military taking over a wing of the workhouse, the building where they normally met. Peter, who chaired the meeting, said it was an 'extraordinary thing to have a loaded rifle – I presume it is loaded – and bayonet pointed into the faces of members'. Warming to his theme, he said the young British soldiers guarding the workhouse were subjected to rough discipline and suffered from overstrain and lack of nerve. 'Therefore,' he argued, 'any man or woman entering that gate is in danger of his or her life.' The matter was referred to the chief liaison officer.[3]

The Kilkenny RIC expressed alarm that the IRA kept on drilling during the Truce and were kidnapping alleged thieves. It pointed out that loyalists were anxious about their future, fearing that any government under Sinn Féin would be a 'leap in the dark'.[4] The IRA in Kilkenny was, by this time, filing comprehensive monthly reports to leaders in Dublin on printed forms that demanded information on, among other matters, the strength of RIC stations, enemy agents and officials, and enemy post offices.[5]

The tensions, both petty and large, simmered as negotiations on the future of Ireland advanced. The Articles of Agreement for a Treaty between Great Britain and Ireland, better known as the Anglo-Irish Treaty, was signed in London on 6 December 1921.[6] It envisaged the establishment of an Irish Free State as a self-governing dominion within the British Empire and provided Northern Ireland with an option to opt out of the Irish Free State, which it later exercised. The Irish side, which included Michael Collins and Arthur Griffith, had plenipotentiary status, meaning that they were empowered to sign the Treaty although it was also agreed that they would check with de Valera before signing. The Treaty was ratified by

Dáil Éireann by 64 to 57 votes on 7 January 1922. The Treaty split Republicans into two groups: those who supported the Treaty and the establishment of an Irish Free State, and those who opposed the Treaty, among whose notable advocates was de Valera, who resigned as president of the Republic after the Dáil had adopted the Treaty.

Shortly after the Treaty was signed, the British government ordered a general amnesty for Republican prisoners and Tom Treacy, James Lalor, Edward Comerford and Peter's brother Larry were among those released. Peter presided at a corporation meeting to celebrate the return of the liberated internees. His carefully worded welcome did not hide his premonition of the looming disaster that lay ahead:

> We all trust and hope that ... the liberty they have fought for, or a very great measure of it, is within our grasp, and that further sacrifices will not be necessary from [this] generation.[7]

Peter sensed that open rancour about the Treaty at local authority meetings could spread to the streets or inflame already heated tempers. Kilkenny citizens waited to see which side Peter would take; the one advocated by his former prison comrade de Valera, or the one supported by Collins and Griffith.

When the issue came up at a meeting of Kilkenny County Council, Peter supported a proposal to go into private session and after two and a half hours of discussion, members issued a resolution to the effect that they saw no alternative to ratification of the Treaty but chaos. They also appealed to de Valera to 'do everything in his power to preserve unity and prevent the appalling consequences of a split'.[8] Peter made two speeches at Kilkenny Corporation meetings about the Treaty, one at which the corporation voted to support the agreement and the other a month later after he had been elected mayor for a fourth consecutive term.

Kilkenny Corporation was one of 328 statutory bodies throughout Ireland to support the Treaty.[9] Peter's address to members at this meeting included what would turn out to be a futile appeal for unity among Republicans, where he had to admit that the long-held dream of a Republic was shattered:

> The plenipotentiaries were given a gigantic task and were up against the ablest politicians in the world and, personally, [Peter] was of the opinion that they accomplished almost a miracle and brought back a really good deal – more than most people expected from England. He knew they didn't bring back a republic and as one who was a republican all his life he was sorry but at the same time he did not think that any republican would be justified in turning down the Treaty. He thought it was the shortest road to Irish independence.

When challenged by another member as to why the Republic was abandoned, Peter, who had been unequivocal in rejecting the terms of the third Home Rule Bill because of the exclusion of Ulster from an independent Ireland, answered with a mixture of world-weariness and pragmatism:

> I am afraid I could not answer that question. If we had the Republic and the Treaty before us, I would back the Republic but we have not. We have the Treaty and the alternative and that is what the Dáil has to deal with.[10]

Members voted to support the Treaty, with one dissenting voice, Alderman J. W. Upton.

Peter used his speech as incoming mayor in 1922 to confess that he had been looking forward to a period of relaxation and to becoming an ordinary member of the corporation until colleagues persuaded him to once again agree to be the city's first citizen. He then turned to the topic of the Treaty again, this time using a mixture of logic and romantic nationalism to try to glean support for it:

> We in Ireland have arrived at a crossroads. No man knows what the future holds for Ireland. We have decided, unfortunately, to break; there seems to be no doubt about that …
>
> The substance of freedom is there, and if we are manful enough to take it up and defy the right of anybody to interfere in the management of our affairs, and if we have a united country as we had in the past, I believe Ireland will attain its destiny along the lines that the Irish people desire to attain it.[11]

One of the leading opponents of the Treaty in Kilkenny was Edward Aylward, officer commanding, 7th Battalion, Kilkenny Brigade. He, like Peter, had sacrificed much for the Republican cause. Aylward's view was that they had not fought so long and so hard for so little. Both sides argued their points with some measure of their own logic. It was not that one side had given up or that another would not; neither was it that one was battle-weary and the other had the taste of blood. Both sides knew what they were doing and the arguments that supported their views, and conflict between them was inevitable. Peter had only one card left to play and on it was written the word 'conciliation'.

There was, however, one last event in the lead up to the Civil War that brought both Republican groups together in celebration: the departure of British forces from most of Ireland. The *Kilkenny People* described the vacation of Woodstock by the British forces as 'the devil's own brigade leave'.[12] Celebrations in Inistioge were heightened by the return the following day of James Hanrahan, who had been arrested at the time of Ernie O'Malley's visit to Kilkenny. The *Kilkenny Moderator* reported that one of the Crossley tenders which transported the Auxiliaries from Woodstock to Kilkenny railway station had written on it in chalk, 'Off to Paradise and Blighty'.[13]

In February 1922 the Black and Tans took what the *Kilkenny Moderator* described as 'their welcome departure' from Kilkenny:

Two of them entered the Irish National Foresters' club early on Thursday evening and before they could be ejected caused a good deal of damage in the billiard room and smashed a large window facing the street. They subsequently marched up the centre of High Street, one of them carrying a brush on his shoulder out of which hung a Union Jack.

Others of them are reported to have interfered with and used insolence towards civilians, and a few fistic encounters took place here and there in the streets.

Great tension prevailed in the city for some hours, lest anything untoward should happen, I.R. [Irish Republican] Police in large numbers were on alert to prevent any disturbance ...

They were driven to the railway station in Crossley tenders, and indulged in a good deal of boisterous singing and shouting on their way through the streets ... There was a large crowd of civilians present at the railway station, and a good deal of 'scrapping' took place between some of them and the Black and Tans but nobody was seriously hurt.[14]

Another line was drawn between the past and the future of Kilkenny with the handover of the military barracks to the IRA. The Kilkenny brigadier, George O'Dwyer, took charge of the building amid triumphal scenes. At a subsequent ceremony for the blessing of the colours, O'Dwyer remarked that on their departure the British forces had broken the flagstaff (as was tradition) before decamping:[15]

> However, better late than never and the republican flag was now flying where the flag of England had previously floated. Inside these barracks they were endeavouring to build up an army that would defend the lives and liberties of the people of Ireland. They were not Free Staters, they were soldiers of the Republic, and they owed their allegiance to the Republic but as an army they held aloof from politics. They left political issues to the people of Ireland to decide and whatever the people of Ireland decided it was the duty of the army to support and not to suppress their will by force of arms. That was democratic doctrine as far as he understood it.[16]

Tensions between pro- and anti-Treaty forces had been raised in other areas over which side should take control of British military garrisons. General Mulcahy (pro-Treaty) described the difficulty he experienced by saying that he and his officer command 'were dealing with a difficult situation where you did not know where loyalty lay and you had to handle the threat of what was a secret society'.[17] The stakes were raised even higher on 14 April, when Rory O'Connor led a force of anti-Treaty militants to take over the Four Courts and other buildings in Dublin and a stand-off ensued.

Sporadic shootings, raids and attacks on property began to be a feature of life in County Kilkenny. Edward Aylward used the start of the general election campaign in Kilkenny in 1922 to outline the anti-Treaty position. At a meeting in Knocktopher, Liam Healy, speaking on Aylward's behalf, was unequivocal:

> The terms of [the] document place the present generation of Irish men and women in the shameful, humiliating conditions of foregoing their nationality and accepting the King of England and his royal imbecile son, their heirs and successors, as the rulers of their ancient land. They were asked by the advocates of the Treaty to repudiate the martyrs who had fallen in the fight for independence in every generation from Wolfe Tone to Pádraig Pearse – to give up the fight now when Britain was defeated and embarrassed all over the world, and had failed by every conceivable form of terrorism and outrage which devilish ingenuity could devise to exterminate the Irish race; to haul down the flag of the Irish Republic and to accept the status of British colonists. Somebody had said that the three things most to be feared were the horns of a bull, the heels of a horse and the smile of an Englishman.[18]

From his base in Callan, Aylward taunted and harried the pro-Treaty forces. He stole motor cars from the local RIC chief Inspector, F. I. Whyte, from wealthy landlords and from Peter:

> Without being unduly sanguine, the mayor of Kilkenny might reasonably have hoped that [with] the departure of the Black and Tans, the Auxiliaries and all the other British forces, he would

be immune, and his family and business would be immune, from the raids and other attentions which were of regular and frequent occurrence for practically six years or, to be accurate, since April 1916 … On Sunday night, his motor garage was broken into and a motor car which had been entrusted to him for repair removed. The car was the property of the [IRA] headquarters, Kilkenny, and repairs, on which his mechanics had been working for nearly a fortnight, were nearly completed. The parts, however, had not been fully assembled, so that the car had to be pushed down the lane which leads from the garage to Parliament Street, and then, it is assumed, towed away by another motor car.[19]

Colonel Commandant J. T. Prout, who led the pro-Treaty South-Eastern Command that included Kilkenny, Waterford and south and mid-Tipperary, received a letter from Aylward the following month and the tone illustrated the man's hostility towards the pro-Treaty side:

I am informed that you sent out troops into our company area [Callan district] recently, Black-and-Tan-like, in search of motor cars taken by us from the arch-fiend C. I. Whyte. Now, according to our republican principles we consider ourselves justified in taking and keeping those cars so far as we are concerned the truce with England terminated when the articles of surrender were accepted … We would consider ourselves justified in treating you as we would treat the mercenary Tans and peelers had Commandant [George O'] Dwyer and the hero (?) lord mayor [Peter DeLoughry] permitted us. We shall accept your interference as a declaration of war and shoot you down in the streets as representatives of the British government. We totally condemn the taking of private cars, but ours are lawful spoils. Therefore, 'beware of entrance to a quarrel'.[20]

In November 1922 another of Peter's cars, a hackney Ford, was held up by three armed members of the anti-Treaty forces at Drangan, County Tipperary, as it was being driven by Richard Dalton from Fethard to Kilkenny with a prisoner 'who was on parole'. Dalton was brought to a house where he met Dan Breen, who asked him where he was going and what he was doing:

> [Dalton] produced a permit and the men said it was a Free State permit. When they saw the name of the owner they said he [Peter DeLoughry] was 'no good' … [Dalton] had never seen them or the car ever since.[21]

Towards the end of April 1922, anti-Treaty forces under Aylward and John Morrissey, officer commanding, 4th Battalion, Kilkenny Brigade, invaded and occupied the RIC barracks in Parliament Street and John Street, as well as Kilkenny prison. An uneasy peace existed that was broken by sporadic gunfire. Prout was keen to keep the peace and negotiated with the anti-Treaty forces to try to calm the atmosphere.

Matters came to a head when the anti-Treaty forces in Parliament Street RIC barracks took possession of the bonded stores in Chapel Lane to search for whiskey that had come from Belfast. (A 'Belfast boycott' had been imposed by Dáil Éireann in response to anti-Catholic rioting and pogroms in the summer of 1920.) The whiskey was later removed to Kilkenny prison. Prout visited the anti-Treaty forces there on Saturday 29 April and issued an ultimatum that if the whiskey was not returned and the building handed back to the control of the prison governor by 5.30 that evening, force would be used against them. By two o'clock in the afternoon, a proclamation to this effect had been circulated by Prout to shopkeepers for display.

Pro-Treaty forces were then deployed at various points throughout the city, including Kilkenny Castle, St Canice's round tower and the Bank of Ireland, High Street. These troops were fully armed and had a Thompson sub-machine gun. Up to 200 soldiers were despatched from Beggars Bush barracks (pro-Treaty) as reinforcements. At around four o'clock, a *Kilkenny Journal* reporter interviewed young soldiers loyal to the anti-Treaty side who informed him that they had just been to confession. One of them gave a message to be delivered to his mother 'in case anything might happen'. At five o'clock, an armed party of Prout's troops from the military barracks was seen coming down the Castle Road. This was when Peter intervened:

> A motor drove up, from which the mayor of Kilkenny alighted and, having spoken to the officer in charge of the army party for a few moments, he drove away in the direction of the military barracks … DeLoughry informed Colonel Prout that the irregular forces were prepared to restore the goods seized but that they would not vacate the prison. Colonel Prout declined to accept these terms and stated there must be complete evacuation.[22]

The *Irish Independent* reported that Peter had been 'working strenuously for peace' throughout the stand-off.[23] This task would have been made more difficult because of his clear pro-Treaty stance, but his efforts paid off. By 5.45 p.m. a report reached Prout that the anti-Treaty forces had all but left the prison:

Colonel Prout went personally to investigate the truth of the statement, and found two of the irregular forces awaiting him to hand over the stores seized.[24]

In its report of the event, *The Times* of London could not resist poking fun at the anti-Treaty forces:

The usual touches of comedy which seem inevitable to all Irish events are not lacking. A report from the Four Courts [anti-Treaty forces] says: 'The vice-commanding officer, Kilkenny brigade, surrendered Kilkenny jail to the Free State forces this evening. He was subsequently placed under arrest by order of his [own] senior officers.' Another comic touch was provided by the discovery that the [whiskey] was not of Belfast manufacture at all, but was the product of Power, Dublin.[25]

It was all over by seven o'clock on Saturday evening, but the following Monday night anti-Treaty forces from Counties Tipperary, Waterford and Kilkenny arrived in the city and joined up with their allies occupying the two RIC stations. Throughout the night, they invaded and stationed themselves at vantage points in the city, including Kilkenny Castle, the workhouse, the workingmen's club, Kieran Street, Smithwick's brewery, the belfry and round tower of St Canice's Cathedral, the Tholsel and Arthur J. Wilsdon's grocery shop in Upper John Street. They also took over the Imperial Hotel, Rose Inn Street, at three o'clock on Tuesday morning. Guests were told they could stay until after breakfast.[26]

Backed by reinforcements from Dublin, Prout began the task of retaking the buildings. An *Irish Independent* reporter telephoned Kilkenny military barracks during the onslaught and an officer there said that 'the shooting was so heavy he could hardly hear anything'.[27] The assault by Prout's pro-Treaty forces began at eleven o'clock on Tuesday morning. During the bombardment of Wilsdon's shop opposite Kilkenny railway station, an ambulance approached on its way to the county hospital, carrying the corpse of a man who had drowned in the Nore. The driver, William Oakes, opened fired on Prout's troops as he drove past and the vehicle was immediately surrounded and Oakes was disarmed.

All the buildings were retaken. One of the most difficult tasks for the pro-Treaty forces was the battle for the Imperial Hotel, which was surrendered late on Tuesday evening. The hotel's owner was praised by the *Kilkenny People* for her bravery: 'Miss O'Neill refused to leave during the siege. She was told there might be fierce fighting but she said she would stick it out. And she did. Her pluck during the trying ordeal is universally admired.'[28] Kilkenny Castle was the last to surrender, at nine o'clock on Wednesday night. George O'Dwyer cut short his honeymoon to take part in the fight against anti-Treaty forces.[29] The assault had lasted from early morning, but its ferocity had not stopped children from 'engaging in, what was to them, an exciting hurling contest in High Street near the city hall' as 'bullets were whizzing past'. On John's bridge, a boy was seen lying in a very dangerous position exposed to the fire from the castle, calmly gathering up the discarded clips of empty cartridge cases; he had his pockets full.[30]

The Earl of Ossory and Lady Ossory had remained in the castle throughout the fighting. When they emerged after the guns had ceased firing, they were applauded by a crowd that had gathered at the front of the castle:

His Lordship acknowledged the demonstration of goodwill by raising his hat.

His Lordship, it was noticed, was minus a collar or tie, and was badly in need of a shave. ...

Asked how his recent guests had behaved, His Lordship emphatically declared, 'They were courtesy itself, and fought with much bravery. I had permission to leave the castle if I chose to do so and was also guaranteed safe escort.'

When the fight was over, the officers and men who had stormed the castle shook hands with the defenders and congratulated them on their great fight.

The Earl of Ossory also showed his admiration for the castle defenders and shook each man warmly by the hand.[31]

More than 100 prisoners were taken into custody. No one had been killed but some on both sides were wounded. A little more than a week later, all the prisoners were released. One of them said that Prout had treated the anti-Treaty soldiers with the utmost courtesy and had told them that he had no harsh words, because in obeying the orders of their superior officers they were fulfilling the first duty of every soldier.[32]

No sooner had the dust of battle settled than Prout received an anonymous letter calling him a traitor. The writer told Prout that there were a few '.45 Webleys oiled waiting for you [and your] brat of a son'.[33] Jack Prout, who was fourteen years old, had, according to the *Evening Mail*, surprised everyone by his reckless daring during the Kilkenny battle. When the correspondent saw him at the military barracks, the boy was armed with two Webley revolvers, and when asked if he could shoot, offered to give a demonstration of his marksmanship. His father did not appear to be worried that the boy's life might be in danger, remarking, 'The threat to murder my son, I disregard, for he is able to protect himself.'[34]

The Times of London used the events in Kilkenny to press home its point that the immediate stable political future of Ireland was in jeopardy:

> The fight that has waged for two days in Kilkenny is by far the most serious that has yet taken place between the rival Irish forces … Kilkenny is the logical conclusion of Mr Roderick O'Connor's heroics in Dublin, and of Mr de Valera's wanton incitement. If Ireland be not rent from end to end it is not the fault of those who have lit the train. It may be, and we trust it is, that Irishmen are beginning to realise whither their country is drifting. If they are, Kilkenny should complete their enlightenment.[35]

A day after the fighting had ceased in Kilkenny, a truce was signed in Dublin by three officers representing both sides. Four members of this committee, including Commandant Dan Breen and Brigadier General Seán Moylan, visited Kilkenny, where they consulted Peter on what had happened and what might be done.[36] It was a futile exercise as bitterness was present in the chests of warriors on both sides.

15

Hatred Simmers, 1922

The DeLoughrys and the Stallards found themselves holding opposing views on the Treaty. However, the two families put their political differences aside and continued to be business partners and socialise together and the children of both families remained the best of friends. This did not stop some of their hard-line friends and relatives questioning the continued connection. When the issue of the Treaty or the Civil War arose, members of both families would tell the questioners that there were more important matters to fight over than politics.[1]

Despite this, they endured what many families had to suffer during and after the Civil War. Peter's wife, Win, a daily communicant, noticed that friends with whom she used to laugh and talk averted their eyes when she made her way to the Black Abbey for mass. Loyal customers faded, never to return. Nanny noticed that during the evening when she sat at the half-opened shop window, passers-by who used to wave to her did not do so anymore; they quickened their step, heads down. Sudden and permanent isolation erupted among brothers, neighbours and in the case of the DeLoughrys, among their 'sisters' in Cumann na mBan.

In Kilkenny city, Cumann na mBan evolved into an anti-Treaty organisation. As a staunch supporter of the Treaty, Win found no reason to remain in the organisation and could have stepped into the background, but instead she decided to establish a branch of Cumann na Saoirse (Freedom Council) in the city for women who shared her views. The organisation was heavily centred in Dublin and it aimed to destroy and counteract 'Irregular' (anti-Treaty forces) propaganda and intelligence work. Anti-Treaty militants kept a close eye on the activities of Cumann na Saoirse, even going so far as to compile lists of the addresses of women connected to the organisation.[2] Win chaired the first meeting in the Tholsel, where members, including the novelist Florence Hackett,[3] announced their 'wholehearted support in the coming [1922 General] Election to those candidates who undertake to use the Treaty for the securing of Ireland's independence'.[4]

A controversy began following Peter's decision to allow the Tholsel to be used by the Kilkenny branch of Cumann na Saoirse for its inaugural meeting:

> One of the ladies of Cumann na mBan, apparently acting under instructions – I don't know whether she was or not – came up here [City Hall] and posted bills on the walls, the windows, and even on the desk and mirrors; you can still see bits of them that could not be removed. I could understand if it was done by girls who were brought up without any ideas in politeness or good breeding, but the particular lady who did this – I would not expect it from her and none of you would if you knew her. She may try to persuade herself that she was actuated by patriotic motives, but I don't know of anything in her past career that could give her any claim to try to criticise other people who have been working in the national movement all their lives. She is more prominent now of course![5]

Peter's remarks are noteworthy in that, as a confirmed conciliator and mediator in the political life of Kilkenny, this is the first recorded instance where he is seen to descend into a petty quarrel, allowing the bitterness of Civil War to invade his psyche by taking swipes at opponents using all the canniness of an experienced local politician. He went as far as to claim that one of the Cumann na mBan members had attended dances where Black and Tans were present.[6]

Three Cumann na mBan members, Siobhán Dooley, Una Egan and Sinéad Stallard, became embroiled in the row with Peter. During the Civil War they were arrested. When they were about to be searched, they protested and were released on the intervention of an officer.[7] Peter's sharp comments prompted Dooley, Egan and Stallard to write to the *Kilkenny People*:

> Sir – With reference to the mayor's 'tolerant and manly statement' [a sub-heading used in the report of Peter's remarks] which appeared in last week's local papers, the 'mutilation' of City Hall was carried out by a section of Cumann na mBan acting under orders, not by 'a member' as stated.
>
> The instruments used to 'mutilate' the assembly room were paste brushes and pins. Anybody who has visited the assembly room within recent years will admit that paste brushes were not out of place there, considering the condition of the wallpaper …
>
> The mayor's allusion to dances is mystifying. Can it be that he refers to a fancy dress ball which was held in Kilkenny since the Treaty was ratified?
>
> There were many worthy citizens present at this function including the mayor himself, and among the pierrots, a British citizen or two who had formerly belonged to the British army of occupation.
>
> Not having been in his own country during the activities,

[he was in Lincoln prison] the mayor could not be expected to know the individual work of Cumann na mBan members. We, therefore, overlook the inaccuracies of his statement in last week's papers.

Signed on behalf of Cumann na mBan,

Siobháin ní Dublaoic,

Una ní Aodagáin

Sinéad ní Stallaird.[8]

In reports from the Cumann na mBan Kilkenny Brigade to its headquarters in Dublin, Cumann na Saoirse was described disparagingly as Cumann na Searchers, a reference to the help members were giving Free State forces with searches.[9] The local Cumann na mBan also lamented their difficulty in raising funds and pinpointed the main obstacle preventing them from doing this: 'Concerts etc. could be got up but as the mayor holds control of places such as theatre, [Town] Hall, this prevents anyone asking for the hire of such places and of course he is very Treaty.'[10]

Peter acted as director of elections in Kilkenny for pro-Treaty Sinn Féin in the campaign for the 1922 general election held on 16 June. The election was held under the provisions of the Treaty, paving the way for the formal establishment of the Free State. Six candidates sought election in the Carlow-Kilkenny constituency. Two anti-Treaty candidates, Edward Aylward and James Lennon, lost. Three pro-Treaty candidates were elected: W. T. Cosgrave, on whose behalf Peter had campaigned vigorously, Denis Gorey (Farmers' Party) and Gearóid O'Sullivan.[11] However, the most first-preference votes by far were cast for the Labour candidate, Patrick Gaffney, whose party had campaigned not for or against the Treaty, but for workers' rights. (The Labour Party later accepted the Treaty. Nationally, pro-Treaty candidates under Michael Collins secured fifty-eight seats to the thirty-six won by Éamon de Valera's anti-Treaty candidates. The pro-Treaty Farmers' Party, led by Kilkenny man Denis Gorey, took seven seats and the Labour Party took sixteen seats.)

In August 1922 the death of Arthur Griffith and the killings, in quick succession, of Harry Boland and Michael Collins left people on both sides bereft of hope, temporarily at least, and consumed by confusion. Peter displayed a sense of desperation when paying tribute to Collins at a meeting of Kilkenny Corporation:

> Those of the members of the Corporation who attended the funeral obsequies in Dublin of Arthur Griffith could not fail to be struck with admiration at the fine physique, manly and soldierly bearing of General Collins as he marched in the sad procession, and certainly his presence and bearing inspired everybody with confidence that although the nation had sustained a great loss by the death of President Griffith, they had in General Collins a man ready and able to step into his shoes. To quote General Collins' own words: 'A malignant fate seems to dog Ireland's footsteps' and that was the way that most people felt when they heard of the appalling calamity that had befallen the nation by his death: they felt that some misfortune was always dogging the fate of Ireland.

Peter said that the greatest tribute would be paid to the dead not 'by encouraging a spirit of pessimism but by looking forward and striving to imitate the spirit of him whom they now mourned, the spirit of him who had always implicit confidence in the final outcome of Ireland's aspirations'.[12]

The leadership vacuum was filled by W. T. Cosgrave, who was elected president of the executive council when the third Dáil met for the first time. The following month Cosgrave enacted the Emergency Powers Bill that provided for the establishment of tribunals which were empowered to impose the death penalty. He did so reluctantly, but the rising wall of bodies from the Civil War and the refusal by anti-Treaty forces to agree to surrender arms under an amnesty forced his hand. The historian Joseph Curran described Cosgrave:

> In his quiet commonsensical way, he made an effective leader. He delegated authority wisely; handled Ministerial disputes even-handedly and was, on the whole, an ideal Chairman. His colleagues valued his advice and steadiness and long before he left office, his competence and wit had made him personally very popular with voters.[13]

Late in 1922, as the Civil War continued to rage, Peter's feeling of desolation expressed following the death of Collins was mixed with anger at the seemingly unending violence. He remained a steadfast supporter of Cosgrave:

> The only thing that is preventing what the people want – peace – is an armed minority that is striving to override the wish of the whole people of Ireland. I don't see anything to hope for from the statements made by those leaders who are fighting against the government and the people; I don't see anything to indicate that they are inclined to be reasonable. The president [Cosgrave] said the other day ... that there would be no humiliating terms imposed on them; still it has not brought forth any expression that would give reason to hope. It is the other way about and

some of the statements made recently are more 'die-hard' than ever.[14]

Peter got an opportunity to advance his political ideas with his election to the upper house of the national parliament, the Senate, being one of thirty members voted in by members of the Dáil.[15] He was joined by another Kilkenny representative, Ellen, Countess of Desart, who took her seat after W. T. Cosgrave had nominated her. The establishment of the Senate was due in part to an assurance given by Arthur Griffith that southern unionists would have representation in a new parliament, a promise fulfilled by Cosgrave after Griffith's death. The make-up of the house was described in an *Irish Times* feature as the most curious political grouping in the history of the Irish state:

> The recreations listed by senators were as intriguing as the senators themselves and ranged from pig-sticking to collecting English china. The *New York Times* remarked that the first Senate was 'representative of all classes'.
>
> In all, seven peers, a dowager Countess, five baronets and several knights were represented. The Senate consisted of thirty-six Catholics, twenty Protestants, three Quakers and one Jew.[16]

Peter and the Countess took their seats in the chamber on 11 December 1922 among other members including Dr Douglas Hyde, Oliver St John Gogarty and W. B. Yeats. While attending the Senate the following day Peter was notified that he had to return to Kilkenny on urgent domestic business: Win had given birth to their sixth child, Peadar.[17]

16

Catholic Church Brimstone, 1923–25

At the beginning of 1923 Peter found himself in a strong position politically. His close friend W. T. Cosgrave was president (prime minister) of the executive council, so he had a direct and close contact with the most powerful politician in the Free State. He remained mayor of Kilkenny for a fifth consecutive year and had embarked on the establishment of a Kilkenny branch of a new political party, Cumann na nGaedheal. In announcing who would be welcome to join the newly formed Cumann na nGaedheal party, Peter said it was 'open to everyone, let him be an Orangeman if he likes'.[1]

When W. T. Cosgrave introduced the Emergency Powers Bill in September 1922, an amnesty issued shortly afterwards elicited little response and military courts came into operation on 15 October. Under this legislation, seventy-seven executions were carried out. Cosgrave explained his reasons:

> Although I have always objected to a death penalty, there is no other way I know of in which ordered conditions can be restored in this country or any security obtained for our troops, or to give our troops any confidence in us as a government. We must accept the responsibility.[2]

Peter was approached by parents on at least two occasions to vouch for young men from the anti-Treaty side brought before the courts and facing a possible death sentence. He wrote letters to the judges pleading for their lives to be spared. The letters show a side to Peter's character that was not always apparent in his public life. On close examination, these letters show that more thought went into them than is immediately apparent. In one letter, written on behalf of Michael McSweeney, he employed the devices of an engineer and a writer where precision fused with rhetoric. Peter employed similar devices when writing on behalf of Martin Medlar, Paulstown, County Kilkenny, where he mixed conversational and formal language to drive home the point that the issue should be seen from the point of view of Medlar's parents, thus placing their son in the more sympathetic context of a 'child' and not a gunman. He concluded his appeal by citing respected members of the community who felt similarly, including Seán Gibbons, chairman of Kilkenny County Council and Dr Edward Dundon, a leading nationalist from County Carlow. Medlar escaped execution and was imprisoned for eighteen months.[3]

The fact that Peter wrote the letter at all, and that the Medlar family felt they could approach him, throws light on a much neglected area of Civil War Ireland. While members of the opposing sides might have disliked or hated each other, this was not the case for everyone. Jim Maher, author of *The Flying Column – West Kilkenny*, notes that while the anti- and pro-Treaty sides were sworn enemies, they had a certain regard for one another. The officer to whom the letter was addressed is likely to have been more impressed that Peter was speaking up for an opponent than by his standing in local and national politics. However, the impact of Peter's communication was obviously given weight by his being a mayor and a senator.

While being a member of the upper house was likely to impress pro-Treaty advocates, the opposite was the case for those maintaining an aggressive anti-Treaty position and whose militants set out on a campaign to burn the houses of southern unionists, particularly those who sat in the Senate. Michael Hopkinson says that 'the worst spell of attacks on unionist property was in the early months of 1923'.[4] By the end of March 1923, thirty-seven senators' homes had been burned to the ground.[5] Desart Court in County Kilkenny, described by *The Irish Times* as 'one of the most beautiful mansions in the south of Ireland', was targeted by militant anti-Treaty Republicans.[6] The mansion was owned by the Fifth Earl of Desart, who succeeded his brother, and was brother-in-law to Ellen, Countess of Desart. As such, the aggressive anti-Treaty faction viewed it as a legitimate target on the grounds of nationalism and as a social protest (against landlordism).

Three men entered the building on the night of 22 February 1923 and, according to the three household staff present, began to hack the furniture with axes and made a heap of the debris. The raiders removed paintings from the walls and added these to the vandalised tables and chairs. They then sprinkled petrol on the pile and set it alight before smashing the windows and doors. When they had left, the gardener attempted to move the grand piano outside but it fell down steps and smashed. The earl's wife, Lady Margaret Joan Lascelles, claimed that the 'tenantry were not above some looting and damaging of the dying house'.[7] The mansion was reduced to a ruin in three hours. However, some goods from the house were salvaged by staff and were later conveyed in two lorry-loads to Kilkenny for transportation via rail and steamer to England. The second consignment was held up by armed raiders and set alight.[8]

The Republican chief of staff, Liam Lynch, was killed on 10 April 1923 and was replaced by Frank Aiken, who called a halt to the struggle. Anti-Treaty forces declared a ceasefire on 30 April.[9] The following month, Aiken ordered members of these forces to dump arms rather than to continue a fight they were incapable of winning. The number of civilians who died is not known; the number of military deaths has been estimated at up to 4,000, although Michael Hopkinson believes this figure to be too high.[10]

As director of elections for Cumann na nGaedheal in the 1923 general election in Kilkenny, Peter was keen not to see a repeat of the 1922 result where the Labour Party candidate had topped the poll well ahead of Cosgrave. The historian Ciara Meehan makes the point that 'most political parties are created to win power through electoral success, but Cumann na nGaedheal – born into the blood of fratricidal conflict – was built by men already exercising power'.[11] In a speech to Cumann na nGaedheal party workers, Peter told them that Cosgrave had decided to 'sink or swim by Kilkenny' and that the constituency (now comprising Carlow-Kilkenny) should be seen to back him as much he had backed it.[12]

Peter left little to chance. During Cosgrave's campaign visit to Kilkenny a week before the election, he scheduled him to speak in Kilkenny city, Castlecomer, Ballyragget, Freshford, Johnstown and Tullaroan, a schedule that involved a sixty-mile journey through the county in one day. The speeches concluded at midnight and a similar canvass was organised for the following day. Peter had also arranged for Judge Daniel Cohalan, a prominent Irish-American and judge of the

Supreme Court of New York, to speak at the rally in Kilkenny city.

The hustings were not an easy experience for candidates on either side. During a speech at the Parade in Kilkenny, Cosgrave was heckled. One spectator shouted: 'De Valera fought and bled for Ireland' to which Cosgrave retorted, 'I say that is not true. He fought for Ireland but he never bled for it (laughter and applause) and what is more he came out of this fight without a single member of his family getting as much as a scratch (applause).' In Castlecomer, Cosgrave replied to another heckler who challenged him about the executions:

> They executed Collins and my uncle and many other good citizens before we executed anyone. We only executed when every appeal to reason failed and when only the strong hand ruled. We govern, and make no mistake about it, I will do it again if necessary.[13]

Cumann na nGaedheal won fifty-eight seats to de Valera's party's thirty-six. Peter had done his work well in the Carlow-Kilkenny constituency: Cosgrave won 17,709 first-preference votes. His nearest rival, Michael Shelly (anti-Treaty), secured 5,641.[14] As the *Manchester Guardian* pointed out during the year, 'Kilkenny proves to be a Free State stronghold.'[15]

In the Carlow-Kilkenny by-election held in March 1925, Peter had to contend with the anger of constituents over a one shilling cut in old-age pension payments.[16] As he was about to speak at a rally, he was heckled. Civic Guards intervened to remove the interrupters.[17]

At another rally, Peter answered a spectator who raised the issue of the pension cut during his address to the crowd:

> If you want to know who cut the old-age pensions, go and ask those people who came out to destroy the country, and if you support the people who caused destruction to the tune of forty or fifty million sterling, there will be no old-age pensions at all.[18]

The Cumann na nGaedheal candidate, Thomas Bolger, won the by-election comfortably.[19]

Peter also continued to enjoy success in local politics. As mayor, he discharged the usual duties of welcoming visiting dignitaries and dealing with infrastructural developments, such as the electrification of Kilkenny city in which he took a great interest, wearing both his engineer's helmet and mayoral chain. He represented the city at a conference of the Association of Irish Municipal Authorities and enjoyed tributes paid by the local government auditor to the running of Kilkenny Urban District Council.[20] Along with the Wicklow TD, Christopher Byrne, Peter succeeded in having a 300-year-old bell returned to the Black Abbey in Kilkenny from Dunlavin in County Wicklow.[21] He was also regularly attending sessions of the Senate, where his contributions were few but varied. He campaigned for the replacement of imperial measurements with the metric system[22] and introduced a bill designed to define more clearly the circumstances in which the holding of an inquest should arise.[23] Peter said he was introducing the bill so that in future it might be easier to identify why an accident had occurred, allowing corrective measures to be put in place to reduce the risk of a recurrence.[24] The bill was eventually enacted as the Coroners (Amendment) Act, 1927.

However, it was in the Senate chamber in 1925 that Peter's downfall from national politics occurred. Between 1923 and 1925 attempts were made to damage him politically with attacks of varying degrees of subtlety and magnitude. He did not help his own cause by changing from his usual careful, if blunt, statements to another style of argument. In one exchange, where Kilkenny was being compared unfavourably with Carlow, Peter said: 'Here in Kilkenny our estimate is lower than in Carlow – a little bit of a county; it is not a county at all!'[25] While headline writers welcomed such contributions, they left Peter vulnerable to attack.

From an early age, Peter had been aware of the power of the Catholic Church in Ireland. The manner in which some local clergy, most notably Bishop Brownrigg, had harried and damned Fenianism and the GAA was a regular feature of his childhood. In adult life, he and Tom Stallard had been the victims of public attacks by the Catholic clergy, in 1916 and 1917 regarding the Sunday opening of their cinema, a battle that he and Tom had won. This may have given Peter a false sense of security. He let his guard down during a discussion about the censorship of films at a meeting of Kilkenny Urban District Council in March 1923. There he stated that the proper censors were members of the public, although he qualified the remark by saying that nothing that would corrupt public morals should be shown. In June of that year he was more emphatic, telling the Senate during a debate on the Censorship of Films Bill that 'I am against this Bill altogether, so far as the censoring of films goes, because I think that the public are the real censors.'[26] The idea that the public should be left to decide on what was good for them was not one supported by the Catholic clergy, whose view was expressed forcefully the following year.

Peter attended a Civic Guard dance at the courthouse in Kilkenny in November 1924. As mayor, he was the first mentioned in the long list of guests from financial, legal and local government sectors that was published in the local press. General Eoin O'Duffy, the chief commissioner, and deputy commissioner Ned Coogan were also present. The fact that there was a bar in operation at the event drew the ire of the Rev. Andrew O'Keeffe, who denounced the dance from the pulpit of St Mary's Cathedral the following Sunday. He told the congregation that the Civic Guards had objected to licences being granted for dances at the Desart Hall because of the noise and riotous behaviour by patrons on the streets afterwards and it was difficult to reconcile the presence of a bar at the Civic Guards' dance with the views they had expressed about Desart Hall a year previously:

> The Rev. preacher said he referred to the matter not so much because there was a bar there, but because it was the cause of drinking excesses. In his opinion, that dance, considering the circumstances under which it was held, scandalised the people of Kilkenny more than any dance had done for a long time. In protesting against it, he had the sanction and approval of his Lordship the Bishop.[27]

The bishop referred to, Dr Brownrigg, was celebrating his fortieth year in the See of Ossory during 1924.

Shortly after Fr O'Keeffe's denunciation from the pulpit, Kilkenny Urban District Council welcomed a delegation from the Kilkenny Vigilance Committee who were trying to get the local authority to use the powers of the 1890 Public Health Act to regulate and, if need be, outlaw public dances where alcohol was being sold. No agreement was reached, but at the end of the discussion Peter raised the issue of Fr O'Keeffe's condemnation:

I refer to references made from the pulpit and reported in the local press about a recent dance held in the courthouse. I happened to be at that dance, and I have no hesitation in saying that what appeared in the public press of what Fr O'Keeffe said from the pulpit could be described as nothing short of a libel … No one can say that the Civic Guards, since they came to Kilkenny – I have as much facilities [*sic*] for observing them as any other man – that they were ever seen under the influence of drink. That could not be said of their predecessors … If the trouble had been taken to consult Chief Superintendent Lynch or Superintendent Feore, I am sure they would put Fr O'Keeffe right on the matter; but the ordinary rights of justice and fair play were not observed.

Fr Walsh said they were in favour of public dances and innocent amusements subject to a little restriction.

Mr Griffin suggested that this part of the discussion should not go to the press.

Senator DeLoughry – I made them deliberately for the press.

Mr Griffin – The reason I asked the press not to report it is that it might appear to the other side as unpleasant.

Senator DeLoughry – They can think what they like.

After the delegation left, the discussion continued. Peter gave the view that 'a lot of busybodies go to the clergy with stories and the clergy listen to them which is the worst feature of it'.[28] The meeting concluded with no action being taken.

By attacking Fr O'Keeffe, Peter was attacking Bishop Brownrigg. His remarks, both blunt and off-hand about the Catholic clergy, were not forgotten.

The issue of divorce would also lead to friction between Peter and the clergy. The 'moral fibre of the new [Cosgrave] administration came under closer scrutiny in November 1922 and

January 1923, when the first petitions for divorce were lodged in the Private Bills office of the Oireachtas'.[29] In Kilkenny, the issue was linked to what the Catholic clergy interpreted as a general decline in public morality. During a sermon at the Black Abbey, Fr Coleman condemned dances, the theatre and the cinema. He criticised 'the scanty clothing of females' and the 'free use of intoxicants'. He said that divorce cases revealed to other classes of society a 'world of hideous evil and shameful infamies'. He complained that 'never were theatres so widespread, never were actors and actresses so numerous'. He described the cinema as a moral danger to both adults and the young which 'brought out the sex appeal, it gave disgraceful scenes from the orgies of the underworld, it placed a halo around daring crime and ungoverned passion'.[30]

Two months later, Fr Coleman singled out Ellen, Countess of Desart, for attack after she had made a contribution to the divorce debate in the Senate in which she said:

> In the name of women I protest against the idea that it is divorce that destroys the sanctity of the home. Surely, the law laid down 3,000 years ago by the greatest legislator, took the more sensible view of the matter. The Mosaic law, as can be read in the Bible, not only permitted divorce but enjoined it. The law recognised that it was the seducer in the home or out of it, not the judge in court or parliament, who breaks up the home.[31]

Fr Coleman described the Countess as one who was well known for her schemes for the social betterment of the people, but:

> The awful revelations of the divorce courts in England alone, not to speak of other countries, showed the utter absurdity of her

contention. She even attempted to prove her point by quoting the Sacred Scriptures … Whatever that lady's private religious view might be, she certainly placed the Mosaic legislation above that of Jesus Christ.

The oblique reference to her being of the Jewish faith was not the only one made by the priest. He told his congregation that 'it was inevitable that the very small minority in Ireland – neo-pagan writers, Protestants of various denominations and Jews – should seek to introduce divorce into this country'.[32]

Cosgrave, early in 1925, proposed to the Dáil that standing orders be revised to rule out the introduction of divorce. However, Lord Glenavy decided to rule Cosgrave's resolution out of order in the Senate:

James Douglas, who had chaired the Joint Committee and drafted the rejected proposal, devised an alternative procedure which would, in effect, have prevented discussion of Divorce Bills without prohibiting their introduction. His resolution requiring a first reading for Divorce Bills in both houses, before consideration in the [Senate] was approved by fifteen senators to thirteen on 11 June 1925.[33]

Peter was not present at the vote because he was lobbying for funds for Kilkenny's structural development. His absence was seized upon by Archdeacon James Doyle, St Canice's, Kilkenny, who wrote a letter to the press demanding an explanation:

Is it true that he did not vote on the 'Douglas motion' and, if the answer be negative, why did he not vote? Is he prepared to give a guarantee that he will, if elected, vote against every attempt that may be made in the Senate to promote, in any way, the legalising of divorce in the Irish Free State?

Peter held the view privately that divorce should be available to those who wished to avail of it, but he did not express this view publicly.[34] As a confirmed Catholic, he argued that divorce was not part of his religious hinterland and that he looked upon the debate in the Senate as of no practical importance. He explained his absence in the chamber during the vote by saying that he had been in Government Buildings attempting to negotiate a loan of £10,000 for the improvement of the Kilkenny water-works. Unwisely, he said that the Douglas motion was simply a debating point 'started by some high-brows in the Seanad more for the purpose of airing their eloquence than for any practical object' and he looked upon securing the money for Kilkenny's waterworks as more important than 'debates on unrealities' in the Senate.[35]

By employing these arguments, he was pouring scorn on the upper house of which he was a member. The less than con-vincing explanation resulted in a second published letter from the Archdeacon in which he argued that the Douglas motion *was* of great importance. He questioned why Peter had not been able to take fifteen minutes out from his meeting at Gov-ernment Buildings to cast his vote 'considering the importance of the issues to be decided at the coming [Senate] Election, any man or woman who has a vote and culpably fails to record it, will – to say the least – do a very bad turn for Ireland. Believe me.' The archdeacon continued:

If Senator DeLoughry's account of his fellow senators be correct, *viz* that 'they go to the Senate more for the purpose of airing their eloquence than for any practical purpose', and that they waste their time upon 'unrealities', the ratepayers may well ask – is it for this we are taxed to provide for each of those senators an income of £300 net per year, that they may waste their time 'airing their eloquence' upon 'unrealities'?

In attempting to defend himself Peter repeated the more cogent points he had made and bemoaned the campaign that had been launched against him:

> I have learned with, I am bound to say, intense regret, not because my personal interests are involved but because I expected a higher standard of honour and fair play from even the least friendly section of my fellow citizens and fellow countrymen that a concerted attack has been made on my candidature for the Senate on wholly false grounds.[36]

At a meeting in the Kilkenny theatre to support Peter's candidature, a letter from Cosgrave was read in which he gave Peter a ringing endorsement, but the damage had been done.

In his address to the assembly, Peter referred to bogus posters that had been put up throughout the city (including on the gates of Catholic churches) regarding the divorce controversy. (The import of these posters is not known, but it is likely they claimed that he supported the introduction of divorce legislation.)

> 'The names of the originators did not appear, because,' Senator DeLoughry said, 'I suppose they were afraid to put their names to it, or perhaps they were ashamed, or perhaps their past record would not bear scrutiny.' (Applause) ... 'I come before you as a

citizen; I lived practically all my life in Kilkenny – I have been before you in public life all my time I have been for the past twenty years on public boards. Most of you knew my father and my grandfather (applause). We belong to this old city of which every one of us are proud. Do you think – does anybody here, even those who may have something against me – think a man can serve twenty years in public life, without walking on somebody's corns, if he acts conscientiously? … I yield to no man – priest or layman – in my loyalty to my religion, but at the same time, I believe we should embrace in this new State and call to its service the intellects and the brains of every citizen.' (Applause).[37]

Along with the other eighteen outgoing senators, Peter nominated himself for re-election in 1925, unlike the previous occasion when he was nominated by TDs. The election was by single transferable vote, with the entire state forming a single nineteen-seat electoral district. Despite early indications that he would be successful, he did not win a seat. What the electorate missed and what Peter failed to drive home in the middle of this controversy was that he had secured the loan of £10,000 for Kilkenny waterworks, equivalent to more than £425,000 today. The *Kilkenny People* reported that while on public grounds 'his defeat is to be regretted, so far as he is personally concerned, it might be regarded as a blessing in disguise'.[38]

Peter now had more time on his hands than he had had for a long time. His heavy workload was further reduced in July 1925 when, after six years in office, he stepped down as mayor and handed over the chain to James Reade of the Labour Party.[39] His successful negotiation for a government loan to fund the city's waterworks was acknowledged publicly by Reade when he was elected mayor of Kilkenny for a second time in 1926: 'Were it not for Ald. DeLoughry, they would have no water scheme – nobody else could claim credit for it.'[40]

Reminders of the past were intruding on his life around this time. The DeLoughry family had been loyal to Parnell. Though he might not have understood it as a child, over time Peter came to appreciate the circumstances of Parnell's downfall through the scandal over his divorce, attacks by the Catholic clergy and the destructive rivalry of nationalist factions. Having gone through similar though less damaging misfortune himself, he was likely to have empathised with Parnell even more in adulthood. Peter had sent a message of welcome to John Devoy, a Fenian from his father Richard's generation, when he visited Ireland in 1924.[41] Another of Richard's contemporaries was John Haltigan. His son Patrick, who had been appointed Reader of the United States House of Representatives, was presented with the freedom of Kilkenny when he visited the city in August 1925. Peter played a prominent part in the ceremony.[42]

The death of the former GAA president James Nowlan in July 1924 was a poignant moment for Peter:

He [Nowlan] was visited by many old friends during his last illness, especially by one of his dearest friends and youngest disciples, Senator Peter DeLoughry. Jim Nowlan and Dick DeLoughry (the senator's father) were workers in the same cause, as was also Jim Nowlan's father and when the two men of the older generation passed away, the friendship cemented by years of close association was continued, and Nowlan, being considerably the elder, took a kind of paternal interest in young Peter DeLoughry when the latter was no more than a boy.[43]

Given that Peter's mother, Bridget, ended her days as an inmate of Kilkenny District Lunatic Asylum, it is noteworthy that during a Senate debate on the Local Government Bill, 1924, Peter put forward an amendment that all mention of the words 'asylum' and 'lunatic asylum' be changed to 'mental hospital'.[44] The amendment was accepted and ratified in the Dáil on 10 March 1925.[45] A more direct reference to Bridget can be found in a letter, dated 27 February 1925, which Peter sent to a cousin in the United States whose mother had just died:

> I need scarcely tell you how sorry we were to hear of your very sad bereavement. Certainly the mother is always the strongest link in the family chain and it is very hard to bear the great loss which a mother's death means … None of us is here for very long and in a few years we shall have taken the same road.[46]

17

Founder Fights Back, 1926–31

Peter's loss of his Senate seat and of the mayoralty did not see a lessening of his work-rate. In fact, Win wrote to a relative in the United States at the end of 1926 apologising for his not corresponding, explaining that he hated to write letters, saying, 'what a busy man he is'.[1]

He became even busier the following year when he contested and won a seat for the Carlow-Kilkenny constituency in the September general election. Bishop Brownrigg, despite his antagonism towards Peter, subscribed £10 to election expenses for Cumann na nGaedheal. In the Dáil, Peter joined the other Cumann na nGaedheal TDs to support the minority administration under Cosgrave. The leader of the opposition (Fianna Fáil) was Éamon de Valera.

The death of Fr Andrew O'Keeffe, elicited a surprising message of sympathy from Peter. The two men had exchanged strong verbal attacks on each other's beliefs over censorship, Peter having practically accused Fr O'Keeffe of committing libel over references to the conduct of guests at a Civic Guards' dance. However, Peter paid tribute to the priest in a manner that was generally unexpected:

He was an outstanding personality in the city. He was a man of very strong views on many social questions but while he held those views strongly we all know and knew he held them honestly … If I might be allowed to introduce a personal note, I would like to say this much: in Fr O'Keeffe, I and my family have lost a very dear and sincere friend. I may be pardoned for reciting a time when things were very black and disturbed, when my premises were locked up and occupied by the Auxiliaries and Black and Tans, when my wife and children were not allowed outside the door, and when anyone who went in was not allowed out – at that time, Fr O'Keeffe was most constant in his visits and attention and care on behalf of my family. I can never forget that for him [*sic*]. He did not do it for any motive other than that prompted by a charitable concern for his parishioners.[2]

Peter's engineering bent led him to become deeply involved in Kilkenny's participation in the Shannon hydro-electric scheme at Ardnacrusha in County Clare, an enormous project undertaken by Cosgrave's government. He met two of the project's engineers, Waldemar Borquist and Thomas Norberg Schulz, in Kilkenny to talk to them about how Kilkenny might profit from the construction.[3] Shortly before the power station was completed, Peter met Cosgrave in the Club House Hotel in Kilkenny and asked him if there was a possibility of Kilkenny getting current from the subsidiary scheme that was to supply Waterford. Cosgrave said that if Peter could 'put up a good case, showing that there is a certain number of traders in Kilkenny anxious and willing to take advantage of that scheme, I believe it will go a far way, but you will want to act very quickly'.[4] Peter issued circulars to traders asking them to put their names down as subscribers. This initiative was seized upon by John Magennis at a corporation meeting as an insult to its members. (However, Magennis did not explain fully his complaint. His accusation that Cosgrave was spiteful is puzzling since it appears that Cosgrave was attempting to help Kilkenny.)

Ald. Magennis – I saw the circular and I say it is a very strange thing that the president or the head of state would lend himself to a vindictive piece of spite – it is the most uncalled for act that was ever guilty by a man supposed to be ruler of the State.

Ald. DeLoughry – I should like Ald. Magennis to dilate a little upon that.

Ald. Magennis – There is no necessity for me to dilate on it at all. You are in full knowledge of the whole thing.

Ald. DeLoughry – It is very easy to make insinuations and not go any further. It is a very cowardly thing to do.

Ald. Magennis – I was never a coward. I never ran away from any position I ever took up.

Ald. DeLoughry – Oh, no! You never ran away from anything in your life!

Ald. Magennis – I never funked.

Ald. DeLoughry – You were never afraid of work in your life? You never did a single day's work for the last twenty years.

The Mayor [James Reade] appealed that no heat be introduced into the discussion.

Ald. DeLoughry – This man is here, always making insinuations. I have tried to keep peaceful and calm, but I cannot put up with that man's insinuations every time he comes up here. Good God! I have worked all my life anyway and I am proud of it and I am able to work still. (To Ald. Magennis) You are

> a working man! You will get all you want of it tonight if you
> want it.
>
> Ald. Magennis – I never got a soft–
>
> Ald. DeLoughry (heatedly) – You won't get anything soft from
> me anyway. If you want any fight you can have it tonight,
> Alderman Magennis.
>
> The Mayor again appealed for calmness.[5]

A year into his Dáil term, Peter built on the electoral success when he again contested local authority elections winning back a seat on Kilkenny Corporation and on Kilkenny County Council.

As an engineer, Peter was keenly interested in radio and had begun selling wireless sets in the early 1920s. His close association with the Civic Guards gave him an opportunity to experiment with the 'new technology' at one of the annual dances in Kilkenny courthouse organised by the force:

> A very pleasing innovation was introduced by the installation of
> a special Marconi amplification set, which enabled the music to
> be heard all over the building. The installation was carried out by
> Messrs R. DeLoughry and Sons, local agents for the Marconi
> Co. and a man sent specially by the Marconi Co. was in charge of
> the equipment during the night.[6]

Peter found that the cut and thrust of debate in the Dáil was not as colourful as that of local authority meetings. He used the national parliament to raise local issues, but also contributed to debates on money-lending, vaccination laws, hawkers' licences and bank holidays. He employed some wit and folksy speech during a debate on wireless broadcasting when he supported a suggestion by Deputy Patrick W. Shaw that horse-racing should be broadcast on radio:

> Mr DeLoughry – I never had the good fortune to be able to pick a winner, so that horse-racing has not a personal appeal. The great masses of the people, however, are deeply interested. I appeal to the parliamentary secretary to consider Deputy Shaw's suggestion that the results of big races in which Irish horses, and particularly Kilkenny horses, compete, should be broadcast … Although the Dublin programmes are excellent, I do not think there is enough of ancient Irish music broadcast. I do not think I ever heard the *Boys of Kilkenny* broadcast from the Dublin station. It is an excellent old Irish song, very popular, and I have not heard it so far.
>
> Mr Seán Lemass: Give us a verse.[7]

Peter and Alderman Magennis continued to launch low blows at each other during corporation meetings. They had been involved in high octane political arguments for the best part of twenty years. Like two boxers they seemed to revel in a scrap. However, there was another side to their encounters. When Magennis stood down as mayor in 1929, having served a year in office, Peter said that he had presided over the meetings with the greatest courtesy and fair play:

> Although Ald. Magennis and himself might differ on many points, still he thought that during his term as mayor they never had any great difference. 'That is about his conduct in the chair,' said Ald. DeLoughry, who added, 'When he is outside he might be a different proposition altogether.' (Laughter).[8]

The damage done to Peter's political career by members of the Catholic Church over the divorce issue did not make him dilute his criticisms of the clergy when they disagreed on issues religious or otherwise. During a meeting of the Kilkenny Technical Schools Committee, one of the administrators, Rev. Bro. Gleeson, proposed cutbacks to the day trades' preparatory school. He suggested changes to the running of classes because there were only two boys in one class. He asked Peter: 'Are you approving of a teacher for two boys? Is the manual teacher employing his time on two boys?' Bro. Gleeson argued that funds should be spent in the country at large and not confined to the city 'to save you [Peter] money by getting in apprentices already trained':

> I believe the money should be spent on the basic industry of the country – agriculture – instead of helping two or three firms in the city to get skilled tradesmen out of the technical school. Ireland's basic industry is agriculture and it should be helped.

Bro. Gleeson's contentions touched a nerve with Peter:

> Even if there are only two boys or three boys there, we ought to give them the best education we can to fit them for the battle of life afterwards … Bro. Gleeson is talking of what he knows nothing about. I am talking of what I know … We are told that agriculture is the basic industry in this country. Are we always to continue as an agricultural country? Are we to be told that agriculture is to be the only industry – that other industries in Ireland are never to be developed? Would it be no use to farmers if there was a hive of industry in Kilkenny to sell in instead of as at present sending their products to the ends of the earth … It

is absolutely out of order to bring forward this argument about agriculture.[9]

The issue of censorship, which had been raised several times at Kilkenny Corporation meetings, re-emerged as a contentious issue in 1931. Members were asked to consider resolutions from the League of the Kingship of Christ demanding censorship of foreign publications and calling for 'drastic measures to cope with the display of films of "unChristian origin and degrading tendencies"'.[10] Peter said that the adoption of the resolutions would damage his business, a politically naïve point that reduced the force of his other argument which was that he was against the level of censorship in existence: 'If [censorship] errs at all, I think it errs on the side of severity.' He said that if he wanted guidance on any Catholic questions he would take it from the bishops and clergy and not 'from any chance organisation of nonentities'. The councillor who raised the issue, Edward Furniss, picked up on this point, quoting a member of the hierarchy who had supported strict censorship. Peter retorted: 'I did not say a bishop or priest, I said bishops and priests.'[11]

Despite his public disagreements with the Catholic hierarchy, Peter maintained a respect for those whose views corresponded with his own interpretation of Christianity and did not abandon his religion because of what he perceived as myopic prelates. He was also aware that not all members of the hierarchy held the same views. In January 1930 he proposed a resolution to award the papal nuncio, Paschal Robinson, the freedom of Kilkenny city. Peter's speech welcoming the nuncio was marked by triumphalism and sincerity:

In the nation's capital, a government chosen by the Irish people is securely established; peace reigns and, spiritually, the people remain unchanged and unchangeable, while in adhesion to the spirit of liberty, which has always been manifested by our race, the principles of civil and religious freedom for all classes are firmly maintained.[12]

* * *

Beneath the laughter, beneath the horrors of the War of Independence, of the Civil War and the animosity that followed, a row simmered between Peter and de Valera over the return of the key that Peter had made in Lincoln jail. During Peter's lifetime, this issue never became public and he confined his attacks on de Valera to his political stance. His brother David recalled the conversation about the escape from Lincoln, when Peter had said: 'I want you to remember that I claim the return of this key as my property', to which de Valera replied, 'The key will be returned to you, without doubt, at some future time in a fitting public manner.' David said the DeLoughry family understood from this that 'the key would be inscribed or something of the kind and we wondered what occasion would be chosen for the presentation'.[13]

An IRA officer, James Fitzgerald, recalled that Harry Boland had given him two files and six keys, including Peter's key, in Manchester on the night of the escape. About a week later in Dublin, Fitzgerald handed Peter's key to Boland on the understanding that it would be given to de Valera. Fitzgerald kept the remaining keys and files.[14]

Following Peter's release from Lincoln prison in March 1919, he set about attempting to acquire the key. On at least two occasions he asked Boland to return the key: once at the Curragh races where Boland is reported to have said, 'Is that all that's troubling you?';[15] and on another unspecified occasion when it's claimed that Boland said: 'You're not interested in de Valera now! I have the key and I am going to keep it.'[16]

On his brother's advice, Peter then turned the focus of his quest to de Valera, to whom he wrote three letters. His sister, Lil, said de Valera did not reply to the first two.[17] According to David, on the advice of friends 'Peter made the tone of the [third] letter "abusive"' and this elicited a reply:[18]

Dáil Éireann
Oifig and Príomh Aire
President's Department

October 19
1921

P. DeLoughry,
6, Albany Terrace,
Ranelagh, Dublin.

A Chara –
The president has received your letter of October 17, and he directs me to say that while he has mentioned the matter to Miss Boland, he hardly thinks it likely that she will give the key until she hears from her brother in America,
Mise le meas
Caitlín Ni Conaill
Runaidhe na Uachtaráin.[19]

Rumours had been circulating that the key had been taken to America; another suggested that it had been given to Terence MacSwiney's sister, Mary. Such was the bitterness engendered by the row that David believed the rumours were made up 'to annoy Peter and keep him from Harry Boland and de Valera for a time'. David also said that he believed de Valera intended keeping his word but that 'realising all the facts, I considered [that] de Valera acted most dishonourably and he fell very much in my estimations as a man of honour'.[20]

According to Lil, Peter again asked de Valera to fulfil his promise shortly after the Treaty was signed in December 1921, but nothing happened. The row was known to other Irish leaders at the time and a journalist using the initials T. M. wrote many years later about his memory of the controversy, claiming that Boland had 'tantalised' Michael Collins by not giving up the key:

> DeLoughry sent repeated reminders about the promise. These seem to have resulted in making Harry Boland retain the key longer than he had intended. He never knew, I think, that his attitude in the matter vexed Collins, but in May 1922, when Mick recalled the subject to me, there was a tinge of bitterness in his speech.[21]

There the matter rested until 1929, when Peter again demanded that de Valera fulfil his promise when they met in the Dáil restaurant. In April 1929, ten years after the escape, de Valera got the key from the Boland family and handed it back to Peter in Leinster House with a letter in Irish in which he explained that he was returning it in fulfilment of a promise. The *Kilkenny People* reported the event: 'Alderman DeLoughry, in reply to a question whether Mr de Valera and himself had a little drink to celebrate the handing over of the key, replied in the negative.'[22]

John McKenna, who had served on Kilkenny Corporation with Peter, recalled many of the events surrounding the controversy and the night Peter brought back the key to Kilkenny: 'He lent it to me to show it to my family, saying "I would not give that key to another living man even for a moment, only yourself".'[23]

* * *

On 2 July 1931, Peter contributed to a debate on the Finance Bill in the Dáil about cinema admissions. He told the House that he was rising to speak because the discussion had centred on Dublin and that he wanted to remind them that there were cinemas in other places.[24] His contribution is noteworthy because it was the last public statement he made. Reports of his declining health had been appearing in the local press since March and he was greatly debilitated by kidney failure. Cait Grace, a family friend, remembers Peter wearing sunglasses (to mask bloodshot eyes caused by the illness) as he continued to serve in the shop.

One of his last letters was to his beloved sister, Lil. He had sent many to her from jails in Ireland and Britain and now he was writing to her from the imprisonment of illness:

Kilkenny, 14 Sept. 1931

My dear Lil,
A line to say I am feeling fine today, thank God. I have

increased eight lbs, everyone was telling me I got fat which I did not believe as I thought they were only saying so to please me so I weighed myself on the scales which I usually do and almost got a fright.

I do not know how to thank you for all your kindness. I enjoyed the rest and the 'putting' [pudding]. I am afraid if I stayed any longer I would be spoiled between you all. Poor Henry should be tired arranging the seats in garden and dancing attendance on me.

I will miss Lelia's walks and talks which I enjoyed very much and which she bore like an ancient martyr.

I hope you can read this. I must finish for post. Convey my thanks to Dalton for his drives etc. and the boys one and all for all their kindness,

Love to all

Yours V. Affectionately,

Peter.[25]

He sought medical advice and assistance from doctors in London but they were unable to help. On 15 October he made his will, leaving his estate to Win, and his signature betrays his weakness, the letters of his surname angling down the page. He died in the presence of Win and Lil and her husband, Henry Mangan, at their home in Dublin on 23 October. He was forty-nine.

Reports of his death were carried in newspapers across the world, including the *Herald-Tribune*, the *Boston Globe* and *The New York Times*. The *Irish Times* report on his funeral mass and burial in Thornback cemetery, two miles outside Kilkenny city, said that 'all along the route of the procession, the sidewalks were lined with people'. The cortège was led by St Patrick's brass and reed band of which he had been a member as a boy.[26]

Local and national politicians, including de Valera, attended the funeral.

Tributes were paid to Peter in the Dáil and in each of the local authority boards on which he had served. At the Kilkenny County Board of Health, Seán Gibbons said that Peter had 'devoted all his time and precious years of his life to the advancement of his country, very often to the neglect of his private business and his own family interests'.[27] Cosgrave wrote that 'politically we have all lost an outstanding figure in Irish public life. Kilkenny has lost one of its most prized citizens.'[28]

E. T. Keane printed a special supplement in the *Kilkenny People*. His obituary was not entirely complimentary and in his usual style, he went more for the truth than for diplomacy:

Either as a senator or a deputy he took very little part in the debates. It was not that he lacked the capacity to speak clearly or forcibly, for few men were more competent to deal with practical issues in a practical way. The truth is that talking for the sake of talking never appealed to him. He never spoke unless he felt he had something to say that was worth saying and that would prove a useful contribution to the discussion.

But there was another reason. Peter DeLoughry could never make a successful politician and he never tried to be one. He had few of the arts and none of the artifices of the politician. When he took a hand in the political game he made the fatal mistake of putting all his cards on the table and he never kept the ace up his sleeve. That was a fatal disqualification.

Notwithstanding that, or perhaps because of it, he was a useful practical member of the Dáil and he never spared himself in his efforts to serve his constituents.[29]

An anonymous writer to the *Connacht Tribune*, described as 'one who knew him', said Peter had the enthusiasm and capacity for self-sacrifice: 'He was too big for personal bitterness, though he held and expressed his opinions strongly, and at his graveside, those whom he supported and those whom he attacked gathered to pay him the last tribute of goodwill.'[30]

Writing in the *Gaelic American*, Patrick F. Cass said:

> Peter's memory will be the guiding spirit of the present young men of Kilkenny and with that spirit and guidance there is great hope for the future. I know his place in the history of Ireland of the past thirty-five years is secure and I hope he will be rewarded in Heaven.[31]

At Kilkenny district court, the state solicitor Dr M. J. Crotty recalled the time that Peter had been a judge in the Republican courts:

> Although he was not a trained lawyer, still with the help of the associates that were here and his own determination, he administered even-handed justice. His straightforwardness and dislike of chicanery and double-dealing made him as trusted on the bench as he was trusted in the councils of this city and of the State.[32]

At a Kilkenny Corporation meeting, J. E. Cole said that Peter's life was 'cast in stormy times but he was a man of peace. His life was gentle, but the elements were so mixed in him that any man could stand up and say of him: "He was a man".'[33] It was a fitting epitaph.

18

No Rest, 1932–70

The story of Peter's key does not end with its maker's death, as it continued to represent the division in Irish society caused by the Civil War.

De Valera was appointed president of the executive council after Fianna Fáil became the largest party in the Dáil in the 1932 general election. In July 1933 he was awarded the freedom of Kilkenny city, yet he did not mention Peter during his acceptance speech to a large crowd. Instead, he told spectators that he felt there was room for more activity in developing the industrial possibilities of the city and gave them an insight into his political thinking:

> The happenings of our own day are fully comprehensible only in the light of days and centuries before our time. So, when we are devising policies or fixing aims for the present generation, we must look to the past as well as to the future to make sure that our policies are wise and our aims attainable. In politics, no mistake is more fatal than contempt for tradition and refusal to learn from history.[1]

De Valera's refusal to continue to reimburse Britain with the 'land annuities' derived from financial loans granted by Britain to Irish tenant farmers to enable them purchase lands under the Irish Land Acts during the previous half century, resulted in the 'Economic War'. Both countries placed unilateral trade restrictions on each other and the damage to the Irish economy was severe.

This had an impact on Win, who was striving to keep the business afloat after her husband's passing. Peter had gone guarantor for many people in Kilkenny. Win was called upon to honour these debts, which she did when called upon to do so, forking out much-needed cash.[2] Letters written by her, nine years apart, show her state of mind before and after Peter's death and how the family members were progressing. The earlier letter was sent to a relative in the United States in 1926:

My dear Anna,

For a long time I have been wondering ought I drop you a line on behalf of your cousin, Peter. You are very good to forgive him so often for not writing you, but I daresay you quite understand what a busy man he is and if there is one thing in the world he hates, it is letter-writing.

I am glad you received his photo alright. It is a very good one of him.

Why on earth do you not come over to Ireland to see us and so many people coming over? Nearly everyone in Kilkenny had a friend home during this year and we had hopes [of] you or some of the O'Briens paying us a visit. We would all be simply charmed to see you.

Well, I do not know if Peter ever told you anything about our family of children. There are three boys and three girls. They are as follows: Dick, Tom, Lily, Sheila, Nessa and Peadar Óg (little Peter). Dick is at school in Newbridge about fifty miles from home. We often motor up to see him. Tom is at the local Christian Brothers' [school] and is doing wonderfully well.

Lily, Sheila and Nessa are going to the Presentation Convent about 100 yards from home. Lily is very clever and a great favourite with the nuns. Sheila is careless and gay and does not bother very much but Nessa is very like Lily and is very attentive to her studies. Then there is little Peter, who has not started school yet. He is only four years and is very frail looking although he is not really delicate.

I intend having their photo taken during the summer in a group and I shall be delighted to let you have one.

With very many thanks for kind remembrances for Christmas.

Wishing you every luck and prosperity for the New Year, joined by all the family,

Yours Sincerely

Win de Loughry.[3]

The second letter, sent to a relative in England in 1935, shows that the family business was thriving thanks, in part, to de Valera's policies:

Dear Connie,

How good of you to acknowledge the shamrock. I am sorry it was late.

All here were very sorry to learn of the death of your dear mother, RIP. There is nothing that can bring such a change in a family as the death of one so dear and near.

I am glad you are keeping fairly fit yourself. It must be lovely to have a nice home in the country. It is my one ambition if God will spare me.

The business which we extended some years before poor Peter's death, RIP, is being conducted by my two eldest sons, Dick and Tom, and they have built up a very successful business in the motor line. We carry out repairs to cars and hire them out. Also we got two petrol pumps installed. My eldest girl (Lily) is in the civil service. She passed very successfully in her two examinations.

The second girl, Sheila, is still going to school. She is rather a wild artist and does not take much pains with her studies. At present she is learning shorthand and typewriting. We hope to make her useful at home in the office.

Nessa comes next (and like Lily) has great application to study so we hope she will be as successful as she (Lily) is.

Peadar Óg (little Peter) is of course the pet of the house. He is twelve years old.

David and Larry are both married with a family of three each, one girl and two boys. Both are living in Kilkenny and do all in their power to help me here with the business and try to make up in a little way for the loss of dear Peter.

The foundry is doing remarkably well, owing to the imposition of tariffs.

Kindly remember me to Cissie.

With very best wishes for your future happiness from all,

Yours Affectionately,

Win de Loughry.[4]

De Valera also had a more direct impact on the family. Win's sons Dick and Tom became members of the United Ireland party. 'The launch of United Ireland/Fine Gael on 8 September 1933 rationalised the anti-Fianna Fáil opposition into a coalition incorporating as an integral part of it the Blueshirt organisation along with the Cumann na nGaedheal and Centre parties.'[5]

The period was marked by civil unrest that arose for several reasons. Maurice Manning cites three main causes: the growing rift between the government and the IRA; the impact of the Economic War; and 'the total distrust of each side for the other in a tension-filled and poisonously bitter environment, at a time when all the pent up and malignant emotions of the Civil War decade were fast coming to a head'.[6] Manning also details one of many stormy rallies at which the leader of the Blueshirts, General Eoin O'Duffy, spoke:

> The military was again called in to restore order at an O'Duffy meeting in Kilkenny on 22 October [1933]. At this meeting, O'Duffy accused every member of the crowd who interrupted of being a communist. He said communism was strongest in Kilkenny outside of Dublin; he knew that they had 300 rifles at their disposal and that there was a 'communist anti-God cell' in nearby Castlecomer.[7]

On 30 November the Garda Síochána raided the houses of leading Blueshirts and members of Fine Gael across the country, including the DeLoughrys. In his report of the incident, E. T. Keane was unforgiving:

> DeLoughry is dead and de Valera is president of the Irish Free State, thanks to DeLoughry and men like him who accepted the Treaty. DeLoughry's widow is trying to keep together for the benefit of herself and her family the business he built up. During the Black and Tan regime, DeLoughry's house was raided nearly every week. At one time, Auxiliaries occupied it for a week and closed down the business. Peter DeLoughry and his brother escaped with their lives … On Thursday morning last about 11.30, a number of detectives visited the residence of Mrs Winifred DeLoughry (widow of the late Alderman Peter

DeLoughry TD) in Parliament Street, and made a most minute search of the premises. Mrs DeLoughry's sons are prominent members of the United Ireland organisation, and the detectives seized and took away a number of documents relating to that movement. The detectives of course only carried out their instructions and acted quite courteously. Peter DeLoughry was a friend and defender of the Civic Guards when other people were attacking and maligning them.[8]

An account of the Lincoln prison escape published in the *Irish Independent* in 1936 reignited the controversy over the key. Testy letters were printed in the national newspapers from Peter's sister, Lil, and from Harry Boland's sister, Kathleen O'Donovan, over the delay in the return of the key to Peter. In a private letter to Mrs O'Donovan, Lil vented her anger, showing that the bitterness had not dissipated:

> The key had been kept in your family for ten years although Mr de Valera had evidently told you of his promise and asked you to give up the key eight years before that … You also stated in your letter that only for Mr de Valera's promise you would not have handed over the key. Even without that promise, I don't think you could have justified such treatment of a man who had worked patiently in prison for several weeks, using the mechanical skill for which he was noted in fashioning that master key.[9]

The Lincoln escape came to prominence again in 1950 when de Valera made a visit to the prison, accompanied by Fenner Brockway. Twenty years later, a biography of de Valera written by Lord Longford and Thomas P. O'Neill was published in which seventeen pages of one chapter are devoted to the

Lincoln escape, but there is no mention of Peter's name or his part in the rescue anywhere in the book.[10] Another of de Valera's biographers, Tim Pat Coogan, said that de Valera not only shaped history, 'he attempted to write it also – or, more correctly, to have it set down as he ordained'.[11]

During his campaign to be elected president of Ireland for a second term, de Valera visited Rothe House in Kilkenny where Peter's key was then lodged. He had never before spoken in detail about the key, whether it had jarred or had worked fluidly. Peter's daughter-in-law, Anna T. (Cissie) De Loughry, was present when de Valera, who was almost blind, asked to have the key put in his hand. He felt it and said, 'You know, it turned like velvet in the lock.'[12]

Endnotes

Abbreviations

BMH	Bureau of Military History, Dublin
BMP	Brendan Mangan papers, held by Brenda Clausard, Dublin
CBS	Christian Brothers School, Kilkenny city
CAC	Churchill Archives Centre, Cambridge, England
CO	Colonial Office, London
DFP	Family papers, held by Pádraigín Ní Dhubhluachra, Kilkenny
DMIPC	Directorate of Military Intelligence, Postal Censor
DDA	Dublin Diocesan Archive
EdeV	Éamon de Valera papers, UCD Archives
GAA	Gaelic Athletic Association
HO	Home Office, London
IRB	Irish Republican Brotherhood
KJ	*Kilkenny Journal*
KM	*Kilkenny Moderator*
KP	*Kilkenny People*
NA	National Archives, Kew
NAI	National Archives of Ireland
NLI	National Library of Ireland
OKR	*Old Kilkenny Review*
RIC	Royal Irish Constabulary
UCD	University College Dublin
WMC	Workingmen's Club of Kilkenny
WS	Witness Statement

1 Iron-Founder Moulded, 1882–95

1   General Register Office, Dublin. Peter was born on 22 April 1882 and christened Joseph John DeLoughry. The reason for altering his Christian name in later life is not known.

2   Anna T. (Cissie) De Loughry, 'Parliament Street 1974', *OKR*, 1:3 (1976), p. 181.

3   *KJ*, 8 November 1884.

4   Griffith's Valuation (updated) 1887, General Register Office, Dublin.

5   *KP*, 31 October 1931.

6   *KM*, 3 February 1892.

7   *KM*, 16 September 1885.

8   *KJ*, 31 October 1931.

9   *KJ*, 20 February 1895.

10 R. V. Comerford, *The Fenians in Context: Irish Politics and Society, 1848–82* (1985), p. 112. See also Owen McGee, *The IRB, the Irish Republican Brotherhood from the Land League to Sinn Féin* (2005).

11 BMP, in a memoir written by Brendan Mangan: 'Bridgid O'Brien had come from Kilkenny to marry him in the USA'. The marriage took place at St James' Church, Newark, on 12 November 1866: marriage record supplied by the Church of Jesus Christ of Latter-Day Saints' family history library, Dublin.

12 *KP*, 23 February 1895. Stephens also held a rally in Jones' Wood on 15 May 1866. However, the *KP* identified the one that Richard had attended: Stephens 'promised to leave for Ireland immediately to lead the revolutionary forces in the battle for freedom'.

13 Griffith's Valuation (updated) 1873, General Register Office, Dublin.

14 *KJ*, 8 April, 22 April and 3 June 1885.

15 *KJ*, 25 August; 6 November 1886. Richard DeLoughry was appointed captain of the WMC hurling team in November 1886, the first recorded captain of a hurling team in the county under the new GAA regime.

16 NA CO 904/68. Despite this, some priests remained involved in GAA clubs in Kilkenny, see Marcus de Búrca, *The GAA, a History* (2000); *KJ*, 23 February 1887.

17 *KM*, 28 October 1891.

18 *KJ*, 6 July 1889.

19 *KJ*, 29 August 1894.

20 *KM*, 18 April 1888; Intelligence notes, NA CO 903/6, B series, 501/9019S.

21 *KJ*, 28 November 1888.

22 *KP*, 31 October 1931.

23 DDA, Dr Abraham Brownrigg to the Archbishop of Dublin, Dr William J. Walsh, 13 December 1890.

24 *KJ*, 11 February 1891.

25 NA CO 904/53.

26 The Confederation club team representing Kilkenny made it to the All-Ireland hurling final in 1893, but was defeated by Blackrock, the team representing Cork. Gerry O'Neill, *Kilkenny GAA Bible* (2005), p. 139. See also Dermot Kavanagh, *A History, Kilkenny Senior Hurling County Finals, 1887–2004* (2004).

27 *KM*, 3 January 1894.

28 Registry of Deeds, Dublin. The *KM*, 18 April 1894, reported that the premises was withdrawn from auction as the highest bid of £150 was not greater than a private offer Richard had made. Though he was named as having attended the auction, his identity as the potential new owner was not given.

29 *KJ*, 22 December 1894.

30 Richard's widow, Bridget, and their daughter, Lil, did not attend the funeral as it was not usual at that time for women to be present at such ceremonies.

31 Obituary notices and his official death record put his age, incorrectly, at 49 years. He died on 18 February 1895.

2   Smoke Rises, 1895–1909

1 Liam Ó Bolguidhir, 'The early years of the Gaelic League in Kilkenny', *OKR* 4:4 (1992), p. 1022.

2 Margaret M. Phelan, 'Ellen, Countess of Desart, 1858–1933', *Conradh na Gaeilge, Comóradh an chéid*, supplement to the *KP*, April 1997, p. 4.

3 The Tholsel is the seat of the city's local authority.

4 *KM*, 17 October 1896.

5   General Register Office, Dublin.

6   *KP*, 12 December 1896.

7   *KP*, 13 March 1897.

8   *KP*, 19 December 1903.

9   MacDonagh taught in St Kieran's College, Kilkenny, from 1901 to 1903.

10   Tom Garvin, *Nationalist Revolutionaries in Ireland, 1858–1928* (2005), p. 78.

11   *KP*, 14 November 1903.

12   *KJ*, 21 December 1901.

13   *KP*, 3 June 1905.

14   *KP*, 4 July 1908.

15   *KP*, 11 January 1908.

16   *KP*, 16 April 1904.

17   *KP*, 9 April 1904.

18   NAI BMH (copy) WS 699. The statement given by Josephine Clarke (*née* Stallard) gives the building where the flag was erected as St Francis Abbey.

19   NAI BMH (copies) WS 1614 (Timothy Hennessy) and WS 1032 (James Lalor).

20   *KP*, 29 July 1905.

21   *Ibid.*

22   *KP*, 5 August 1905 and 28 October 1905.

23   *KP*, 9 December 1905.

24   *KP*, 23 December 1905.

25   *KM*, 15 November 1905.

26   *KM*, 18 April 1906.

27   James J. Comerford, *My Kilkenny I.R.A. Days* (1978), p. 182.

28   *KP*, 31 October 1931.

29   *KP*, 5 January 1907. The report gives Peter DeLoughry's address as Manchester.

30   *KP*, 20 January 1906.

31   General Register Office, Dublin.

32   *KP*, 27 April 1907.

33   *KP*, 18 April 1908.

34   *KP*, 21 November 1908.

35   *KP*, 28 November 1908.

36 *KP*, 12 December 1908.

37 *KJ*, 31 October 1908.

38 *KP*, 27 November 1909.

39 *Ibid.*

40 *KJ*, 27 November 1901 *et seq.*

41 *KP*, 6 September 1899; 17 October 1908.

42 *KP*, 16 December 1906.

3   Flames Shoot, 1909–14

1   Ó Ceallaigh (1882–1966) became second president of Ireland, 1945–59.

2   NAI BMH (copy) WS 513 (Thomas Furlong). Pat Corcoran was elected deputy head centre. The meeting was also attended by Furlong, Tom Hennessy, Ned McSweeney, Tom Stallard and MacDermott. According to a British secret service document (NA CO 904/14 Précis re Secret Societies) MacDermott, Seán Milroy and Andrew O'Byrne attended a big GAA event in Kilkenny in aid of the Stephens' memorial on 17 July 1910.

3   NAI BMH (copy) WS 513 (Thomas Furlong).

4   NA CO 904/82.

5   Rev. J. Canon Doyle, St Canice's.

6   *KP*, 22 October 1910.

7   *KP*, 9 November 1910.

8   *KP*, 5 November 1910.

9   *KP*, 7 January 1911.

10 *KP*, 21 January 1911.

11 *KP*, 28 January 1911.

12 *KP*, 31 October 1931.

13 *KP*, 18 February 1911.

14 General Register Office, Dublin.

15 Hansard, 30 April 1883, vol. 278, c. 1434.

16 Institut Pasteur, Paris.

17 *KJ*, 13 January 1892.

18 *KM*, 9 January 1892.

19 General Register Office, Dublin. Thomas Murphy died on 13 December 1886 shortly after birth; James died under two years of age on 6 October 1887.

20 General Register Office, Dublin.

21 A department store in Kilkenny city.

22 General Register Office, Dublin.

23 Recollection of Win Dunne, granddaughter of Peter and Win DeLoughry, in conversation with the author.

24 David and Larry appeared in two further productions in Kilkenny of Henry Mangan's *Robert Emmet* in 1910 and 1912, *The West's Awake* by Malachi Muldoon in 1913 and *The Poor of New York* by Dion Boucicault two years later. Countess Markievicz was so taken by Larry's interpretation of the role of Dermot O'Dowd in her husband's play *The Memory of the Dead* that she asked him to play the part in a production in Cork Opera House in 1913 in which she also acted. Such was the impression that he made during his performances in Cork, that she asked him to join her Independent Dramatic Company's production of the play on a tour of the United States, an invitation he was inexplicably unable to accept.

25 *KP*, 27 November 1912. Michael O'Rahilly used The O'Rahilly, which is a celticised version of his name.

26 *KJ*, 2 February 1913.

27 *KP*, 29 November 1913.

28 *KP*, 22 November 1913.

29 *KP*, 4 November 1911.

30 *KP*, 20 April 1912.

31 *KJ*, 24 July 1912.

32 Peter DeLoughry attended the inaugural meeting of the Boy Scouts, Kilkenny command, in Rothe House on 21 July 1912 and seconded the proposal to establish a troop in the city.

33 *KJ*, 27 November 1912.

34 *KP*, 29 November 1913.

35 *KP*, 31 January 1914.

36 *KP*, 27 April 1912.

37 *KP*, 31 October 1931.

38 *KJ*, 25 May 1912. Simon Pure is a character from a play entitled *A Bold Stroke for a Wife* (1717) by Susannah Centlivre (1669–1723). Keane is accusing Peter of being superficially or hypocritically virtuous.

39   *KP*, 6 July 1912.

40   *KP*, 30 March 1912.

41   *KP*, 21 January 1911.

42   *KP*, 9 December 1911.

43   *KP*, 3 June 1911.

44   *KP*, 13 December 1913.

45   *KP*, 9 March 1912.

46   *KJ*, 27 May 1911.

47   *Ibid.*

48   *Irish Independent*, 12 April 1912.

49   *KP*, 1 January 1916.

50   *KP*, 14 June 1914.

51   *Ibid.*

52   *KP*, 31 January 1914.

53   *Ibid.*

4   Fire Spreads, 1914–16

1   Charles Townshend, *Easter 1916, the Irish Rebellion* (2005), p. 36.

2   *KP*, 14 March 1914.

3   NA CO 904/92.

4   *KP*, 11 April 1914.

5   *KP*, 20 June 1914.

6   *KP*, 2 May 1914.

7   *KP*, 9 May 1914.

8   NAI BMH (copy) WS 590 (Thomas Treacy).

9   NA CO 904/120/4, Précis of information – Crime Branch Special.

10   *KP*, 1 August 1914.

11   Comerford, *My Kilkenny I.R.A. Days*, p. 186.

12   This street was known at the time as King Street. It is now Kieran Street.

13   The building has reverted to its original name.

14   NAI BMH (copy) WS 590 (Thomas Treacy). A witness statement given by Edward Halley of Callan, NAI BMH (copy) WS 1642, recounted how Peter was involved in another confrontation, though one less hostile, in the summer of

1915 in Ballybur where, in the company of local Volunteers, he challenged Fr P. H. Delahunty, Callan, who was then a Redmondite supporter.

15 NA CO 904/95.
16 *Ibid.*
17 NA CO 904/97.
18 *Ibid.*
19 NA CO 904/120.
20 NAI BMH (copy) WS 1614 (Timothy Hennessy). Others from Kilkenny who took part in the training were: Pierce Brett, Ned Comerford, Timothy Hennessy, Martin Kealy, James Lalor.
21 NA CO 904/26.
22 NA CO 904/120/4.
23 NAI BMH (copy) WS 513 (Thomas Furlong).

5   Kilkenny, 1916

1 The business was located at 1 Parliament Street. Tom Stallard was appointed manager. The business moved to the Kilkenny theatre in the 1920s, a move helped by Ellen, Countess of Desart.
2 *KP*, 18 March 1916. The row between Peter, Tom Stallard and the local clergy flared up again towards the end of 1917 when lengthy letters by both parties were published in the *KP* on 15, 22 and 29 December 1917.
3 NAI BMH (copy) WS 1032 (James Lalor).
4 *KP*, 29 January 1916.
5 NAI BMH (copy) WS 590 (Thomas Treacy).
6 *Ibid.*
7 NA CO 904/26.
8 Recollection of Pádraigín Ní Dhubhluachra.
9 Commercial travellers were commonly agents of secret societies and political parties.
10 NAI BMH (copy) WS 590 (Thomas Treacy).
11 NAI BMH (copy) WS 268 (W. T. Cosgrave).
12 NAI BMH (copy) WS 699 (Dr Josephine Clarke).
13 NAI BMH (copy) WS 685 (Mrs Bulmer Hobson).
14 NAI BMH (copy) WS 355 (Kitty O'Doherty).

15 The Swan is a village close to the Kilkenny boundary.

16 NAI BMH (copy) WS 590 (Thomas Treacy); James Lalor recalled an incident after they had completed their business in Wolfhill colliery: 'I remember this incident distinctly by our visit to Kelly's Hotel, Portlaoise the next day. We had been out all night and were very hungry as we had no breakfast. When we got to the hotel it was too early for dinner so we ordered tea with steak and onions for the three of us. The waiter stared at us in a strange manner, but passed no remark. He served the meal to which we did justice, but still we noticed that he continued to stare at us in a strange way. Subsequently it dawned on us that the day was Spy Wednesday and, of course, a fast day. Our ordering and eating steak on that day must have shocked the poor waiter.' NAI BMH (copy) WS 1032 (James Lalor).

17 *Sunday Independent*, 23 April 1916. MacNeill's countermanding order was prompted by the arrest of Bulmer Hobson, the capture of Sir Roger Casement and his failure to deliver German arms, MacNeill's eventual acceptance that the Dublin Castle Document was a forgery and, more than all these, the belief that the Rising had no chance of military victory.

18 NAI BMH (copy) WS 590 (Thomas Treacy).

19 *Ibid.*

20 His surname is given as Lyddon in some witness statements.

21 NAI BMH (copy) WS 590 (Thomas Treacy).

22 Pat Corcoran, Patrick St; Edward Comerford, Wellington Square; James Lalor, Friary St; Tom Furlong, Michael St; Pierce Brett, Blackmill St; Larry DeLoughry, Parliament St; Thomas Neary, Poulgour; William Stephens, c/o Burke's, High St; Denis Barry, the Monster House; John Lalor, Goose Hill; John Kealy, John St; Patrick Parsons, Wolfe Tone St; Anthony Mullaly, Parnell St; Patrick Burke Senior, Wolfe Tone St; James Madigan, Abbey St; Joseph Coyne, Bishop's Hill; Michael Ryan, Bishop's Hill; Charles Smith, Maudlin St; Maurice Higgins, Upper John St; William Denn, Talbotsinch; Michael Purcell, High St; Laurence Walsh, Dunmore; Stephen O'Dwyer, Patrick St; Michael O'Dwyer, John St; Thomas Stallard, Parliament St; and Thomas Treacy, Dean St.

23   Seán Gibbons, Ballylarkin, Freshford; Martin Kealy, Blanchfields
        Park; John Harte, Blanchfields Park and James Carrigan, Clara.
24   NAI BMH (copy) WS 590 (Thomas Treacy).
25   NAI BMH (copy) WS 1032 (James Lalor).
26   NAI BMH (copy) WS 590 (Thomas Treacy).
27   NAI BMH (copy) WS 1006 (Martin Kealy). The *KJ*, 12 August
        1916, reported that the circumstances of Kealy's death were
        raised in the House of Commons. Michael Meagher MP, North
        Kilkenny, told the House that as Kealy was being marched to the
        railway station under fixed bayonet, local doctors had implored
        the military doctor to examine him to see if he was fit for the
        journey. Matthew Keating MP, South Kilkenny, told members
        that those responsible for Kealy's death must be identified and
        punished 'for they are a disgrace to the [British] Army'.
28   NA CO 904/99.
29   *Royal Commission on the Rebellion in Ireland, minutes of evidence
        and appendix of documents* (1916). The transcript of Inspector
        Power's evidence states that he found a '3.03 [*sic*] Lee Enfield'.
30   NA CO 904/26.
31   *KP*, 20 May 1916.
32   NA CO 904/120.
33   Stallard was treated for a poisoned hand after he had been
        transported to Dublin. Larry may be saying that Stallard was
        the only one who really suffered.
34   BMP.
35   H. H. Asquith (1854–1928), British prime minister 1908–16.
36   BMP.
37   NA HO 144/1455/313106/57a (20 June 1916).
38   www.theeasterrising.eu, accessed 20 February 2008.

6   Phoenix Flame Rekindled, 1916–18

1   *KP*, 5 August 1916.
2   Brian Feeney, *Sinn Féin – A Hundred Turbulent Years* (2010),
       pp. 60–1.
3   NAI BMH (copy) WS 1093 (Thomas Treacy).
4   *Royal Commission on the Rebellion in Ireland, minutes of evidence
       and appendix of documents* (1916).

5   NA CO 904/101, October 1916.

6   NA CO 904/120.

7   NAI BMH (copy) WS 1093 (Thomas Treacy). Treacy and his wife set up a drapery business in Parliament Street after his release.

8   *KP*, 25 November 1916.

9   NAI BMH (copy) WS 1093 (Thomas Treacy).

10 *KP*, August 1916.

11 Comerford, *My Kilkenny I.R.A. Days*, pp. 70–1.

12 *Ibid.* Comerford also recalled that, on one occasion, he and a friend went into an upstairs room filled with sacks of corn, large wooden crates, piles of old furniture and a coffin that had been used as a prop in a play. Their access was blocked by a pram, which one of them pushed to one side. The coffin also rolled out of the way. A Volunteer in another room shouted at them to be quiet and asked if their intention was to wake up Dame Alice Kyteler, who had been accused of witchcraft in the city in the fourteenth century and after whom the building is now called.

13 NA CO 904/101.

14 *KP*, 28 October 1916.

15 Dr Edward Thomas O'Dwyer (1842–1917) took a strong stand against General Maxwell after the Rising.

16 NA CO 904/101.

17 *KP*, 24 February 1917. The only fourteen-year-old schoolboy with the surname of DeLoughry in Kilkenny at this time was James DeLoughry of Blackmill Street, a cousin of Peter. In 1916 James and his brother, Richard, were members of Fianna Éireann, an Irish Republican youth movement (DFP).

18 General Register Office, Dublin.

19 *KP*, 18 November 1916.

20 *KP*, 10 November 1917.

21 *KP*, 24 November 1917.

22 *KP*, 23 March 1918.

23 These names are taken from lists supplied by Thomas Treacy in his witness statement and by Jim Maher in his book *The Flying Column – West Kilkenny 1916–21* (1987), p. 2.

24 Maher, *The Flying Column*, p. 2.

25 NAI BMH (copy) WS 1032 (James Lalor). The meeting at Barry's Hotel took place on 8 April, Easter Sunday, 1917. Lalor, Patrick Corcoran and Martin Kealy were among the Kilkenny delegates who attended.

26 *KP*, 23 September 1916. Before 17 August 1916, time in Ireland was set twenty-five minutes behind Greenwich Mean Time. After this date, the marking of time in Ireland was made to coincide with that of Britain.

27 *KP*, 18 November 1916.

28 *KP*, 6 January 1917.

29 *KP*, 26 August 1916.

30 *KP*, 28 October 1916.

31 *KP*, 27 January 1917.

32 *KP*, 10 February 1917.

33 NA CO 904/102.

34 NA CO 904/103.

35 *KP*, 12 May 1917.

36 *KJ*, 13 June 1917.

37 NA CO 904/103.

38 *KP*, 30 June 1917. Alderman Joseph Purcell is variously reported in the Kilkenny newspapers as siding with Sinn Féin at some meetings and with the Irish Parliamentary Party, of which he was a member, at others. Purcell was an eccentric and volatile figure who swapped allegiance every now and then, not because of the way the political wind was blowing, but because he revelled in explosive argument.

39 NAI BMH (copy) WS 1032 (James Lalor). De Valera polled 5,010 votes in East Clare to Lynch's 2,035.

40 *The Times*, 16 July 1917.

41 *KM*, 21 July 1917.

42 NA CO 904/103.

43 *KJ*, 21 July 1917.

44 Comerford, *My Kilkenny I.R.A. Days*, p. 65.

45 NA CO 904/103.

46 *KJ*, 15 August 1917.

47 NA CO 904/104.

48 NA CO 904/105.

49   NAI BMH (copy) WS 1093 (Thomas Treacy).
50   *KP*, 11 May 1918.
51   *KP*, 20 April 1918.
52   *Ibid.*
53   *Ibid.*
54   Florence Hackett, 'The Irish insurrection – Easter week in Kilkenny, April 1916', *OKR* 3:1 (1984), p. 22; *Irish Independent*, 14 April 1949; NAI P133/14.

7   The Road to Lincoln, 1918

1   NAI BMH (copy) WS 1093 (Thomas Treacy). Treacy was living at 15 Dean Street at this time.
2   Feeney, *Sinn Féin*, p. 99.
3   *KP*, 25 May 1918.
4   BMP.
5   *KP*, 25 May 1918.
6   *Ibid.*
7   NA CO 904/24/1.
8   BMP.
9   UCD Archives EdeV papers P150/613.
10   NA CO 904/186.
11   *KP*, 25 May 1918.
12   NA CO 904/106.
13   *KP*, 1 June 1918.
14   BMP.
15   *KP*, 8 June 1918.
16   *KP*, 15 June 1918.
17   *KP*, 22 June 1918.
18   NA CO 904/106. This report for the month of June 1918 is notable in that it marked the first time that Cumann na mBan in Kilkenny was listed in a local RIC report as a separate entity. One branch is recorded with thirty members.
19   *KP*, 6 July 1918.

8   Life in Lincoln, 1918

1   Darrell Figgis, *A Second Chronicle of Jails* (1919), p. 42.

2   Lincoln is a cathedral city and the main county town in Lincolnshire. From the mid-nineteenth century it changed from being a market town to an industrial centre. During and after the First World War it was important as a centre for tank production. The prison lies on the eastern edge of the city.

3   Figgis, *A Second Chronicle*, p. 57.

4   *Ibid.*, p 58.

5   *Ibid.*

6   Lord Longford and T. P. O'Neill, *Éamon de Valera* (1970), p. 78.

7   Figgis, *A Second Chronicle*, p. 58.

8   *Irish Independent*, 3 January 1964.

9   From a transcription of a recorded interview given by Seamus Ua Duibne (Dobbyn), supplied by his youngest daughter, Bláthnaid Ó Brádaigh. Tape 2 f. 13.

10   Seán Etchingham, *Irish Independent*, 23 January 1919.

11   At a similar event in Gloucester prison, de Valera had beaten other prisoners in a mile-long race, Longford and O'Neill, *de Valera*, p. 78.

12   The Aidan Heavey collection, the Aidan Heavey Public Library, Athlone, County Westmeath.

13   DFP.

14   Seán Etchingham, *Irish Independent*, 23 January 1919.

15   From a transcription of a recorded interview given by Seamus Ua Duibne (Dobbyn), supplied by his youngest daughter, Bláthnaid Ó Brádaigh. Tape 2 f. 16.

16   Seán Etchingham, *Irish Independent*, 23 January 1919.

17   Longford and O'Neill, *de Valera*, p. 78.

18   Alice S. Green, *The Making of Ireland and Its Undoing 1200–1600* (London, 1908).

19   Seaside resort in County Waterford, a popular summer retreat for the DeLoughrys.

20   BMP.

21   NA HO 144/1496/362269. DMIPC Ninth report, 14 July 1918–15 March 1919.

22   NA HO 144/1496/362269. DMIPC Fifth report, 15 December–31 December 1918.

23   NA HO 144/1496/362269. DMIPC Second report, 1 November–16 November 1918.

24 *Ibid.*

25 NA HO 144/1496/362269. DMIPC Seventh report, 15 January–31 January 1919.

26 NLI, Seán O'Mahony papers Ms. 24, 458.

27 *Ibid.*

28 *Ibid.*

29 UCD Archives, EdeV papers P150/612.

30 DFP.

31 Longford and O'Neill, *de Valera*, p. 78.

32 Of the sixty-nine Sinn Féin candidates returned (four were elected to represent two constituencies each), thirty-six were in prison. Of these, the Lincoln prisoners who won and their constituencies were: Colivet (Limerick city), de Valera (Clare South, Mayo East – lost in West Belfast), Etchingham (Wicklow East), McCabe (Sligo South), MacSwiney (Cork County mid) and O'Mahony (Fermanagh South). Under a deal brokered by Cardinal Logue, Sinn Féin agreed not to contest Down South; Tyrone North East, where Milroy ceded to Thomas Harbison, Irish Party; Donegal East, where O'Flaherty ceded to Edward Joseph Kelly, Irish Party; and Armagh South.

33 *Irish Independent*, 23 January 1919.

34 NA HO 144/1496/362269. DMIPC Fifth report, 15 December –31 December 1918.

35 Maher, *The Flying Column*, p. 7.

36 *KP*, 21 December 1918.

37 UCD Archives EdeV papers P150/612.

38 De Valera returned the postcard to Lelia in 1954 by which time she was a nun, having taken the name Sister Petra in memory of Peter, but he kept the handball in his desk and looked upon it as a lucky token.

39 BMP.

40 *KP*, 4 January 1919.

41 *KJ*, 25 January 1919.

9   Escape from Lincoln – Thoughts Emerge, 1918–19

1   Archibald Fenner Brockway (1888–1988) was a British anti-war activist, journalist and politician. He was vocal in his opposition

to conscripted military service and acted as a prominent pacifist during the First World War.

2 *Labour Leader* was the newspaper that Brockway had edited before his imprisonment.

3 Fenner Brockway, *Inside the Left* (2010), pp. 112–19.

4 CAC, FEBR Box 1 Item #13/10.

5 *Sunday Independent*, 14 November 1954.

6 From a transcription of a recorded interview given by Seamus Ua Duibne (Dobbyn), supplied by his youngest daughter, Bláthnaid Ó Brádaigh. Tape 2 f. 13.

7 NA HO 144/1496/362269. DMIPC Second report, 1 November–16 November 1918.

8 *Ibid.*

9 NA HO 144/1496/362269. DMIPC Fourth report, 1 December –15 December 1918.

10 NA HO 144/1496/362269. DMIPC Seventh report, 15 January–31 January 1919.

11 DFP, unfinished account of Lincoln escape by Peter DeLoughry (n.d.) handwritten on 4 fs.

12 Diarmaid Ferriter, *Judging Dev* (2007), p. 33.

13 From a transcription of a recorded interview given by Seamus Ua Duibne (Dobbyn), supplied by his youngest daughter, Bláthnaid Ó Brádaigh. Tape 2 f. 5.

14 UCD Archives EdeV papers P150/615.

15 From a transcription of a recorded interview given by Seamus Ua Duibne (Dobbyn), supplied by his youngest daughter, Bláthnaid Ó Brádaigh. Tape 2 f. 6.

16 UCD Archives EdeV papers P150/615.

17 From a transcription of a recorded interview given by Seamus Ua Duibne (Dobbyn), supplied by his youngest daughter, Bláthnaid Ó Brádaigh. Tape 2 fs. 6–7.

18 UCD Archives EdeV papers P150/615.

19 The postal censor had noted in his second report that 'McGarry does not appear to be in the habit of using code' – NA HO 144/1496/362269. DMIPC Second report, 1 November–16 November 1918.

20 UCD Archives EdeV papers P150/615.

21 For example in this communication, de Valera rendered the English word 'files' as 'feidhls' to make it look like an Irish word.

22 'Trustworthy' is an alternative translation of 'fidelem'.

23 A crease in the letter has made some words difficult to discern. However, the overall meaning is clear without them. The 'letter to that woman, whose home I have indicated' is Seán McGarry's wife. His home is represented in the postcard sketch where he is grappling to get a big key into his front door.

24 UCD Archives EdeV papers P150/615. The 'S' represents John O'Mahony's first name in Irish, Seán, which he used on occasion.

25 UCD Archives EdeV papers P150/615.

26 *Ibid.*

27 *Ibid.*

28 Andrew Brasier and John Kelly, *Harry Boland – A Man Divided* (2000), p. 87.

29 NAI BMH (copy) WS 274 (Liam McMahon's account).

30 NAI BMH (copy) WS 847 (Patrick O'Donoghue).

31 UCD Archives EdeV papers P150/615 (de Valera's account).

32 T. Ryle Dwyer, *Michael Collins, the Man who Won the War* (2009), p. 104.

33 Desmond Ryan, *Unique Dictator: a Study of Éamon de Valera* (1936), p. 89.

34 UCD Archives EdeV papers P150/620.

35 UCD Archives EdeV papers P150/620 (letter from Gerald Boland to de Valera).

36 UCD Archives EdeV papers P150/620 (escape of de Valera and others from Lincoln jail in February 1919, draft notes by Fintan Murphy).

37 UCD Archives EdeV papers P150/615.

38 The first 's' is a mistake; the correct spelling is 'epistolam'. It appears someone subsequently put a circle around that 's'.

39 Correct spelling should be 'intellegat'.

40 Correct spelling should be 'oportet' which, with the accusative 'me' + infinitive = (literally) 'it is my duty that I be'. Together with the last two footnotes, which suggest errors in spelling in the Latin used, this suggests that the composer/writer of the

text was not highly skilled in the use of Latin and might not have been Samuel O'Flaherty.

41   UCD Archives EdeV papers P150/615.

42   A sign posted on the prison walls warned visitors that the penalty for helping anyone to escape was two years' imprisonment.

43   UCD Archives EdeV papers P150/620 (escape of de Valera and others from Lincoln jail in February 1919, draft notes by Fintan Murphy).

44   UCD Archives EdeV papers P150/615 (de Valera's account).

45   *Sunday Press*, 8 October 1950, in an article by Liam MacGabhann.

46   UCD Archives EdeV papers P150/615 (de Valera's account).

10 Escape from Lincoln – Peter's Key Turns, 1919

1   Seán Milroy, *Memories of Mountjoy* (1917), p. 1.

2   NAI BMH (copy) WS 274 (Liam McMahon's account).

3   NA HO 144/1496/362269. DMIPC Seventh report, 15 January – 31 January 1919.

4   *Irish Independent*, 23 January 1919.

5   Piaras Béaslaí, *Michael Collins and the Making of a New Ireland* (1926), vol. 1, p. 265.

6   UCD Archives EdeV papers P150/615.

7   *Irish Independent*, 19 July 1926.

8   NA HO 144/1496/362269. DMIPC Seventh report, 15 January – 31 January 1919.

9   *Irish Digest*, January 1942, 'De Valera escapes from Lincoln jail' condensed by Desmond Ryan from a 2RN radio series compiled and compered by Noel Hartnett, p. 87.

10   UCD Archives EdeV papers P150/615.

11   UCD Archives EdeV papers P150/620 (Frank Kelly's account).

12   UCD Archives EdeV papers P150/620 (Liam McMahon's account).

13   UCD Archives EdeV papers P150/615.

14   UCD Archives EdeV papers P150/620 (transcribed interview with Harry Boland by anonymous writer).

15   UCD Archives EdeV papers P150/615.

16   This letter was written in Irish. The translation by Dr Martin

Holland gives precedence to the idiomatic thrust of the language (such as *ye* for *you* plural) while striving to retain the essence of the tone and the spirit of its expression.

17 This is a curious error by de Valera. The new moon or dark moon was the most suitable for an escape. This dark moon was present on the Friday night (31 January 1919). There would not have been much of a change in the days that followed. However, when de Valera warns that it would be another fortnight before another suitable moon would become available, he was wrong. At that time, 14 February 1919, the full moon or bright moon would have been in the sky, which would have made an escape more risky. The next new moon or dark moon would not arrive until 2 March 1919. De Valera may have become so engrossed in his observations that he became muddled in the detail or perhaps he was imposing a make-believe deadline by lying about the moon phases to force his co-conspirators into action.

18 UCD Archives EdeV papers P150/615.

19 UCD Archives EdeV papers P150/620.

20 *Sunday Independent*, 5 May 1929.

21 From a transcription of a recorded interview given by Seamus Ua Duibne (Dobbyn), supplied by his youngest daughter, Bláthnaid Ó Brádaigh. Tape 2 f. 10.

22 *Sunday Independent*, 5 May 1929.

23 Laurence Lardner also directly helped Peter with this work.

24 *KP*, 9 January 1936 (letter by close friend of Peter, John McKenna).

25 *Sunday Independent*, 5 May 1929.

26 UCD Archives EdeV papers P150/615.

27 Fitzgerald means either RIC or British soldiers. The Black and Tans were not in Ireland at this time and the term – even though it was sometimes used for regular British forces – was not coined until after their arrival in March 1920.

28 *Irish Independent*, 13 January 1936.

29 UCD Archives EdeV papers P150/620 (escape of de Valera and others from Lincoln jail in February 1919, draft notes by Fintan Murphy). Murphy also explained that Collins checked each rung of the ladder, rejecting one, which Murphy kept as a

souvenir.

30 NAI BMH (copy) WS 847 (Patrick O'Donoghue).

31 *Ibid.*

32 *Ibid.*

33 From a transcription of a recorded interview given by Seamus Ua Duibne (Dobbyn), supplied by his youngest daughter, Bláthnaid Ó Brádaigh. Tape 2 f. 19.

34 De Valera was expected to be one of those to attempt to escape. McGarry's position in the IRB made him an obvious choice. Dobbyn was to have been among them but was asked by O'Mahony if he would mind if Milroy took his place. Dobbyn said that Milroy was 'on the verge of a nervous breakdown' and 'very down in the dumps'. He readily agreed to Milroy joining de Valera and McGarry.

35 *Irish Independent*, 3 March 1964.

36 Brockway, *Inside the Left*, p. 117.

37 BMP. In a letter from David deLoughry to Lil Mangan, 8 December 1938.

38 *Irish Independent*, 3 March 1964.

39 NAI BMH (copy) WS 847 (Patrick O'Donoghue).

40 UCD Archives EdeV papers P150/620 (Frank Kelly's account).

41 De Valera also used socks to dampen any sound of his footsteps: see Longford and O'Neill, *de Valera*, p. 85.

42 *Irish Independent*, 3 March 1964.

43 UCD Archives EdeV papers P150/615 (de Valera's account).

44 *Sunday Press*, 8 October 1950, in an article by Liam MacGabhann.

45 Accounts vary as to whether Boland or Collins attempted to open the outer gate.

46 UCD Archives EdeV papers P150/615 (de Valera's account).

47 *Sunday Press*, 8 October 1950, in an article by Liam MacGabhann.

48 UCD Archives EdeV papers P150/620 (transcribed interview with Harry Boland by anonymous writer).

49 Womens' Auxiliary Army Corps.

50 *Sunday Press*, 8 October 1950, in an article by Liam MacGabhann.

51 UCD Archives EdeV papers P150/620 (transcribed interview with Harry Boland by anonymous writer).

52 *Irish Independent*, 3 March 1964.

53 Longford and O'Neill, *de Valera*, p. 86.

54 From a transcription of a recorded interview given by Seamus Ua Duibne (Dobbyn), supplied by his youngest daughter, Bláthnaid Ó Brádaigh. Tape 2, fs. 17–8.

55 Brockway, *Inside the Left*, p. 117.

56 From a transcription of a recorded interview given by Seamus Ua Duibne (Dobbyn), supplied by his youngest daughter, Bláthnaid Ó Brádaigh. Tape 2, f. 18.

57 *Irish Independent*, 3 March 1964.

58 Brockway, *Inside the Left*, p. 117.

11 Escape from Lincoln – Aftermath, 1919

1 Paddy O'Donoghue was also with the three escaped prisoners.

2 UCD Archives EdeV papers P150/620 (escape of de Valera and others from Lincoln jail in February 1919, draft notes by Fintan Murphy).

3 The governor was in fact one rank above captain, Major Goldie-Taubman.

4 *Irish Independent*, 3 January 1964.

5 *The Sydney Morning Herald*, 4 February 1919.

6 *The New York Times*, 4 February 1919.

7 *Star*, 5 February 1919.

8 *The New York Times*, 2 March 1919.

9 NA HO 144/1496/362269. DMIPC Ninth report, 14 July 1918–15 March 1919.

10 *The Irish Times*, 5 March 1919.

11 David Fitzpatrick, *Harry Boland's Irish Revolution* (2004), p. 116. Fitzpatrick's biography includes a thorough and masterly account of the Lincoln escape from its inception through to its aftermath.

12 *Irish Independent*, 7 February 1919.

13 *Sunday Independent*, 16 February 1919.

14 *Irish Independent*, 6 February 1919.

15 Longford and O'Neill, *de Valera*, p. 88.

16   NAI BMH (copy) WS 274 (Liam McMahon's account).

17   NA HO 144/1496/362269. DMIPC Ninth report, 14 July 1918–15 March 1919.

18   BMP.

19   *Irish Independent*, 11 March 1919.

20   Recollection of Lelia Mangan in an interview with Gemma McCrohan on *Telling Times*, a six-part documentary series broadcast on RTÉ Radio One, 8 June–13 July 1989.

21   Cosgrave had won the seat in a by-election in 1917. The constituency was altered for the 1918 general election when Kilkenny City was amalgamated with Kilkenny North.

22   Recollection of Pádraigín Ní Dhubhluachra, Kilkenny, in conversation with the author.

23   *KP*, 15 March 1919.

24   *KM*, 15 March 1919.

25   *KP*, 15 March 1919.

26   The Irish Volunteers came to be known as the Irish Republican Army (IRA) during 1919.

27   NAI BMH (copy) WS 1208 (Daniel J. Stapleton).

28   NAI BMH (copy) WS 1614 (Timothy Hennessy).

29   NAI BMH (copy) WS 1032 (James Lalor).

30   NAI BMH (copy) WS 1093 (Thomas Treacy).

31   *KP*, 5 April 1919.

32   *KP*, 22 March 1919.

33   *KP*, 5 April 1919.

34   *KP*, 22 March 1919.

35   UCD Archives P133/14.

36   *KM*, 29 March 1919.

37   NA CO 904/110.

38   *KM*, 28 May 1919. Fr Michael O'Flanagan (1876–1942) a native of County Roscommon, was vice-president of Sinn Féin.

39   Feeney, *Sinn Féin*, p. 123.

40   NA CO 904/110.

41   *KP*, 1 November 1919.

12 War of Independence, 1920

1   NA CO 904/111.

2 Born 4 January 1920.

3 NAI BMH (copy) WS 1101 (Martin Cassidy).

4 NAI BMH (copy) WS 1032 (James Lalor).

5 *Irish Press*, 19 December 1936.

6 NA CO 904/24/3.

7 DFP.

8 *KP*, 27 March 1920.

9 *KP*, 20 March 1920.

10 NAI BMH (copy) WS 1093 (Thomas Treacy); for accounts of engagements by Kilkenny battalions, see Maher, *The Flying Column*.

11 *KP*, 26 June 1920.

12 NAI BMH (copy) WS 1093 (Thomas Treacy).

13 *KP*, 12 June 1920.

14 NAI BMH (copy) WS 966 (John Walsh).

15 In an article 'Patrick Corcoran: a postscript' based on information provided by Anna T. (Cissie) De Loughry and her daughter, Padraigín Ní Dubhluachra, *OKR*, 48 (1996), p. 7.

16 *KJ*, 21 August 1920.

17 *KP*, 6 November 1920. The death by hanging of Kevin Barry, who was seventeen years old, outraged public opinion. He had been arrested for his part in an ambush on a British army truck in Bolton Street, Dublin, on 20 September 1920.

18 NAI BMH (copy) WS 1093 (Thomas Treacy).

19 NA CO 904/113.

20 NAI BMH (copy) WS 1271 (Patrick Dunphy).

21 Brigadier General F. P. Crozier, *Ireland for ever* (1971), p. 95. The other dangerous areas were: Clare, Cork, Dublin, Galway, Kerry, Limerick, Mayo and Meath.

22 *Ibid.*, pp. 95–6.

23 NA CO 904/113.

24 Richard English, *Ernie O'Malley, IRA Intellectual* (2006), p. vii (preface).

25 Ernie O'Malley, *On Another Man's Wound* (2002), p. 70.

26 *Ibid.*, p. 240.

27 *Ibid.*, p. 243.

28 *Irish Press*, 15 December 1936. This reference to O'Malley's

delayed arrival is taken from a statement written by members of the Kilkenny Brigade following publication of Ernie O'Malley's book *On Another Man's Wound* in 1936. The statement was printed in editions of the *Irish Press* from 15 to 19 December 1936 and signed by Patrick Bryan, John Joseph Byrne, Seán Byrne, Éamonn Comartún, James Lalor, Joseph Rice and Thomas Treacy.

29 Comerford, *My Kilkenny I.R.A. Days*, p. 280.
30 *Irish Press*, 15 December 1936.
31 Comerford, *My Kilkenny I.R.A. Days*, p. 282.
32 Maher, *The Flying Column*, p. 51.
33 O'Malley, *On Another Man's Wound*, p. 245.
34 *Irish Press*, 16 December 1936.
35 Novel by H. G. Wells. O'Malley's own account differs slightly from that given by the Kilkenny Brigade, in that he makes no mention of reading the novel on the evening he arrived at the house.
36 *Irish Press*, 17 December 1936.
37 O'Malley, *On Another Man's Wound*, p. 248.
38 Maher, *The Flying Column*, p. 53.
39 NA CO 904/113.
40 Maher, *The Flying Column*, p. 54.
41 *Irish Press*, 17 December 1936.

13 Fire Turns Inwards, 1920–21

1 O'Malley, *On Another Man's Wound*, p. 256.
2 Maher, *The Flying Column*, p. 54.
3 NAI BMH (copy) WS 980 (Edward Aylward).
4 O'Malley, *On Another Man's Wound*, p. 264.
5 *KP*, 22 January 1921.
6 *Manchester Guardian*, 21 January 1921.
7 DFP.
8 *KP*, 22 January 1921.
9 *Irish Press*, 18 December 1936.
10 This is a reference to O'Malley, who gave the name Bernard Stewart on his arrest. Peter, while writing private notes here, maintained the use of O'Malley's pseudonym. He misspelt the surname in his notes.

11   DFP.

12   *KJ*, 25 December 1920.

13   *Ibid.*

14   DFP.

15   *KP*, 22 January 1921.

16   *KM*, 5 February 1921.

17   Recollection of Nessa Dunne (*née* DeLoughry).

18   *KM*, 19 February 1921.

19   *KP*, 19 February 1921.

20   Recollection of Jack DeLoughry, Talbotsinch, Kilkenny.

21   *KP*, 22 January 1921.

22   UCD Archives P133/14.

23   *KJ*, 2 March 1921.

24   UCD Archives P133/14.

25   Peter had by this time installed an electric unit in the house, making it the first in Kilkenny to use such power for domestic purposes.

26   *The Irish Times*, 11 February 1969.

27   *KP*, 4 February 1922.

28   NA CO 904/114.

29   O'Dwyer later became chief superintendent of An Garda Síochána.

30   O'Malley, *On Another Man's Wound*, p. 377. Within two weeks of the arrests of the Kilkenny Irish Republican Army leaders, a successful ambush was carried out on a joint British military and police patrol at Ninemilehouse near the county boundary with Tipperary. Eight British soldiers and an RIC man were killed in two further attacks on reinforcements from Clonmel. An ambush in Friary Street in Kilkenny city in February 1921 was foiled when a young girl screamed. The following month a Black and Tan was killed as members of the 7th Brigade shot their way out of Garryricken House after being surrounded by British forces. See Maher, *The Flying Column*.

31   *Irish Press*, 18 December 1936.

32   Maher, *The Flying Column*, pp. 92–3.

33   George O'Dwyer emerges as one of the most intriguing figures in Kilkenny from this period. His son, Liam O'Dwyer, said that

to some extent his father led a charmed life. George O'Dwyer returned to Ireland in 1916 from New South Wales where he had been managing a fruit farm. He travelled home on a ship that formed part of a convoy of three. The vessels on the bow and stern sides were torpedoed. His ship escaped attack. Once, while he was on the run, he was asleep in a house in North Kilkenny, when he felt a hand grip his shoulder. When he woke, his shoulder was in some pain. He got up, opened the window and heard the engine of a Crossley tender. O'Dwyer hastily left the house. Shortly afterwards it was surrounded by British forces and thoroughly searched. O'Dwyer returned to the house the following day to thank the owners for alerting him but they said they hadn't. O'Dwyer said afterwards, with a twinkle in his eye, that it was the spirit of Sam McAllister who, in February 1799, drew fire from British forces besieging his hideout in Doirenamuc in County Wicklow that allowed Michael Dwyer, an ancestor of George, to get away. During the Civil War, while de Valera was on the run, O'Dwyer heard that he was hiding out in Cappahayden in County Kilkenny. O'Dwyer believed that if he told his superior, Major General Prout, about this, de Valera would have been executed. O'Dwyer decided not to say anything and wondered afterwards how much that decision had altered the course of Irish history.

34   NA CO 904/113; CO 904/114; CO 904/115.

14 Treaty and Civil War, 1921–22

1   *KJ*, 23 July 1921.
2   *The Freeman's Journal*, 21 July 1921.
3   *KP*, 8 October 1921.
4   NA CO 904/116.
5   BMH Ref. No. A/0718 (Kilkenny Brigade, November 1921).
6   BMP. Peter's brother-in-law, Henry Mangan, in his capacity as city accountant of Dublin Corporation, accompanied the delegation to London. In an unpublished essay entitled 'The boy historian', one of Henry's sons, Brendan, wrote that his father's role as a financial assistant in the drafting of proposals

concerning taxation funds and refunds allowed him to witness many interesting sessions of the negotiations. He had many anecdotes from this experience, especially concerning Michael Collins, whom he much admired as a forthright spokesman.

7   *KP*, 17 December 1921.
8   *KP*, 31 December 1921.
9   Michael Hopkinson, *Green against Green* (2004), p. 35.
10 *KP*, 7 January 1922.
11 *KP*, 4 February 1922.
12 *KP*, 28 January 1922.
13 *KM*, 21 January 1922.
14 *KM*, 18 February 1922.
15 Edmond Mulrooney from Dunbell provided the barracks with its flagstaff made from an ash sapling he had cut near his home.
16 Captain M. Mullagh and Lieutenant L. Condon, 'History of Stephens' barracks, Kilkenny', *OKR*, 3:3 (1986), p. 261. See also Tom Lyng, *Castlecomer Connections* (1984), p. 162; *KP*, 11 February and 20 April 1922; *KM*, 29 April 1922.
17 Quoted in Hopkinson, *Green against Green*, p. 62.
18 *KP*, 25 March 1922.
19 *Ibid.*
20 *KJ*, 29 April 1922. The '(?)' is Aylward's caustic reference to Peter, questioning his standing in the community.
21 *KP*, 28 June 1924. Peter was awarded £110 compensation for loss of the car at a court in Tipperary on 23 June 1924. He also received £125 compensation from the British government in November 1925 for loss and damage he incurred from British military forces, *KP*, 5 December 1925.
22 *KJ*, 6 May 1922.
23 *Irish Independent*, 1 May 1922.
24 *The Irish Times*, 1 May 1922.
25 *The Times*, 1 May 1922.
26 *Irish Independent*, 3 May 1922.
27 *Ibid.*
28 *KP*, 6 May 1922.
29 Lyng, *Connections*, p. 175.
30 *KM*, 6 May 1922.

31   *KJ*, 6 May 1922.

32   *KJ*, 13 May 1922.

33   *Ibid.*

34   *KM*, 13 May 1922.

35   *The Times*, 4 May 1922.

36   *The Times*, 6 May 1922.

15 Hatred Simmers, 1922

1   Recollection of Nessa Dunne, Dublin, daughter of Peter and Win DeLoughry, in conversation with the author.

2   Cal McCarthy, *Cumann na mBan and the Irish Revolution* (2007), pp. 189–91.

3   Florence Hackett (1884–1963) novelist, short story writer and playwright.

4   *KP*, 22 April 1922.

5   *KP*, 29 April 1922.

6   *Ibid.*

7   *KJ*, 6 May 1922.

8   *KP*, 13 May 1922.

9   McCarthy, *Cumann na mBan*, p. 190.

10 BMH Captured documents, Lot 34.

11 *KP*, 24 June 1922.

12 *KP*, 26 August 1922.

13 Quoted in Stephen Collins, *The Cosgrave Legacy* (1996), p. 34.

14 *KP*, 25 November 1922.

15 The Senate was also known as the first Seanad.

16 *The Irish Times*, 29 July 2008, in an article by Elaine Byrne.

17 *KP*, 16 December 1922.

16 Catholic Church Brimstone, 1923–25

1   *KP*, 28 July 1923.

2   Hopkinson, *Green against Green*, p. 181.

3   Medlar was arrested on 26 January 1923 and released in July 1924. As a Fianna Fáil candidate, he was elected to the Dáil in 1957 and remained a TD until his death in 1965. The other case concerned Michael McSweeney, Vicar Street, Kilkenny,

who was charged along with two others with carrying out an armed raid on the Home Rule Club in Kilkenny. A letter from Peter vouching for McSweeney's good character was read in court. The judge referred to Peter's defence of McSweeney's character in his summing up. McSweeney was given a stiff fine and spent a few hours in custody; *KP*, 8 November 1924; DFP; Jim Maher, in conversation with the author.

4   Hopkinson, *Green against Green*, p. 195.

5   *The Irish Times*, 29 July 2008.

6   *The Irish Times*, 3 March 1923.

7   G. Mauresceaux, 'Desert Court and its occupants', *OKR* (1974), p. 24.

8   *KJ*, *KM*, *KP*, 3 March 1923; *KP*, 31 March 1923.

9   Hopkinson, *Green against Green*, pp. 256–7.

10 *Ibid.* p. 273.

11 Ciara Meehan, *The Cosgrave Party: a History of Cumann na nGaedheal, 1923–33* (2010), p. xii.

12 *KP*, 28 July 1923.

13 *KP*, 25 August 1923.

14 *KM*, 1 September 1923.

15 Quoted in *KP*, 28 April 1923.

16 The by-election was required because Seán Gibbons (Cumann na nGaedheal) resigned his seat and joined the Farmers' Party.

17 *KP*, 7 March 1925. The Civic Guards were established in early 1922 to replace the RIC. The force was renamed the Garda Síochána in 1922 but 'Civic Guards' remained the popular name until the 1960s.

18 *KP*, 7 February 1925.

19 *KP*, 14 March 1925.

20 *KP*, 24 June 1924.

21 *KP*, 8 August 1925.

22 *KM*, 26 May 1923.

23 *KP*, 9 May 1925.

24 Senate debates, vol. 5, 20 May 1925.

25 *KP*, 24 January 1925.

26 Senate debates, vol. 1, 7 June 1923.

27 *KJ* and *KP*, 13 December 1924.

28 *KP*, 20 December 1924.
29 David Fitzpatrick, 'Divorce and separation in modern Irish history', *Past and Present*, 114 (1987), p. 188.
30 *KP*, 4 April 1925.
31 Senate debates, vol. 5, 11 June 1925.
32 *KP*, 4 July 1925.
33 Fitzpatrick, 'Divorce and separation', p. 191.
34 Recollection of Nessa Dunne, Dublin, daughter of Peter and Win DeLoughry, in conversation with the author.
35 *KP*, 5 September 1925.
36 *KJ*, 12 September 1925.
37 *KP*, 19 September 1925.
38 *KP*, 17 October 1925. In Peter's campaign literature for the Senate election, he was listed as having been mayor of Kilkenny, vice-chairman of Kilkenny County Council for three years and chairman of the following bodies: the Poor Law Guardians, Kilkenny County Board of Health, Kilkenny County and City Joint Technical Committee and the Board of Governors of Kilkenny mental hospital.
39 *KP*, 4 July 1925. Peter, who was first elected mayor while in Lincoln prison, had held the office for six years and five months (23 January 1919–30 June 1925). His campaign literature for the 1925 Senate election wrongly stated that he had been mayor for seven years.
40 *KP*, 3 July 1926.
41 *KP*, 2 August 1924.
42 *KP*, 29 August 1925.
43 *KP*, 5 July 1924. Peter presented a portrait of Nowlan to the corporation shortly after this. The image still hangs in the main debating chamber in the Tholsel, Kilkenny.
44 Senate debates, vol. 4, 28 January 1925.
45 Dáil debates, vol. 10, 12 March 1925.
46 Family papers of Patricia DeLoughrey, Boston.

17 Founder Fights Back, 1926–31

1 Family papers of Patricia DeLoughrey, Boston.
2 *KP*, 2 April 1927.

3   *KP*, 18 October 1924.

4   *KP*, 28 September 1927.

5   *Ibid.*

6   *KP*, 9 February 1929.

7   Dáil debates, vol. 29, 16 May 1929.

8   *KP*, 29 June 1929.

9   *KP*, 28 September 1929.

10   The League of Kingship of Christ was one of several groups established by extreme Catholics to campaign against intemperance and immorality. Members of these organisations felt obliged to protect Christians from books, films and newspapers that they considered unsuitable.

11   *KP*, 4 January 1931.

12   *KP*, 25 January 1930.

13   BMP. In a letter from David deLoughry to his sister, Lil Mangan, dated 8 December 1938.

14   *Irish Independent*, 29 November 1938.

15   BMP. In a letter from Lil Mangan to Harry Boland's sister, Mrs Kathleen O'Donovan, dated 12 December 1936.

16   BMP. In a letter from David deLoughry to his sister, Lil Mangan, dated 8 December 1938.

17   BMP. In a letter from Lil Mangan to Harry Boland's sister, Mrs Kathleen O'Donovan, dated 12 December 1936.

18   BMP. In a letter from David deLoughry to his sister, Lil Mangan, dated 8 December 1938.

19   BMP. Harry Boland was appointed by the Dáil ministry as a salaried American representative. He left for New York on 2 October 1921.

20   BMP. In a letter from David deLoughry to his sister, Lil Mangan, dated 8 December 1938.

21   *Irish Independent*, 5 November 1938.

22   *KP*, 4 May 1929.

23   *KP*, 11 January 1936.

24   Dáil debates, 2 July 1931.

25   BMP.

26   *The Irish Times*, 26 October 1931.

27   *KP*, 31 October 1931.

28 *KJ*, 31 October 1931.
29 *KP*, 31 October 1931.
30 *Connacht Tribune*, 31 October 1931.
31 *Gaelic American* (New York), 7 November 1931.
32 *KP*, 31 October 1931.
33 *KJ*, 31 October 1931.

18 No Rest, 1932–70

1   *KP*, 1 July 1933.
2   Recollection of Nessa Dunne, Dublin, daughter of Peter and Win DeLoughry, in conversation with the author.
3   Family papers of Patricia DeLoughrey, Boston, in a letter dated 29 December 1926.
4   Family papers of Geoff and Eileen Cartwright, Sheffield, England.
5   John M. Regan, *The Irish Counter-revolution, 1921–36* (2001), p. 341.
6   Maurice Manning, *The Blueshirts* (2006), p. 106.
7   *Ibid.* pp. 104–5.
8   *KP*, 2 December 1933.
9   BMP. In a letter from Lil Mangan to Mrs Kathleen O'Donovan, dated 12 December 1938.
10 Longford and O'Neill, *de Valera*, pp. 77–93. The omission of Peter's name does not cast into a bad light either Longford or O'Neill who had to work under a strict template set out by de Valera. In my opinion, the standing, as historians, of both Longford and O'Neill remains towering.
11 Tim Pat Coogan, *De Valera – Long Fellow, Long Shadow* (1993), p. 2.
12 Anna T. (Cissie) De Loughry, 'Remembering Lincoln prison escape', *OKR*, 2:5 (1983), p. 469. Peter's key is now in the care of the National Museum of Ireland, kept at Collins Military Barracks, Dublin.

References

Archives

Aidan Heavey Collection, Athlone, County Westmeath

British Library, Collindale

Bureau of Military History, Dublin

CBS Kilkenny

Churchill Archives Centre, Cambridge, England

The Church of Jesus Christ of Latter-Day Saints (Mormon) Family
    History Library, Dublin

Diocese of Ossory, Registry of Baptisms

Dublin Diocesan Archive

General Register Office, Dublin

H. M. Stationery Office, London

Institut Pasteur, Paris

Jesuit Library, Milltown Park, Dublin

National Archives of Ireland

National Archives, Kew, England

National Library of Ireland

NUI, Maynooth

Parliamentary Archives, Westminster

Registry of Deeds, Dublin

University College Dublin

Manuscripts in private possession

DeLoughry family papers – Kilkenny (courtesy of Pádraigín Ní
    Dhubhluachra)

Brendan Mangan papers (courtesy of the Mangan family)

Family papers of Eileen and Geoff Cartwright, Sheffield
Family papers of Patricia DeLoughrey, Boston

Newspapers

Connacht Tribune, Daily Express, Daily Independent, Daily Telegraph, Evening Mail, The Freeman's Journal, Gaelic American, Irish Independent, Irish Press, The Irish Times, Kilkenny Journal, Kilkenny Moderator, Kilkenny People, Leinster Leader, Manchester Guardian, Nation, The New York Times, Star, Sunday Independent, Sunday Press, The Sydney Morning Herald, The Times

Bibliography

Béaslaí, Piaras, *Michael Collins and the Making of a New Ireland* (Dublin, 1926)

Brasier, Andrew and John Kelly, *Harry Boland – A Man Divided* (Dublin, 2000)

Brockway, Fenner, *Inside the Left* (Nottingham, 2010)

Collins, Stephen, *The Cosgrave Legacy* (Dublin, 1996)

Comerford, James J., *My Kilkenny I.R.A. Days* (Kilkenny, 1978)

Comerford, R. V., *The Fenians in Context: Irish Politics and Society, 1848–82* (Dublin, 1985)

Coogan, Tim Pat, *De Valera – Long Fellow, Long Shadow* (London, 1993)

Crozier, F. P., *Ireland for ever* (Trowbridge and London, 1971)

De Búrca, Marcus, *The GAA, a History* (Dublin, 2000)

Dwyer, T. Ryle, *Michael Collins, the Man who Won the War* (Cork, 2009)

English, Richard, *Ernie O'Malley, IRA Intellectual* (Oxford, 2006)

Feeney, Brian, *Sinn Féin – A Hundred Turbulent Years* (Dublin, 2010)

Ferriter, Diarmaid, *Judging Dev* (Dublin, 2007)

Figgis, Darrell, *A Second Chronicle of Jails* (Dublin, 1919)

Fitzpatrick, David, *Harry Boland's Irish Revolution* (Cork, 2004)

Garvin, Tom, *Nationalist Revolutionaries in Ireland, 1858–1928* (Dublin, 2005)

Green, Alice S., *The Making of Ireland and Its Undoing 1200–1600* (London, 1908)

Hopkinson, Michael, *Green against Green* (Dublin, 2004)

Kavanagh, Dermot, *A History, Kilkenny Senior Hurling County Finals, 1887–2004* (Kilkenny, 2004)

Longford, Lord and T. P. O'Neill, *Éamon de Valera* (London, 1970)

Lyng, Tom, *Castlecomer Connections* (Kilkenny, 1984)

Maher, Jim, *The Flying Column – West Kilkenny 1916–21* (Dublin, 1987)

Manning, Maurice, *The Blueshirts* (Dublin, 2006)

McCarthy, Cal, *Cumann na mBan and the Irish Revolution* (Cork, 2007)

McGee, Owen, *The IRB, the Irish Republican Brotherhood from the Land League to Sinn Féin* (Dublin, 2005)

Meehan, Ciara, *The Cosgrave Party: a History of Cumann na nGaedheal, 1923–33* (Dublin, 2010)

Milroy, Seán, *Memories of Mountjoy* (London, 1917)

O'Malley, Ernie, *On Another Man's Wound* (Dublin, 2002)

O'Neill, Gerry, *Kilkenny GAA Bible* (Kilkenny, 2005)

Regan, John M., *The Irish Counter-revolution, 1921–36* (Dublin, 2001)

Ryan, Desmond, *Unique Dictator: a Study of Éamon de Valera* (London, 1936)

Townshend, Charles, *Easter 1916, the Irish Rebellion* (London, 2005)

Articles, pamphlets, journals

De Loughry, Anna T. (Cissie) 'Parliament Street 1974', *OKR*, 1:3 (1976), pp. 175–89

— 'Remembering Lincoln prison escape', *OKR*, 2:5 (1983), pp. 468–70

De Loughry, Anna T. (Cissie) and Padraigín Ní Dubhluachra, 'Patrick Corcoran: a postscript', *OKR*, 48 (1996), pp. 7–8

Fitzpatrick, David, 'Divorce and separation in modern Irish history', *Past and Present*, 114 (1987), pp. 172–96

Hackett, Florence, 'The Irish insurrection – Easter week in Kilkenny, April 1916', *OKR*, 3:1 (1984), pp. 17–23

Mauresceaux, G. 'Desart Court and its occupants', *OKR* (1974), pp. 21–5

Mullagh, Captain M. and Condon, Lieutenant L., 'History of Stephens' barracks, Kilkenny', *OKR*, 3:3 (1986), pp. 256–66

Ó Bolguidhir, Liam, 'The early years of the Gaelic League in Kilkenny', *OKR* 4:4 (1992), pp. 1014–26

Phelan, Margaret M., 'Ellen, Countess of Desart, 1858–1933', *Conradh na Gaeilge, Comóradh an chéid*, supplement to the *Kilkenny People* (April 1997), p. 4

Power, CI P. C., evidence, 27 May 1916, *Royal Commission on the Rebellion in Ireland. Minutes of evidence and appendix of documents* (London, 1916), pp. 83–5

Ryan, Desmond, 'De Valera escapes from Lincoln jail', *Irish Digest*, xi:3 (Dublin, January 1942), pp. 85–8

Websites

www.debates.oireachtas.ie

www.irish-roots.ie

www.irishtimes.com

www.oldnewark.com

www.theeasterrising.eu

www.turtlebunbury.com

Index

A

Act of Union 43
Aiken, Frank 238
Ancient Order of the Hibernians 58
Anglo-Irish Treaty 13, 214–217,
    220, 228–232, 260, 269
Arbour Hill barracks 202
Ardnacrusha, County Clare 252
Articles of Agreement. *See* Anglo-
    Irish Treaty
Asgard 58
Ashe, Thomas 90, 91, 98
Ashton-under-Lyne, England 148
Asquith, Herbert 78
Association of Irish Municipal
    Authorities 190, 240
Asylum Lane, Kilkenny 70
Auxiliaries 191, 192, 195–200, 202,
    203, 205–207, 209, 211, 218,
    220, 252, 269
Aylward, Edward 199, 217,
    220–222, 231

B

Ballytrain, County Monaghan 193
Banba Hall 59
Barrow, River 190
Barry, Kevin 191
Barry's Hotel, Dublin 86
Bateman, James 205
Bateman, Michael 205
Bateman, Thomas 205
Béaslaí, Piaras 146
Beecham, Sir Thomas 157
Beecham's Opera House 157
Beggars Bush barracks 202, 223
Belfast 112, 222, 224
Bewley's restaurant 177, 178
Birmingham 35
Birmingham prison 110

Bishop of Ferns 62
Black Abbey, Kilkenny 228, 240
Black and Tans 14, 156, 191, 199,
    200, 205, 206, 208, 218–221,
    230, 252, 269
Blanchfield's eel house 190
Blueshirts 268, 269
Blythe, Ernest 80
Boland, Gerald 136, 137
Boland, Harry 13, 14, 15, 135,
    136, 143, 146–151, 154–157,
    159–162, 168, 169, 172, 258,
    260, 270
    assassination of 232
    Lincoln key controversy 259
Bolger, Thomas 240
Bollard, D. W. 74
Borquist, Waldemar 252
Borris, County Carlow 64, 65, 70
Boyd Barrett, Dr J. 91
Breen, Dan 222, 227
Breslin, John 18
Bridge Street, Worksop 167, 168
British Royal Navy 40
Brixton prison 191
Brockway, Fenner 119–121, 145,
    158, 163, 164, 270
Brockway, Lilla 120, 145
Brownrigg, Bishop Abraham 19, 21,
    22, 38, 39, 62, 115, 241–243, 251
Brugha, Cathal 64, 65
Buggy, Miss 186
by-election, Carlow-Kilkenny, 1925
    239, 240
by-election, East Clare, 1917 88
by-election, Kilkenny, 1890 21
by-election, Longford South 1917
    87
by-election, North Roscommon,
    1917 86
by-election, Waterford, 1918 92

Byrne, Christopher 240
Byrne, J. J. 210
Byrne, Seán 195

C

Cahill, T. B. 85
Callan, County Kilkenny 60, 220, 221
Campaign Against Immoral Literary Garbage 47
Cantwell, Thomas 39, 53, 54
Capuchin Friary, Kilkenny 205
Carlow 64, 65, 241
Carlow-Kilkenny constituency 231, 238, 239, 251
Carnegie free library 38
Carnsore Point, County Wexford 60
Carrickmacross, County Monaghan 110
Carroll, John 200
Carson, Sir Edward 55, 109
Casement, Sir Roger 55, 81
Cashel, County Tipperary 46
Cass, Patrick F. 264
Cassidy, Martin 185
Castlecomer, County Kilkenny 35, 41, 185, 191, 238, 239, 269
Castlecomer Road 29
Castledermott, County Kildare 26, 201
Castle Document 66, 67
Castle Road, Kilkenny 223
Cavan 185
Cave Hill 56
Censorship of Films Bill 241
Champion Davies & Co 111
Chapel Lane, Kilkenny 222
Chaplin, Charlie 42
Chief Liaison Officer 213, 214
Childers, Erskine 58
Christchurch Place, Dublin 137
Christian Brothers School, Kilkenny 25, 267
Civic Guards 239, 241–243, 251, 254, 270
Civil War 13, 14, 16, 162, 218, 228, 230, 233, 236, 258, 265, 269

ceasefire 238
  Kilkenny truce 227
Clare 14, 88, 95, 98, 123, 185
Clarke, Dr Josephine 65, 66
Clarke, Thomas 66–69
Clear, Frank 194
Clomanto, County Kilkenny 60
Clonmantagh, County Kilkenny 33
Clonmel, County Tipperary 63
Close, Jim 99
Club House Hotel, Kilkenny 252
Cole, J. E. 264
Coleman, Fr (Black Abbey) 244
Coleman, Richard 176
Colivet, Michael 99, 113, 114, 176
Collins, Con 146
Collins, Michael 13–15, 86, 94, 130, 134, 135, 138, 146, 148–150, 153, 155–157, 159–162, 166, 168, 169, 172, 186, 214, 215, 232, 233, 239
  assassination of 232
  Lincoln key controversy 260
Comerford, Edward 58, 84, 86, 179, 180, 195, 199, 202, 215
Comerford, James J. 32, 57, 84, 194, 195
Confederation club 34
Conlan, Martin 134
Connolly, Thomas 55
conscription 60, 61, 92–94, 96, 100, 108, 119
Coogan, Ned 242
Corbett, Éamon 99
Corbett Wilson, Richard 45
Corcoran, Maggie 109, 148
Corcoran, Pat 31, 34, 58, 61, 64–66, 70, 86, 117
  death and impact on Peter De-Loughry 190
Corcoran, Seán 99, 109, 123, 148, 154, 162, 163
Cork City Hall 186
Cork jail 183, 184
Coroners (Amendment) Act, 1927 240
Cosgrave, W. T. 14, 65, 88–91, 115, 178, 186, 231, 233–235, 238,

239, 243, 245, 247, 251–253, 263
  freedom of Kilkenny 182
Cotter, Seamus 99, 109, 113
Croke memorial, Archbishop 186
Crooksling sanatorium 136
Crozier, Brigadier General F. P. 192
Cuffe, Captain Otway 25, 28, 32
Cullen, Tom 137, 148, 149
Cumann na mBan 65, 67, 83, 85, 89,
  91–93, 143, 180, 209, 228–231
  proclaimed 182
Cumann na nGaedheal 235,
  238–240, 251, 268
Cumann na Saoirse 229, 231
Curran, Joseph 233
Cusack, Dr Bryan 110
Cusack, Michael 18

D

Dáil Éireann 135, 146, 179, 186,
  188, 215, 216, 222, 233, 234, 245,
  250, 251, 254, 260, 261, 263, 265
Dalton, Richard 222
Daly, P. T. 79
Dardis, Leo 86
Davin, Maurice 18
Davis, Thomas 56
Davitt, Michael 18, 21
Dawson Cusack, Paul 99, 106, 110,
  113, 121, 159, 162, 173
de Blagdh, Earnán. *See* Ernest
  Blythe
de Búrca, P. F. 99, 110, 111, 130, 149
Deere, Cornelius 79
Defence of the Realm Act 100, 103,
  178, 182
Delahunty, Fr P. H. 60
De Loughry, Anna T. (Cissie) 271
DeLoughry, Bridget, née O'Brien
  250
  death 26
  marriage 18
  return to Ireland 19
deLoughry, David 23, 27, 28, 42, 43,
  60, 74, 83, 184, 258–260, 268
  fire-fighting 29
  hotel commandeered 203
  Lincoln key controversy 259

DeLoughry family home
  as bomb factory 185, 191
  raid by Auxiliaries, 1920 191
DeLoughry, Francis 23, 26, 32
  death 43
DeLoughry, John, brother 23, 25,
  27, 33
  death 33, 34
  marriage 33
DeLoughry, John, nephew 205
DeLoughry, Larry 23, 27, 28, 34,
  42, 49, 60, 63, 64, 75, 84, 96,
  118, 184, 202, 203, 205, 206,
  208, 268
  amateur acting 28, 43, 180
  arrest, 1916 73
  arrest, 1921 205
  Gaelic League 25
  letter to British authorities 203
  Michael Collins 94
  re-arrested, imprisoned in Bere Island,
    1921 208
  release from prison, 1922 215
  release from Wakefield prison 77,
    94
DeLoughry, Lily 85, 178, 266–268
de Loughry, Nessa 185, 266–268
DeLoughry, Peadar 234, 266, 268
DeLoughry, Peter
  advancement in IRB 38
  against executions 236, 237
  apprenticeship 25
  arrest, 1916 71
  arrest, 1918 97
  arrest, December, 1920 200
  birth 17
  British secret service report on 98
  campaign against motor permits 182
  Catholic Church 21, 62, 245–247,
    257
  cleanliness 172
  confirmed as mayor of Kilkenny, 1919
    178
  confrontation with governor of Lin-
    coln prison 172
  conscription 94
  contribution to Dáil debates 254
  Coroners (Amendment) Bill 240
  de Valera's promise to return Lincoln
    key 159

director of elections, 1922 general election 231
director of elections, Cumann na nGaedheal 238
East Clare by-election 88
education 25
elected chairman, Board of Guardians 101
elected mayor of Kilkenny, 1st term 150
elected mayor of Kilkenny, 2nd term 184
elected mayor of Kilkenny, 3rd term 204
elected mayor of Kilkenny, 4th term 216
elected mayor of Kilkenny, 5th term 235
elected mayor of Kilkenny, 6th term 248
elected to Kilkenny County Council, 1920 188
election to Dáil 251
election to Senate, 1922 234
emigration 33
entry to politics 39
Ernie O'Malley's impressions of 195
father's death 23
film censorship 241, 257
final contribution in the Dáil 261
financial damage to business 83, 206, 257
fire-fighting 29
forging Lincoln master key 154
Gaelic League 25
general election, 1923 238, 239
home rule 43, 44
illness and death 262
industrial relations mediator, Stathams 181
influence of folklore 56
interest in radio technology 254
involvement in attack on Hugginstown RIC barracks 188
IRB leader 31, 38
Irish speaker 178
joins Volunteers 55
judge of republican courts 188
Kilkenny by-election, 1917 88, 90
Kilkenny Sinn Féin leader 180
Kilkenny waterworks 248
Lincoln prison escape, planning 126

Lincoln quartermaster election 112, 113
local elections, 1928 254
making will 262
marriage 40
mediator in Civil War 223, 224
metric system 240
Michael Collins 186
mother's death 26
nicknamed Peadar 106
on divorce 14, 243–247, 256
on saving Ernie O'Malley's life 202
poor health 202, 203, 261, 262
release from Arbour Hill, January 1921 204
release from Lincoln prison 177
reported in *Manchester Guardian* 201
return to Kilkenny from Lincoln prison 166, 170–175, 178, 179
return to public life, 1921 213
row with Cumann na mBan 230
support for Anglo-Irish Treaty 216
Terence MacSwiney 190, 191
treatment of by Black and Tans 200
Waterford by-election, 1918 92
DeLoughry, Richard, brother 23, 26, 33
DeLoughry, Richard, father 17–21, 23, 92, 102, 248, 249
attitude to Britain 19
death 23
emigration to United States 18
Fenianism 18
GAA 19
marriage 18
political associations 18
return to Ireland 19
DeLoughry, Richard, son 41, 85, 178, 266–268
DeLoughry, Sheila 85, 178, 266–268
DeLoughry, Thomas Francis 43, 85, 178, 266–268
DeLoughry, Thomas, grandfather 248
DeLoughry, Win 40–42, 75, 77, 79, 85, 96, 98, 100, 108, 114, 116, 118, 178, 180, 185, 190, 203–206, 208, 228, 234, 251, 262, 266–268
childhood 40, 41

Cumann na mBan 85, 93, 180
Cumann na Saoirse 229
garda raid on her home 269
marriage 40
Department of Agriculture and
Technical Instruction 86
Derby, England 103
Desart Court 237
attack on by anti-Treaty forces 238
Desart, Earl of 237
Desart, Ellen, Countess of 25, 28,
32, 38, 234, 237
and divorce 244
election to Senate, 1922 234
freedom of Kilkenny city 39
Desart Hall 64, 242
de Valera, Éamon 13–15, 88, 89, 90,
97–99, 101, 103–106, 113–116,
120, 122–131, 133, 135–138,
140–142, 144–146, 149, 150,
214, 215, 227, 232, 239, 251,
258–260, 263, 265, 267–271
arrival in Dublin after Lincoln prison
escape 175
freedom of Kilkenny city 265
Lincoln key controversy 259–261
Lincoln prison escape, 3rd attempt
150–152
Lincoln prison escape, 4th attempt
154, 155, 157–162
Lincoln prison escape, aftermath 166,
170–175, 178, 179
Devoy, John 249
Dicksboro hurling club 74
Dobbyn, James J. 99, 104, 106, 112,
113, 121, 123, 154, 157, 162, 163
Lincoln prison escape, 1st attempt
126, 127
Donnegan, Margaret 33
Dooley, Siobhán 230
Douglas, James 245
Douglas motion 245, 246
Dowling, Joseph 95
Doyle, Archdeacon James 245, 246
Doyle, Very Rev. J. Canon 39
Drangan, County Tipperary 191,
193, 222
Drury Lane theatre orchestra 43
Dublin Castle 22, 29, 37, 38, 45, 72,

82, 83, 134, 145, 176, 199, 202,
203, 211
Dublin Corporation 28, 203
Dublin Lock-out 47
Dublin Metropolitan Police 209
Dublin United Tramway Company
47
Dunbell, County Kilkenny 29
Dundon, Dr Edward 65, 70, 236
Dún Laoghaire (Kingstown) 111,
156, 177
Dunlavin 240
Dunphy, Patrick 191
Durham jail 103, 104
Dwyer, Michael 31, 34

E

Economic War 266, 269
Edward VII 30
Egan, Una 230
Ellsworth, Billy 175
Emergency Powers Bill 233, 235
Emmet, Robert 43
Etchingham, Seán 99, 104–106, 114,
121, 123, 142–146, 149, 175

F

Farmers' Party 231, 232
Feeney, Brian 81, 95
Feore, Supt. Seán 243
Fethard, County Tipperary 222
Fianna Fáil 251, 265, 268
Figgis, Darrell 79, 98, 103, 104
Finance and Leases Committee,
Kilkenny Corporation 45
Finance Bill, 1931 261
Fine Gael 268, 269
First World War 49, 58, 74, 104,
114, 119, 124, 125
Fitzgerald, James 155, 156, 258
Fleming, Éamon 69
Foresters' club, Kilkenny 218
Four Courts 220, 224
French, Lord 109
Freshford, County Kilkenny 238
Frizelle, George, RIC 50, 51, 64, 74

Furlong, Thomas 38, 61, 70
Furniss, Edward 257

G

Gaelic Athletic Association (GAA)
18, 19, 22, 23, 25, 28, 39, 43, 105,
183, 241, 249
Gaelic League 25–28, 36, 39, 48, 63
proclaimed 182
Galbally, County Limerick 60, 63
Garda Síochána 269
General election, 1918 114, 182
General election, 1922 220, 229,
231
General election, 1923 238
General election, 1926 251
General election, 1932 265
Geraghty, George 148
German Plot 95, 97, 99–101, 103,
121, 176, 179
general release order 176
Gibbons, Seán 33, 236, 263
Gleeson, Rev. Bro. 256
Glenavy, Lord 245
Gloucester prison 96–98, 100, 103,
176
Glover, James 43
Gogarty, Oliver St John 234
Goldie-Taubman, Major (governor
of Lincoln prison) 125, 144,
145, 151, 154, 172
Goolds Cross, County Tipperary 79
Goosehill, Kilkenny 41
Goresbridge, County Kilkenny 30
Gorey, Denis 231, 232
Government Buildings, Dublin 246
Gowran Park races 189
GPO, Dublin 158
Grace, Cait 261
Graiguenamanagh, County Kilkenny
189, 200
Gravesend, Kent 174
Green, Miss R. 148
Green's bridge, Kilkenny 20
Greenvale, Kilkenny 28
Griffin, Mr (Kilkenny UDC) 243
Griffith, Arthur 33, 79, 87, 89, 91,

98, 99, 146, 186, 214, 215, 232,
234

H

Hackett, Florence 229
Haltigan, Patrick 249
Hanrahan, Andrew 196
Hanrahan, James 196, 197, 199, 218
Hanrahan, Mrs 197, 198
Hanrahan, Thomas 196, 198
Healy, Liam 220
Henderson, Arthur 203
Hennessy, Timothy 31
High Street, Kilkenny 225
Hipwell, Rev. Fr Patrick 30
Hobson, Bulmer 42, 44, 66–68
Hobson, Claire 67
Holland, Edward 196, 197, 199, 202
Holland, Rev. P. 74
Holohan, Fr 78
Holyhead, Wales 137, 177
Home Rule 21, 43, 48, 52, 55, 56,
58, 61, 74, 216
House of Commons 32, 40, 173,
174
Howth, County Dublin 58
Hoyne, H. M. 84, 91
Hugginstown RIC barracks 187,
188, 191
attack on 188
Hyde, Dr Douglas 27, 42, 234

I

Imperial Hotel, Kilkenny 224, 225
influenza pandemic (Spanish flu)
176, 177
Inistioge, County Kilkenny 196,
199, 218
Irish club. See Volunteer Hall
Irish Guards pipers' band 85
Irish National Aid and Volunteer
Dependants' Association 85
Irish Parliamentary Party 18, 33–35,
52, 56, 63, 86–89, 92, 93, 101,
114, 115, 117
Irish Republican Army (IRA) 63,

155, 179, 181, 185, 188–190,
192, 194, 204–206, 210–212,
214, 219, 221, 258, 269
military innovations 191
Irish Republican Brotherhood (IRB)
31, 37–39, 44, 52, 58, 69, 105
Irish Volunteers 42, 55, 57–61,
63–65, 69–71, 74, 84, 85, 88, 96,
98, 105, 135, 148, 180, 182, 189,
193

J

Jenkinson, James 40
John's bridge, Kilkenny 225
Johnson, Marie 208
Johnson, R. 111
Johnson, Thomas 208
Johnstown, County Kilkenny 238
John Street, Kilkenny 29, 203, 222
John Street, Upper, Kilkenny 71,
224

K

Kavanagh, Fr James 129, 131, 134,
138, 142, 143, 146, 150
Kealy, John 71
death 72
Kealy, Martin 72, 86
Kealy, Rev. M. 74
Keane, E. T. 15, 25, 31, 35, 39, 45,
46, 50, 52, 74, 76, 82, 86–89, 91,
97, 100, 101, 102, 115, 117, 118,
178, 180, 182–184, 186, 263, 269
Peter DeLoughry's mayoral campaign,
1919 115
Kearns, Rev. Fr J. 197, 198
Keating, Matthew 43, 78, 115
Keaton, Buster 42
Kelly, Frank 135, 136, 150, 153, 159
Lincoln prison escape, 1st attempt
136
Kelly, J. 92
Kelly, Jack 200
Kelly's Hotel, Lincoln 153
Kenna, Edward 48, 50, 56
Kenworthy, Commander 203
Kerwick, Daniel 49

Kieran Street, Kilkenny 57, 59, 64,
224
Kilbricken, Callan, County Kilkenny
85
Kilcullen, County Kildare 202
Kilkenny Castle 30, 223–226
Kilkenny Cinema Company 62
concerts 84
Kilkenny Corporation 18, 20, 26,
29, 30, 35, 36, 39, 43, 45–48, 52,
56, 73, 74, 86, 93, 117, 118, 182,
190, 191, 208, 213, 215, 217, 232,
253–255, 257, 261, 264
Treaty debate 216
Kilkenny County Board of Health
263
Kilkenny County Council 14, 30,
35, 188, 215, 236, 254
Treaty debate 215
Kilkenny courthouse 31
Kilkenny District Court 264
Kilkenny District Lunatic Asylum
26, 205, 250
Kilkenny Industrial Development
Association 32, 35, 36
Kilkenny jail 71
Kilkenny Journal 18, 20, 44, 223
Kilkennymen's Association, New
York 43
Kilkenny military barracks 61, 201,
219
Kilkenny Moderator 26, 27, 178, 218
Kilkenny National Guard 29
Kilkenny North constituency 115,
178
Kilkenny People 15, 27, 28, 30, 33, 39,
50, 52, 56, 74, 81–86, 89, 98, 101,
116, 181, 199, 200, 206, 218, 225,
230, 248, 263
and Lincoln key controversy 260
foundation of 25
Kilkenny South consituency 115
Kilkenny Technical Schools Com-
mittee 256
Kilkenny Theatre 28
Kilkenny Urban District Council
99, 213, 240–242
Kilkenny Vigilance Committee 242

Kilkenny woollen mills 32
Killarney, County Kerry 46
Kilmacow, County Kilkenny 31
Kilmanagh, County Kilkenny 211
Kingstown. *See* Dún Laoghaire
Kirkwood, Colonel John 192
Knocktopher 78, 220
Kyteler's Inn 59

L

Labour Party, Ireland 182, 184, 208,
    231, 232, 238, 248
Lalor, James 31, 63, 69–71, 79, 86,
    88, 183, 185, 186, 192, 194, 195,
    215
  arrest, 1920 188
Lalor, Jane 41
Lalor, Patrick 41
Land Act, 1870 34
land annuities 265
Lardner, Laurence 99, 122
Larkin, James 47
Lascelles, Lady Margaret Joan 237
League of the Kingship of Christ
    257
Leddon, James 70
Leeds 129, 143
Leinster House 260
Lelia 262
Lemass, Seán 255
Lennon, James 231
Lennon, Michael J. 99, 106, 121,
    125, 157–159, 162, 164, 172
Limerick 47, 70
Limetree, Cuffesgrange, County
    Kilkenny 57
Lincoln 137, 166, 167, 169, 173
Lincoln prison 11, 13, 14, 98, 99,
    103–108, 116, 118, 119, 121,
    126, 171, 176, 178, 180, 182, 186,
    187, 231, 258, 270, 271
  aftermath 171, 172, 175, 176
  Christmas 115
  escape, 1st attempt 125–141
  escape, 2nd attempt 142–150
  escape, 3rd attempt 150–152
  escape, 4th attempt 153–165
  escape plans 124

grand opera 113
  prisoners stand in election 114
  quartermaster election 112
Lincoln Road, Worksop 167, 169,
    170
Lincoln train station 103
Lloyd, Harold 42
Local Government Bill, 1924 250
Local Government Board 40
Longford 90, 110
Longford, Lord 270
Longford South constituency 87, 98
Long Wood, Kilkenny 57
Lynch, Liam 193, 238
Lynch, Patrick 88

M

MacBride, Major John 81
Mac Curtáin, Tomás 80, 186, 204
MacDermott, Seán 34, 38, 61,
    66–69, 81
MacDonagh, Thomas 27, 55, 63, 66,
    81, 98
MacNeill, Professor Eoin 58, 60, 66,
    67, 69, 70, 88, 89, 101, 108
MacSwiney, Mary 260
MacSwiney, Nan 144
MacSwiney, Terence 99, 114, 144,
    186, 190, 191, 204
Magennis, John 48, 52, 53, 63, 86,
    89, 90, 93, 101, 252–255
Magennis, Joseph 87
Mallow, County Cork 193
Manchester 33, 34, 44, 134, 139,
    140, 143, 148, 150, 153, 156, 160,
    166, 168, 171, 172, 258
Manchester Martyrs 19, 20, 36, 44, 63
Mangan, Henry 32, 42, 78, 107, 177,
    203, 262
  marriage 28
Mangan, Lelia (Sr Petra) 115, 177,
    262
Mangan, Lil (Mary Elizabeth) née
    DeLoughry 26, 28, 42, 77, 96,
    100, 106, 107, 116, 175, 177, 203,
    204, 208, 259–262, 270
  marriage 28

Manning, Maurice 268, 269
Mansion House, Dublin 98
Marconi company 254
Market Yard, Kilkenny 58
Markievicz, Countess 88, 182
   freedom of Kilkenny 83
Mater hospital 91
Maxwell, General J. G. 83
Mayo East constituency 123
McCabe, Alasdair 99, 109, 111, 114,
   120, 121, 158, 162, 163
McCan, Pierce 79, 176, 187
McCarthy, Dan 89
McCarthy, John 35
McCarthy, Justin 40
McCullough, Denis 79
McGarry, Seán 13, 99, 105, 112,
   125, 126, 128, 129, 136, 137, 141,
   142, 146, 150, 158, 159, 161, 162,
   166, 170–172, 174, 175, 178
McGrath, Joe 148
McKenna, John 208, 213, 261
McKenna, Patrick 87
McMahon, Joe 185, 187
McMahon, Liam 134, 142, 143,
   150, 153, 168, 172
McMahon, Mrs Liam 153
McSweeney, E. 34
McSweeney, Michael 236
Medlar, Martin 236
Meek, Head Constable 20
Mellows, Barney 148
Mellows, Liam 61
Michael Street, Kilkenny 55
Midland Hotel, Manchester 143,
   157
Military Service Bill 92
Milroy, Seán 13, 79, 88, 89, 91, 98,
   99, 105, 112–114, 120, 121, 128,
   142, 146–148, 158, 159, 161,
   162, 166, 170–172, 174, 175,
   178, 182
   Lincoln prison escape, 1st attempt
      128
Modane, France 174
Monahan, Philip 99, 114
Moore, Rev. Philip 58
Morrissey, John 222

Mosaic law 244, 245
motor permits, campaign against
   182
Mountjoy prison 191
Moylan, Seán 227
Mulcahy, Richard 136, 137, 180,
   185, 187, 192, 194, 219
Mullinavat, County Kilkenny 129
Mulrooney, Mary 41
Murphy, Ellen, née Kelly 40, 41
Murphy, Fintan 136–138, 148–150,
   156, 157
   account of Lincoln prison escape
      166–171
   involvement in Lincoln prison escape,
      first attempt 139, 140
Murphy, John 41
Murphy, Laurence 41
Murphy, Thomas (Win DeLoughry's
   father) 40, 41
Murphy, Thomas (Win DeLoughry's
   brother) 41, 185, 188
Murphy, William Martin 47

N

National Defence Fund 93
National Volunteers 14, 58, 60, 63
Newbridge, County Kildare 266
New Ross, County Wexford 76, 200
New York 18, 43, 174, 239
Neylon, District Inspector 96
Ni Conaill, Caitlín 259
Norberg Schulz, Thomas 252
Nore, River 20, 225
North Dublin Union Board of
   Guardians 40
Nowlan, James 34, 52, 53, 71, 76,
   178, 182
   arrest and imprisonment 183
   death of 249

O

Oakes, William 225
Oakley Road, Dublin 156
Oath of allegiance to Dáil 179
O'Brien, Patrick 32, 33, 43, 57, 76,
   88

Ó Ceallaigh, Seán T. 38, 146, 173
O'Connell, J. J. 'Ginger' 60, 61, 64, 65, 70, 71, 73, 74
O'Connor, Rory 219, 227
O'Connor, T. P. 44
O'Dea, Head Constable 96
O'Doherty, Kitty 67, 68
O'Donoghue, Paddy 134, 142, 143, 149, 153, 156, 157, 159, 161, 166, 168
O'Donovan, Kathleen 270
O'Donovan Rossa, Jeremiah 18, 61
O'Duffy, General Eoin 193, 210, 242, 269
O'Dwyer, George 194, 209, 210–212, 219, 221, 225
  skill as military leader 212
O'Flaherty, Samuel 99, 114, 121
O'Flanagan, Fr Michael 89, 182
O'Grady, Standish 27, 28
O'Keeffe, Rev. Andrew 242, 243, 251, 252
O'Keeffe, P. J. 20, 25, 26
O'Kelly, Lieutenant Edward 63, 66
O'Mahony, John 87, 91, 98, 99, 105, 110, 111, 114, 122, 138, 150, 158, 162
  Lincoln prison escape, 1st attempt 128–133, 136, 138
O'Malley, Ernie 192–197, 199, 200, 201, 202, 209–212, 218
  attempt by Auxiliaries to kill him 202
  criticism of Kilkenny Brigade 195, 210
O'Mara, James 115
O'Meara, W. F. 186
O'Neill, Shane 101
O'Neill, Thomas P. 270
O'Phelan, Fintan 31
O'Rahilly, The 42, 44, 57, 81
O'Reilly, Colonel Joe 156
Ormonde Road, Kilkenny 41
O'Ryan, Nelly 123
Ossory, Diocese of 22, 242
Ossory, Earl of 225, 226
Ossory, Lady 225
O'Sullivan, Mrs 150, 153

P

Parade, Kilkenny 101, 117
Paris 19, 41, 173, 174
Paris peace conference 135, 142, 146, 149, 173
Parliament Street, Kilkenny 42, 64, 66
Parnell, C.S. 18, 21, 22, 36, 97, 99, 101, 249
Pasteur Institute 41
Paulstown, County Kilkenny 60
Pearse, Pádraig 66, 68, 84, 98, 220
Pigott, Richard 99
Plunkett, Count George 86, 87, 98, 146
  freedom of Kilkenny 83
Plunkett, Joseph 64, 81, 83
Poor Law Guardians 41, 89, 93, 101, 213
Portlaoise 70
Potter, Michael L. 48, 49
Power, Pierce. C. 59, 60, 72, 73, 74, 82, 83, 84, 85, 86, 89, 91, 92, 99, 100, 101, 184
Powers whiskey 224
Price, Major Ivor 83
Private Bills office 244
Prout, Colonel Commandant J. T. 221, 222, 223, 224, 225, 226
Prout, Jack 226
Public Health Act, 1890 242
Purcell, Joseph 31, 34, 48, 52, 53, 54, 74, 87

Q

Quinn, Mary Bridget 'Nanny' 42, 96, 178, 205, 206, 208, 228

R

Ramsbottom, Patrick 70
Reade, James 248, 249, 253, 254
Reading jail 79–81, 99, 186
Redmond, Johanna 43
Redmond, John 43, 56, 58, 59, 63, 87
Republican Police 188, 189, 218

Rice, Joe 202

Richmond barracks 72, 77–79

Richmond Place, Dublin 67

Richmond prison 18, 74

Rising, 1916 62–67, 69, 70, 72–75, 78, 82–85, 87, 88, 90, 98, 190, 193

Robinson, Paschal, papal nuncio 257

Rose Inn Street, Kilkenny 224

Rothe House 17, 23, 25, 57, 63, 180, 195, 199, 271

Roughan, James 195, 199, 202

Rowe, Rev. J. 58

Royal Irish Constabulary (RIC) 19, 20, 22, 29, 31, 38, 47, 48, 50, 55, 59, 60, 64, 70, 73, 74, 82–84, 87, 95, 96, 117, 179, 181–185, 187–193, 205, 209, 211, 214, 220, 222, 224

and Volunteer movements 55, 60

Ruane, Thomas 99, 122, 162

Russell, Sem 137

S

Scallop Gap 64, 65

Scott, Canon 147

Sears, William 123

Shannon hydro-electric scheme 252

Shaw, Patrick W. 255

Sheehy, Joe 123

Sheffield 137, 166–171

Sheffield Road, Worksop 167, 168, 170

Shelly, Michael 239

Shore, Robert 194

Shortt, Edward 174

Shouldice, Frank 148

Sinn Féin 32–35, 38, 56, 58, 59, 66, 73, 83, 86–93, 95–102, 104, 111, 114, 115, 117, 134, 135, 137, 172, 173, 176, 180, 182–184, 186, 189–191, 193, 214, 231

1918 general election 114

and buy Irish campaign 35

growth in Kilkenny 91

Irish language classes, Kilkenny 180

National Food Scheme 85, 98

proclaimed 182

Sinn Féin club, Kilkenny 87, 101, 183

Sinn Féin office, Parliament Street 180, 183

Skeeter Park, Cleariestown, County Wexford 70

Slater, John 86, 93

Slevin, RIC 31

Smithwick, R. H. 52, 53

Smithwick's brewery 181, 182, 224

Stallard, George 31, 62

Stallard, Peter 30

Stallard, Sinéad 230

Stallard, Tom 29, 30, 34, 43, 48, 52, 62, 64, 65, 69, 70, 76, 91, 186, 194–196, 208, 241

Stapleton, Daniel J. 179

Statham's motor garage 181

St Canice's Cathedral 223, 224, 245

Stephens, James 18, 19, 36, 43, 90

escape from Richmond prison 18

St John's Ward 39, 117

St Kieran's College 35, 36, 74

St Patrick's brass band 20, 118, 262

St Patrick's church choir 40, 41

Strangman, Dr Mary 50, 51

Sullivan's brewery 181

Sweetman, John 32

T

Talbotsinch, Kilkenny 189

Talty, Kathleen 143, 153

Temperance Hotel, Kilkenny 203

Tholsel 26, 50, 87, 180, 213, 224, 229–231

Thomastown, County Kilkenny 33, 34, 38, 91, 199, 200, 201

Thorne, Cocoa works 111

Thurles, County Tipperary 186, 187

Tipperary 221, 224

Tolch's oil engine 23

Tone, Theobald Wolfe 56, 61, 220

Tramore, County Waterford 108

Treacy, Tom 57–59, 64, 65, 69–71, 73, 74, 79, 82, 83, 86, 88, 92, 95,

183, 185, 187, 188, 191, 192, 194, 195, 215
  arrest, 1920 188
  comes 'off the run', 1919 179
Treann na Gaeilge 107
Trevelyan, Sir George 40
'Trusty' 120
Tullaroan, County Kilkenny 238

U

Ua Duibne, Seamus. *See* Dobbyn, James J.
Ulster Volunteers 55
United Ireland Party 268, 270
United Irish League 29, 56, 90
Upton, J. W. 217
Usk prison 137, 142, 148, 149, 176

V

Versailles, Treaty of 182
Victoria Hotel 90
Volunteer Hall 57, 59, 64, 70, 84, 95
Volunteers 58

W

Wakefield prison 72, 74, 75, 77, 81, 94
Walsh, Fr 243
Walsh, John 190
War Office, British 79, 176
Warren, Fr 78
Warren, Mick 78
Waterford 32, 50, 63, 199, 221, 224, 252
Waterford by-election, 1918 92
Waterloo Cup 175
Waverly Hotel, Lincoln 146
Westinghouse Engineering Works 33
Wexford 15, 38, 60, 62, 64, 70, 72
Wexford Volunteers 64, 65
Wilsdon, Arthur J. 224, 225
Wimbourne, Lord 63
Wolfhill colliery 69
Woodenbridge, County Wicklow 58
Woodstock House 192, 195, 196, 198, 200, 206, 207, 218
Worksop 157, 166–168, 170
Wragby Road, Lincoln 132, 159, 161